PICKING, POLITICKING, AND PONTIFICATING

Dear Richard,

Thank you for helping me find some clarity in a confusing world.

Your friend,

Mike Ball

Picking, Politicking, and Pontificating

*How an Ex-Cop
Legalized Cannabis While
Fighting Corruption*

MIKE BALL

SLING AND STONE PRODUCTIONS
Madison, Alabama

Produced for Sling and Stone Productions,
Madison, Alabama
by NewSouth, Inc.
Montgomery, Alabama

ISBN 978-1-0880-7131-1 (trade paper)
ISBN 978-1-0880-7137-3 (ebook)

Printed in the United States of America

To my father Leldon and my wife Karen,

Conduits of perfect love

Contents

The Unseen Hand

In 2015, I made a brief presentation to the national summit of the Foundation for Excellence in Education about the essential role teachers played in helping me overcome my traumatic youth. The Foundation's annual meeting was hosted by Dr. Condoleezza Rice and held in Denver that year. Dr. Rice was standing in for the Foundation's president, former Florida Governor Jeb Bush. Governor Bush was unable to host that year because of potential conflicts arising from his presidential campaign. A few minutes before my presentation to the group, I had the opportunity for a private chat with Dr. Rice in the green room.

Our conversation meandered toward the effect of music in early childhood brain development and how it positively affects social and academic growth. Although I am a shade-tree musician and she is a classically trained pianist, it seemed evident that our musical efforts during our formative years had played an integral role for both of us.

Dr. Rice discussed how music activates the brain to recognize various sounds and progressions, organizing them in a manner pleasing to the ear. But music does much more than bring pleasure. It trains the mind to organize sounds in a manner that makes sense to the listener, converting noise into music. As it does this, it also enhances the ability of the mind to more efficiently perform many other functions, such as learning other languages or mathematics. The conversation concluded with a consensus that music is an important brain exercise that should not be overlooked as a key component of a quality education. While she talked about her proud parents asking her to play piano for guests when she was a little girl in Alabama and how music helped her overcome shyness and develop social skills, I admired the peaceful wisdom that exuded from this accomplished woman. She was adorned with a cloak of humble confidence that I recognized as a garment worn by those who have been awed by the presence of something much bigger than any of us. My thoughts drifted to the Master Composer/Conductor/Musician who had chosen her for a life of service and prepared her for it by using her parents as a conduit of His perfect love. Love is the power that helps us find our place in his great orchestra. Love calms the noisy chaos of this world.

As Dr. Rice reminisced about her upbringing, I pondered about the One who had chosen and prepared her for a journey. Although my childhood was much less stable and far outside the realm of academia that surrounded her, I had felt the same touch on my life. Regardless of the difference in circumstances and outcome, our common bond was the boundless grace that found us both.

Hearing the beautiful music of Maestro's symphony is one thing but being a willing instrument is quite another. Random sounds make noise, but music is deliberate, not accidental. The Master's touch was on Dr. Rice's life began long before she was born. Her parents even had the foresight to name her "Condoleezza," an Italian musical term meaning "to perform with sweetness," a name consistent with the spirit she exudes.

I believe the Unseen Hand was already preparing for her path when it planted a seed in the mind of a sharecropper's son in Eutaw, Alabama, to invest the cotton he had saved into tuition at Stillman Institute, a private Presbyterian school in Tuscaloosa. It was one of the few places available in 1919 in Alabama where a black man could get a college education. When his cotton money ran out, John Wesley Rice Sr. was able to complete his education with a scholarship obtained by entering the ministry. His passion for the Lord and for education passed through his son John Jr.—who later became dean of students at Stillman College—and then on to John Jr.'s daughter, Condoleezza.

After I took my seat on the flight home, I resumed reading *Miracles* by C. S. Lewis. I'd started the book on the way to the conference and enjoyed reading his explanation of miracles as part of a vast developing whole instead of individual random isolated coincidences or hocus-pocus. By seeking and recognizing their connections, we discover that many of them relate to one another like a score of music within a symphony. If our ears are spiritually receptive and listening for it, we can detect the wonderful creative riffs inserted with perfect timing at unexpected moments by the Master's unseen hand. Faith begins blooming when we learn to recognize the genius of the perfectly timed variations and twists masterfully inserted in real time as the composition unfolds. I cannot think of a more rational explanation for the incredible music filled with creative embellishments than divine intervention by a supernatural musician/composer.

I usually read C. S. Lewis slowly, reading a little and thinking a lot, so I can savor it and give it time to permeate my mind's palate; but this time I read much faster, as though I was on a timeline to get it read, absorbing it quickly and thoroughly, devouring it like a starving man scarfing down a biscuit.

The book describes miracles as a sudden temporary interference from the supernatural realm into the natural world that alters the course of events, causing them to bend in the direction of God's will. It's like we are piloting an aircraft when something unexpectedly takes over the controls for a moment, alters the course then gives it back to us. The duration of the intervention is often very brief before it recedes back into its supernatural realm where it resides; allowing us to resume physical control, but on the altered path. We have no idea when, why, where, or how it is going to happen; however, by learning to look for these supernatural interventions, we discover they are far more common than we would have ever expected. But if we don't believe it possible, we won't look for it. If we don't look for it, we won't see it; and if we don't see, we can't truly believe.

When I finished reading the book, my mind was flooded by memories of "coincidences" throughout my life that reinforced my belief in the amazing force that guided it all. Some call the "coincidences" God-winks, and that works for me. As I meditated about the clusters of those incidents I'd witnessed during the previous days, a clean-cut, professional-looking young man was reading some type of technical-looking book in the seat next to me. During most of the flight, we barely spoke. He read his book, and I read mine. I was barely aware of either his presence or the plane's descent as I contemplated the validity of what I'd been reading.

As the wheels almost touched the runway, the young man in the seat beside me suddenly perked up and said, "We're going back up! we're going back up! What's going on?" startled by the jet engines revving up as the plane began to ascend. The pilot had aborted the landing.

I calmed the young man down by telling him that I didn't think that it was anything to be concerned about. I speculated that the pilot was probably circling out of an abundance of caution because the approach was not just right, or something was near the runway, like maybe a dog. I told him about the fighter jets that frequently aborted landing on the USS *Nimitz* when I served in the Marine Corps. Since I was trying get him not to worry, I didn't mention that I'd never been on a commercial flight that aborted a landing; but I'm sure it's not uncommon. As the plane circled and we chatted, I asked him how his trip to Denver went and he began to share.

He said it had been a terrible business trip. His boss had been very negative toward him, and he couldn't think of any reason for it. It seemed that every idea the young man proposed during the trip was dismissed out of hand, and everything he attempted or did was a failure. Blame for everything that went wrong during the trip seemed to be laid at his feet whether he deserved it or not. It was evident this intelligent, conscientious young man was unaccustomed to being scapegoated and stigmatized, but as someone who has attracted the attention of bullies for many years, I had quite a bit of experience on the matter.

I pointed out that the problem may have little to do with him or his job performance, but to know for sure, he must first take an honest look at himself. I shared how I do it when I sense a spiritual attack. It almost always revolves around some type of bullying behavior, and although there is nothing that we can do to change those people, we always control our reaction to their poor behavior.

The power of a positive, thoughtful reaction to overcome a negative, irrational action is greater than we can imagine. The key to doing that is by first resisting the urge to be discouraged by someone else's bad behavior. Little mention was made of religion during our encounter, although much of what I shared with him came straight from the seventeenth-century theologian/philosopher Jonathan Edwards's essay on undiscerned spiritual pride.

We barely noticed the wheels touching the runway as the plane safely landed. As we disembarked, he asked me for a business card, and I gave him one. I did not think about the encounter again until I checked my email the next day, and read the following message:

From: ███ ███
Sent: Saturday, October 24, 2015 10:10 AM
To: Mike Ball
Subject: Great Meeting You
Hi Mike,

It was a pleasure meeting you on the plane yesterday. Your message could not have been better received. I was just returning from a pretty brutal business trip in terms of personal attacks aimed at me. I am, in fact, a believer and my strategy has always been to force myself to relax and empty my mind when I feel feelings or think thoughts of anger, pride, fear, weakness, and anything negative toward myself or others (regardless of the circumstances). It has worked extraordinarily well in my life and has made me a confident person. However, this last trip was particularly intense as I had to deal with a relentless storm of negativity. I remember thinking to God: Am I the only one in the world who makes an effort to maintain harmony with other people, avoid being prideful, and avoid being angry and controlling my temper and is it worth it if no one else is doing it? Because up until now I almost felt like that. So, my faith was being tested last week and then out of nowhere you provided me with pretty much the perfect message of encouragement because if it worked for you throughout your life, it can work for me too. You mentioned providing further advice to me if I emailed you so I wanted to email you and thank you for your uplifting words. I have never met anyone else who truly thinks the way you do.

If I don't hear from you, I wish you all the best in your endeavors within the legislature.

Best,
███ ███

The aborted landing had not only provided an opportunity for me to give some encouragement to that young man at a time when he was struggling through a spiritual assault, but his email affirmed to me that what had occurred was precisely what I'd read about on the flight. We cannot know how that aborted landing may or may not have altered the course of the lives of the hundred or so other passengers on that flight. However, for that young man and me, it was one of those many supernatural course adjustments, most of which go unnoticed.

Had we not ascended again, we would not have had that conversation. To me and him, it was a supernatural interference that altered the natural course of events and strengthened our faith. It appeared to others as if it must be a perfectly natural occurrence like a pilot error or something in the runway. Maybe I wouldn't have noticed it if I'd not been reading *Miracles*. Just because we don't see them doesn't mean they aren't happening all around us.

That encounter with the young man planted a seed in my mind that others like him might benefit from the insight I've gained over a lifetime marked by either a continual series of supernatural course adjustments or an uncanny run of alternating bad and good luck. I have wavered at times between the two mutually exclusive perspectives, and even tried to have it both ways, but a house divided cannot stand. Luck is random and the almighty God is purposeful. Believing in one excludes the other.

My life has been an arduous but interesting and eventful race. Every obstacle throughout the course seemed to be fashioned specifically to push my limits, while preparing me for the next one that was waiting just outside my view. If I'd seen the next obstacle too soon, I'd have surely given up. As I look back over the entire course, hindsight reveals order and purpose to what seemed random and chaotic as it happened.

After overcoming the challenges of a tragic childhood followed by a lifetime of service as a marine, a state trooper, criminal investigator, and state legislator, my faith has wavered many times but never failed. The end is in sight, and the homestretch looks clear. I just need to tell the story the best that I can so that those who listen might benefit from recognizing the subtle, but powerful Unseen Hand that works in favor of those who suffer and against those who inflict suffering, deriving good from even the worst circumstances. Maybe seeing the fingerprints of that Unseen Hand in my life will help you see them better in yours.

Picking, Politicking, and Pontificating

PART I

Early Life

CHAPTER I

Welfare Case

It's normal for a mother to have an intrinsic desire to respond to the needs of her baby and to have maternal instincts to sense its needs. It's normal for a mother to have a spiritual bond with her child that is never broken. It's normal for a mother to love her children more than herself and to do without to provide for them. It's normal because it is what mothers are for.

My earliest memory is of my mother performing a normal motherly task in response to a normal babyhood need. In my mind, I can see her face and hear her cheerful chatter while she changed my messy pants. There's nothing dramatic about a mother changing her baby's pants. I don't know why I would remember that more than sixty years later, but it is a good memory and I'm glad I did. Maybe it's because so many dramatic events in my childhood commanded my attention, this one little memory sticks to remind me that despite her flaws, she loved me and cared for me. She did her best while coping with the severe mental illness that created unnecessary drama, not just for her, but also for those she loved most. We seldom appreciate that the best things are usually the ordinary.

My mother, Ethel Faulkner, the youngest of ten children, was born in Alabama in 1933 to Wayne and Velma Faulkner. Acutely poor, the Faulkners reminded me of the Ma and Pa Kettle characters from the 1940s and 1950s films, in both personality and physical characteristics. Grandma Faulkner was a strong-willed woman, while Grandpa Faulkner had a more laid back, pleasant countenance. Both were deeply religious Pentecostals, but Grandma's faith had a harsh tone while Grandpa's seemed more loving. He was small in stature but large in spirit.

Sometime around 1950, my mother met my daddy, Leldon Ball, at a tent revival and soon married him. About the same time, the Faulkners began migrating to California—like Beverly Hillbillies but with no money. My mother was left behind in Hartselle, Alabama, with my sister Linda and my daddy Leldon. She struggled to cope with the hardships and insecurity of caring for her fledgling family.

Her undiagnosed mental illness exacerbated the difficulties that surround being a young mother and wife. One day while Daddy was at work, she left home for Stockton, California, with my sister in tow. She may not have known she was pregnant with me when she fled, but a few months later I was born at the San Joaquin County Hospital near Stockton.

Neither Mother nor Daddy ever gave me a reason why she left that made any sense to me. I don't think they even knew. When either mentioned the other to me, it was with fondness, affection, and regret. I've never heard of any arguments or major disagreements between them, and nothing in the divorce she filed two years later yields a clue for her leaving. Neither she nor Daddy ever told me much about it, other than that she wasn't happy. They didn't know much about the nature of her debilitating mental illness.

As a child, I knew something about my mother made her different from others. I knew she loved me, but it never seemed that I had her full attention. It was as if her thoughts were imprisoned inside her mind, and she could only share the ones that escaped. It took a conscious effort to control her mind and make it function. She never seemed completely at ease but was always uncomfortable and restless, struggling with the simplest of tasks. She was cheerful most of the time, but something always seemed to be hidden behind her smile.

When something unexpected arose, it became especially difficult for her to settle her mind down enough to cope with it. It was as if her mind was in a race against itself, and she couldn't slow it down enough to think. It would spin faster and faster until it spun out of control, like a car with the accelerator stuck to the floor with the steering wheel locked in a sharp turn, circling faster and faster, until it spun out or ran out of gas.

Mother remarried while I was still a baby. David Brodehl couldn't have children of his own, but he was a good father to Linda and me. He had a good job at Sharpe Army Depot, a defense distribution center near Stockton, and provided a good living for the family. We lived the middle-class

American dream of the 1950s in a comfortable three-bedroom home with a big, fenced-in backyard.

Mother played a few chords on the guitar, and she loved to sing. Our best times were singing together. She self-medicated with music long before her mental illness was even diagnosed. She didn't understand the therapeutic effects on the chemistry of her brain from playing music, but she knew it helped ease her troubled mind. Music may not be a magic cure for mental illness, but it can give temporary relief to those who suffer, like my mother. Music is also an important part of a healthy spiritual regimen, like regular physical exercise and a healthy diet is for the body.

Mother's side of the family was partial to hillbilly music, and my stepdad's folks favored the Lawrence Welk style. I loved it all. My stepdad's parents were of German ancestry and had migrated to California from North Dakota. Grandma Brodehl let me bang on the piano at their house and Grandpa Brodehl occasionally played one of the harmonicas from the box under the piano bench.

Gospel hymns seemed to be everyone's favorites. I remember the smiling faces when I sang "The Old Rugged Cross" at the East Side Assembly of God. Public approval is addicting, especially for a five-year-old.

My stepdad and I explored the canal and levee behind our house, with our cocker spaniel Skippy tagging along. When someone left the back gate open and Skippy left, my heart broke. We searched for hours trying to find Skippy, with no success.

I grieved for days, until my stepdad brought home a guinea pig. The guinea pig was a poor substitute for Skippy, but at least it stopped my incessant moping. Losing Skippy was my first experience with grief. It is understandable why so many people are afraid to love. The more you love, the more intense the grief when it is gone.

One day my stepdad brought home a twenty-inch Schwinn Spitfire bicycle. It was blue with white trim and training wheels. My feet could barely touch the pedals, but before long I was riding up and down the driveway and the sidewalk. When he noticed that I was riding well, he removed the training wheels. I tried at first to get him to put them back on, but he insisted that I would like it better with the training wheels off. He held his hand on the back seat and helped me learn to ride without the training wheels. He was right, it was better. Self-improvement almost always comes by overcoming fear and taking a risk, but the fear and risk fade when we know there is an unseen hand handy to steady us and catch us if we start to fall.

My stepdad and I went to the car dealer in Stockton to pick out a car. Mother and Linda were excited when we got home with our brand new 1960 fire-engine red Seneca. He decided to try to teach Mother to drive, but it was mission impossible. She couldn't simultaneously manage all the tasks necessary to drive a car. She needed to look out the windshield and watch the road, steer the car, operate the pedals, and listen to my stepdad's instructions all at once. It was just too much.

Just sitting under the steering wheel made her panic. She would look down and watch her foot as it moved from the brake to press the accelerator, startled when the car lurched forward. Then she'd raise her head and look out the windshield but forget to keep her foot pressed on the accelerator causing the car to slow down. When she looked down at her foot to press the accelerator, the car would veer off course.

When my stepdad told her to look out the windshield, she'd panic when she saw the car was swerving out of the lane and jerk the steering wheel and overcorrect. When my stepdad told her to stop, she'd panic, look down at her foot and slam the brake. They did the routine over and over until we all agreed that some people just shouldn't drive.

Our family trips in that Dodge included Micke Grove Zoo and Pixie Woods, an enchanted forest-themed attraction with interesting and fun things for a five-year-old. Our adventures included a trip to the river for a picnic and swimming. Once, while swimming in the river, I waded out too far, barely able to keep my chin above the water with my toes stretched and barely touching bottom. I bobbed up and down and trying to use my toes to move me toward the shore but kept pushing myself in the wrong direction. I panicked went under the water and unable to get to the surface. Just when I thought I was about to drown, my stepdad's big hand grabbed my arm and pulled me to safety. It would not be the last time that I would be rescued by an unseen hand in the nick of time.

When Linda tried to tell me that he wasn't my real daddy, I argued with her and refused to believe it. She said our real daddy was a man named Leldon Ball who lived in Alabama, but I wanted no part of him. Linda made me angry when she called me Mikey Ball. I wanted to be called Mikey Brodehl. But when I started kindergarten, they called me Mikey Ball.

During my first-grade year, a foul wind blew into our idyllic home and swept the joy away. I don't know what caused it, but the atmosphere grew heavy with anger and resentment. The relationship between my mother and stepdad became confrontational, and bickering filled the once-peaceful air. When the bickering receded, sadness swept in.

When the trouble came, Linda comforted and protected me. Mother was in and out for days at a time, leaving Linda and me with our stepdad. When she left our formerly happy home, I begged to stay with my stepdad, but it was no use. We became a dysfunctional family of nomads.

I've lost count of how many different schools I attended in the second and third grades or in how many other people's homes we stayed. We stayed not only with Mother's brothers and sisters but with different acquaintances in several cities in central California. We stayed for a few months with one of my aunts in Seattle. Sometimes we'd stay for a few days, sometimes a few weeks, and other times a few months, but it was always a temporary arrangement.

Sometimes Mother might manage to rent a place of our own, but it never lasted long. Keeping her mind under control became more difficult and she had several mental crashes causing Linda and me to be left with different people for days or weeks at a time. Linda seemed to accept the situation and watched out for me as well as she could. She had remarkable emotional maturity for a child forced to grow up quickly.

During one of Mother's worst times, Linda and I were placed in a foster home. Linda got along fine with the other children, but I didn't. I was scrappy and fought with other children. One fight was bad enough that a social worker was summoned, and I was taken to another foster home out in the country.

It was the first time that I had been separated from Linda, and it was miserable. The separation lasted a few months until mother was doing better. When we got out of foster care, Mother had already rented a three-room apartment above a garage in a dodgy neighborhood. She had also acquired a live-in boyfriend who didn't care much for me or Linda. I think he thought of us as intruders. He had a "tough guy" air that I've since learned to associate with men who frequently find their way to prison. Once Mother called my Uncle Wayne to get the boyfriend to leave. When Uncle Wayne arrived, the boyfriend went after him with a butcher knife, and the fight was on.

The apartment was trashed, and Uncle Wayne worked him over pretty well, managing to take the knife from him with only a cut on his shirt. Uncle Wayne had always seemed friendly and easy-going. Until that day I had no idea what a beast he could be, but he was a good beast. When the police came and took the creep away, Mother fell apart. Again.

At that time, I was an eight-year-old urchin with a knack for mischief, including vandalism, petty theft, and fights. One day, a group of us was playing along the railroad tracks when I got the idea that it might be fun to chuck rocks at cars from the railroad overpass above East Harding Way. Linda tried to talk me out of it, but I was determined. We were breaking windshields of cars passing beneath the overpass when the police showed up. I got away, but Linda, who hadn't thrown any rocks and had tried to talk us out of it, gave herself up. Being a good girl, she ratted me out.

When Linda came riding up in the back of police car, I was already home, sitting on the couch watching TV and acting like nothing had happened. It pushed Mother over the edge and she had another nervous breakdown. When the ambulance came and took her back to the hospital, Linda and I were taken to Mary Graham Hall, a facility on the campus of the San Joaquin County Hospital.

The aging, barracks-style red brick building had the look and feel of a prison, but the staff was kind, and the food was good. It might seem odd, but I liked the institutional setting better than foster homes because there didn't seem to be any favorites. I celebrated my ninth birthday there with chocolate cake.

The facility had a tall fence wrapped around the perimeter of a playground. Through the fence links, I could see people lingering on the grounds of Ward 10 of the San Joaquin County Hospital, where my mother was being detained. Every day, I strained to catch a glimpse of her and maybe get a wave, but I didn't see her again until it was time to say goodbye.

The social worker assigned to our case realized the importance of stability in a child's life and located our father in Alabama. Until then, Leldon Ball was unaware that he had a son. Although he had started a new family with a wife and a three-year-old daughter, he agreed to take custody of us. Fortunately our social worker was crafty enough not to give him too much information about me. He might have had second thoughts had he known what he was getting into.

When our social worker came to Mary Graham Hall and told Linda and me that we were going to Alabama and live with our father, I didn't want to leave Mary Graham Hall and my mother over at Ward 10. I didn't believe in Leldon Ball any more than I believed in Santa Claus. I didn't believe in anyone except Linda. She was the only one who hadn't let me down, except maybe for the time she ratted on me to the cops. Of course, that was understandable. Having a real father seemed like a fairytale, but when the case worker showed me the plane tickets, I started thinking that Leldon Ball might be real.

Our social worker took Linda and me to say goodbye to Mother before driving us to the San Francisco Airport for our flight to Birmingham. I had just turned nine, and I would not see my mother again for many years. I have struggled with conflicting feelings about her. It is difficult to love and resent someone simultaneously. I had reasons to resent her, but I also had good reasons to love her. It took a long time to overcome the resentment and learn to love and honor her as I should.

Vestiges of resentment at my mother for my dysfunctional childhood lingered for years until I began to understand the nature of the debilitating illness that afflicted her. Only then could I truly appreciate her good heart and the love she had for us. Severe mental illness didn't stop her from being a good person, but it did make it difficult for her to have loving interactive relationships. To her credit, she had a positive outlook most of the time and taught me to have one too, even under the worst circumstances, and she taught me persistence. She might have made many bad decisions that put her in many bad situations, but she managed to make the best of it,

"Happier times with my mother and sister Linda"

and she taught me to do the same. She was kind-hearted and looked for the good in others. She was not mean or vindictive, and I don't remember her ever being cruel to me or anyone else. Even when she was out of her mind, I was never afraid of her.

There is a great deal of unwarranted fear because of a lack of understanding about mental illness. Mental illness has many permutations of which only a relative few are dangerous. Learning to understand her mental illness helped me purge the resentment from my soul but I still didn't have the kind of natural love for my mother that most people seem to have. I didn't gain that until I learned many years later about her being encouraged to have an abortion when she found out that she was pregnant with me after she had left my father. She already had a three-year-old daughter, had no job and no husband, and being an unwed mother in 1954 carried a stigma that it does not carry in the twenty-first century. Although she was mentally ill and not very strong-willed, she resisted the urging to abort me.

My mother had her weaknesses and faults. Linda and I were rightly taken from her because she was legally declared to be an unfit mother. Despite that, I am grateful to her for the one decision that to me supersedes all her weaknesses and poor decisions: she chose to let me live. My gratitude for that obliterated the lingering resentment that had been a heavy load to bear.

Replacing resentment with gratitude has helped me understand the role of my difficult childhood as an integral part of preparation for a life of service. The empathy it gave me for those who are rejected and struggle to fit in later helped me fulfill my duties as a state trooper, investigator, and legislator.

It taught me that what feels bad to us is not always bad for us. It could be that what little I have achieved as an adult was not despite Ethel Faulkner being my mother, but because she was my mother, a mother who believed and taught me to believe. Commandment number five, check.

CHAPTER 2

Sweet Home Alabama

In September 1963, soon after my ninth birthday, Linda and I were greeted at the Birmingham Airport by a gaggle of newfound relatives that included Daddy, my stepmother, Claudine, my half sister, Angie, and Daddy's brother Stanley and wife Lucille and their six children. I had never seen a picture of Daddy or even been given his physical description but I immediately recognized him. The gentle warmth that glowed in his eyes reflected the love and kindness that filled his heart. It had a magnetic effect that drew me into his outstretched arms. Leldon Ball wasn't a figment of my older sister's imagination. He was very real, and the depth of his character, wisdom, and most of all, his love was outside the realm of imagination.

Our new home was a shabby little three-room house, wrapped with blueish-gray asphalt rolled-siding with pieces peeling away, covered with a tin roof. The house had a kitchen, bedroom, living room, and a shack out back that functioned as a toilet. The unfinished wood floors in the living room and bedroom and the kitchen floor were covered with worn linoleum. A coal heater in the living room ostensibly provided heat—in the winter we were almost always too hot or too cold, depending upon one's proximity to the heater. It wasn't much of a house, but it was a fine home.

The tiny house guaranteed that we were a close-knit family. Daddy and Claudine slept in the bedroom, Linda and Angie slept on a bed in the living room, and I slept on the couch. Claudine was an excellent cook and made sure that we had a full breakfast every morning and a big supper every night. We were a stable, happy family, living well in our wonderful little home.

Grandpa and Grandma Ball lived next door in a modest but much nicer house, encased in pink drop siding. They even had an indoor bathroom and a black rotary dial telephone.

If a film producer needed someone to fill the role of a sweet, rural,

Southern grandmother, Grandma Ball would have fit the bill. Her appearance reminded me of Granny Clampett from *The Beverly Hillbillies*, but not her personality. Grandma Hattie Mae Ball had the same humble spirit as Daddy. The kids in the neighborhood could count on Grandma for a drink or a snack, and if needed we could go to her for sympathy and care to make the little hurts better. She always had a dip of snuff handy in case of bee stings. She was a gentle soul most of the time, but once I did manage to her get mad. Grandma loved her flower beds, and I trampled one, destroying it. She was livid and swatted my bottom with the ruined flowers and was chewing me out good when she suddenly stopped, dropped the flimsy flowers, and went back in the house. A little while later she came outside with some delicious fried apple pie, being extra nice to me. Her eyes were red. I thought she might have been crying, and not over a few trampled flowers. I wished she wouldn't have given it another thought. I wasn't hurt, and I needed the swat. From then on, I steered clear of her flower bed. Grandma Ball was the epitome of sweetness, and I never wanted to break her heart again.

I was enrolled in the fourth grade at the Hartselle Elementary. My teacher was Miss Emily Alexander, a sweet but serious veteran educator who had been trying to retire for ten years. But she couldn't say "no" to the people who kept begging her to stay one more year (Alabama Governor Kay Ivey reminds me of her). The school year was already under way when I joined the class, but I've never had much problem with classroom work. However, I did have some behavior issues. I had a hard time staying seated at my desk and keeping quiet when I should be listening.

More than once, Miss Alexander grabbed my ear and led me by it into the cloakroom and make me sit in there alone for a few minutes until I settled down. She seldom used the paddle, but when the ear-pulling and the time out lost effect, she would use the paddle. Of course, I got paddled.

As a recent immigrant from California where corporal punishment was not applied, I was dumbfounded Miss Alexander had done such a thing. Not only were my ears and bottom sore, but my wounded ego made my temper flare. That was the final straw, I was going to tell Daddy.

When I got home from school that day, I was seething as I told Daddy what my brutal teacher had done. He listened with empathy, convincing me that he understood and was ready to set her straight. To my happy surprise, he readily agreed to call her. We went next door and used Grandpa's telephone. Daddy told me to look up her number and dial it. When the phone started ringing, I handed him the receiver, listening with anticipation as Miss Alexander was about to get her comeuppance.

Daddy began the conversation with a pleasant tone. "Miss Alexander, this is Leldon Ball, Michael told me you paddled him today and I just wanted to call and thank you. I was wondering if there might be anything that I needed to do at home. No? Well, keep up the good work and if you need me to do anything else, please let me know." I was disgusted at how he gushed as he expressed his gratitude to her for efforts with me.

It was a conspiracy. He wasn't even angry as he smirked at me while hanging up the telephone. His grin injured my pride more even more than Miss Alexander had my tender ears and stinging bottom. Sometimes love hurts.

Daddy loved to play his guitar and my stepmother Claudine loved to listen. She had bought a 1958 Gibson J-50 guitar from the Bank Street Pawn Shop with $150 that she scraped together working at a meat-packing plant. Daddy played the guitar often, strumming chords while we sang along. Simple folks love simple music, and he loved bluegrass, country, and gospel. Joyfully singing along with him was another component of our spiritual bonding.

I was fascinated by that guitar. It slept in a brown chipboard case in a corner of the bedroom. I sneaked into the bedroom almost every day and opened one of the latches so I could stick my hand inside and stroke my fingers across the strings to release that mellow Gibson tone and soothe my willing ears. Daddy eventually caught me with my hand in the case and took the big Gibson out. He sat me in the middle of the bed and let me strum it a while as he watched. Then he left it laying in the middle of the bed and told me to leave it alone.

I wanted to obey, but that big, beautiful guitar kept popping up in my mind. I just couldn't stop thinking about it. It became the object of my affectionate daydreams. I reflected upon its classic design and the mesmerizing grains of its spruce wood protected by its clear, smooth, natural finish.

I relived the feel of my hands sweeping over gentle slope of its mahogany waist and the touch of its flat mahogany back pressed against my stomach. I envisioned the six steel strings as evenly spaced power lines emerging from a hole under the bridge pin, on a journey that stretched across the bridge, above a gaping sound hole and a black rosewood track inlaid with twenty steel speed rails and seven white dots, ending their journey wrapped around their respective capstans protruding from the headstock with its distinctly Gibson shape and logo.

How could I have resisted such a temptation? It wasn't long before I began sneaking into the bedroom and sitting in the middle of the bed, strumming and desperately trying to get something out that didn't sound like noise until Daddy eventually caught me red-handed. To my surprise, he wasn't angry. It was like he had hoped I would disobey him. That was the day that I began to learn to play guitar. He showed me how to hold the pick in my right hand and where to put the fingers of my left hand. Over the next few days, I learned three chords: G, C, D. He gave me permission to play his guitar anytime, but only while sitting on the middle of the bed. This time, I obeyed. I was finally learning to play guitar, but Daddy had played me. He was a subtle genius.

The next Christmas, Santa Claus brought me a little guitar. I hadn't believed in Santa Claus in past years, but I was strongly reconsidering my decision. I could take that guitar wherever I wanted, even outside. I took it everywhere, playing my chords over and over without knowing how they related to a song. G, C, D; G, C, D; G, C, D. Eventually, Grandpa Ball taught me a song:

The Little Brown Jug

(G)Me, my wife, and a (C)bobtailed dog,
(D)Tried to cross a river on a (G)hollow log,
The log did break, and (C)we fell in,
(D)We got wet up (G)to our chins.
(G)Ha, ha, ha, (C)you and me,
(D)Little brown jug, how (G)I love thee.

Ha, ha, ha, (C)you and me,
(D)Little brown jug how (G)I love thee.

I played constantly. Linda and Angie tried to flee the incessant bombard-
ment of their eardrums from the ceaseless pounding of my guitar strings,
but I could usually find them. My stepmother didn't mind at all. Budding
musicians need people like Claudine. Although she didn't play music, she
loved it. She was the chief patron of my attempted music, the chief encourager
and co-conspirator of my musical crimes, much to the chagrin of my sisters.

I was hungry to expand my repertoire of songs. When she heard a song
she liked, she wrote the lyrics in a spiral notebook for me to learn. She
enjoyed my attempts at music, while others tolerated it. Barely. Musicians
need people like Claudine.

Uncle Duff was Grandpa's brother. He worked at the sawmill with
Daddy. He was a spry old coot with an active sense of humor. Uncle Duff
played the piano with his own inimitable style, a sort of hybrid boogie with
an odd syncopation. You couldn't listen to him play without tapping your
foot. He had a great ear and could play about any tune you want to sing,
but only if you sang in the key of B-flat.

When Angie was six, Claudine found a used piano in the want ads and
cleared out a spot for it in our crowded little house. Daddy, Uncle Duff,
Angie, and I got into the flatbed truck and drove across town to pick up
Angie's piano. After a struggle to load the piano on the flatbed, we started
home with Uncle Duff and me riding in the back to keep the piano from
shifting. When we approached downtown Hartselle, Uncle Duff couldn't
resist the opportunity to give a performance for the folks crowding the
sidewalks on a Saturday afternoon. As we rode through town on the back
of that flatbed, he rocked out with a rousing rendition of the old gospel
favorites "Keep on the Firing Line" and "I'll Fly Away." I was glad to see
the folks on the sidewalk laughing and pointing at us. It didn't occur to me
that they must have thought that we were a bunch of rubes. That would
have taken the joy out of it.

The piano became part of our family. It got a regular workout from
Daddy, Linda, Angie, and me. Angie took lessons, learned to read music,

and became quite proficient at the piano. She worked her way through college giving piano lessons and playing at events.

When we went to church, Daddy always sat in the back. Once I asked him why. He dropped his head and said, "Because I'm not worthy." At the end of every service, when the preacher asked, "With every head bowed and every eye closed, if you're not saved and want me to pray for you, would you just slip up your hand?" Daddy always raised his hand, even though

"Daddy at the piano. The little sign over his head says it all"

he believed. It puzzled me then, but not now. Daddy had faith in God, not himself.

Leldon Ball was unable to pass by a stranded motorist on the side of the road. Once we were on our way to the sawmill when he stopped his log truck to check on a man on the side of the road looking under the hood of his car. Daddy quickly figured out the problem and realized he needed a part. He bought the part at the nearby NAPA store and in a few minutes had it installed. The car started right up.

The man offered to pay but Daddy as usual refused to take the money. The more the man insisted on trying to pay, the more Daddy refused to accept it. When we were back in the truck riding to the sawmill, I asked why he wouldn't take the money. Daddy said that he didn't help people for money, he helped people because they needed help. If Daddy had taken the man's money, he would have been paid. He said by not taking the money, the Lord would pay, and the Lord pays in ways better than money.

It shouldn't matter one way or the other, but since this was in mid-1960s Alabama, it is worth mentioning that it was a black man having car trouble that day. It should serve as a reminder that during a time when Alabama was dominated by ugly politics and repressive culture there were still good people of all races trying to do as well as they could toward one another. Daddy wasn't impressed much with politics or politicians, with good reason. Lawyers didn't impress him either. For about the same reason.

I learned about his distaste for lawyers one day when we were checking in on an elderly widow from a prominent family. While Daddy listened, she asked what I wanted to be when I grew up. "A logger," was my reply.

The widow was more than ninety years old and hard of hearing. She thought I said "lawyer" and responded with approval, having had family members engaged in the practice of law. Rather than try to correct her, I went along with it. As we drove away, Daddy told me, "I don't want you to be a lawyer. Lawyers are professional liars. They twist the truth to make it help whoever pays them. It doesn't matter to me what kind of work you do, as long as you grow up to be an honest man who respects the truth." I am pretty sure my political career would have been less demanding and more successful had he not told me that.

Daddy's quiet, unpretentious strength epitomized moral fiber that comes from having a moral compass pointing in the right direction and having faith to follow it, regardless of the consequences.

Our tiny house in Hartselle became even more crowded when my half-brother Randy was born in 1965. Daddy bought five acres a few miles west of Hartselle on which to build a larger house that could accommodate his growing family. He bought the materials and paid for them as he went along because he didn't believe in debt. We did most of the work ourselves. We started working on it in 1965 and when we finally moved into it 1968, it was paid for.

At the new house, I had my own room, where Daddy let me keep his guitar—the little guitar that I had gotten that first Christmas had fallen apart from my merciless pounding. We even got a black and white television, and I could watch *The Glen Campbell Goodtime Hour* and *The Johnny Cash Show* while playing along on that Gibson.

There was more room at our new home, and we were happy. But the truth is that we were just as happy in the little three-room shack next door to Grandma and Grandpa Ball. Where you live don't matter as much as who you live with. A house is a dwelling place. A home is where love dwells, and a family is the conduit of that love. Leldon Ball might not have been impressive by most people's standards, but he understood love. That made him special. And if I could be like him, I could be special too.

CHAPTER 3

Leldon Ball

Leldon Ball and his brother Stanley owned and operated Ball Sawmill on Railroad Street in Hartselle. Like many family businesses, it was loosely organized. Uncle Stanley had the primary responsibility for the office, supplies, the log yard, and the lumber yard, while Daddy took the lead for the operation of the sawmill and most of the supervision of the workers. The sawmill operated part-time, and logging was done part-time.

Daddy was a hard worker and usually initiated what we were going to do, while Uncle Stanley seemed to be agreeable to whatever Daddy wanted. I don't remember ever seeing them have a dispute. But I'm sure they did because they were brothers.

Ball Sawmill obtained logs several ways. They purchased logs from independent loggers or bought timber on the stump and logged it themselves. Sometimes if a customer needed lumber and had a tract of timber, they contracted us to do the entire operation from cutting down the trees to delivering the lumber.

Compared to modern automated and well-equipped logging operations, our methods were quaint. Daddy cut the trees with his Homelite chainsaw. He was masterful with a chainsaw and understood every component and knew how to make them work together for peak performance. He could file an edge on chainsaw teeth that made them glide through wood like a knife through soft butter.

I loved to watch him with his chain saw in the woods. He'd approach a tree, look up toward its top, nod in the direction it was going to fall, and put the saw into it. It always fell where he nodded. I usually held a measuring stick close to the fallen tree and he cut it into logs, trimming off branches as he went. In no time, we'd have logs scattered all over the woods.

Although we had a couple of tractors, we snaked the logs out of the woods with mules because most of the time the logs could be out of woods and lined up at the log pile before a path could be cleared for the tractor. I was fascinated by the Farmall B-series tractor that he kept at the sawmill. It was once bright red, but time had faded it into dingy pink. I drove that old tractor around the sawmill yard for hours. Daddy had warned me not to go past third gear, but I tend to push boundaries. It wasn't long before it was in fourth gear and running wide open. Eventually, I ran it in the ditch and messed up the front end. My disobedience got me a whipping.

During the first year or two with my daddy, I got lots of whippings. I understand why some folks might frown on such a thing, but he was not a violent or abusive man. I earned every whipping, and he never struck me in anger. He didn't punish me immediately; instead, he talked to me

Grandma and Grandpa Ball with my Daddy and Uncle Stanley. They didn't know it, but about this same time, I was born in California.

about whatever I had done and why it was not acceptable. He wasn't as concerned about punishment or wielding his authority as much as making sure I understood his moral code.

Sometimes he told me that I would get a whipping before bedtime. I would be on my best behavior the rest of the day while I thought about what I had done and whatever lesson he was teaching me. He often "forgot" about the whipping by bedtime. Other times, he remembered but talked about it some more, sometime accompanied by a story about one of his experiences, letting me off the hook if he thought the moral lesson was soaking in. He never said "This hurts me more than it does you," but it was true. I could see it in his eyes. Nothing hurt me worse than seeing disappointment in his eyes.

My cousin Jimmy and I snaked the logs out of the woods with our mules, Ella and Ida. I worked Ella, and Jimmy worked Ida. Ella was old, and Ida was in her prime. Ida was bigger and much stronger than Ella. Ella was docile and was easy to ride, while Ida was defiant. She wouldn't put up with anyone sitting on her back. Trying to sit on her back would be a mistake.

Despite the disparity in size and age, Ella could work circles around Ida. She knew how to snake logs. Once she saw where we wanted the logs piled, she didn't need to be driven, because she knew what needed to be done and seemed committed to doing it as expeditiously as possible. All I had to do was hook the tongs in the end of a log and give her the "giddyup" and she could navigate the most efficient course to the log pile. She watched ahead while she was pulling a log. If she saw an obstacle ahead, she sometimes stopped and gave some thought for a few moments before efficiently and sometimes creatively maneuvering the log past it. When she got to the log pile, she lined the log up alongside the others and patiently waited until I got there to unhook the log. That old mule had an uncanny understanding of leverage and motion. Most of the time, we were both better off if I stayed out of her way. If my help was needed, she let me know by staring at me.

Ida required constant attention and working her was a struggle. Usually, it's not the biggest, strongest, or proudest ones that accomplish the most. It's those who approach tasks with a cooperative mindset.

To load the logs, we used a side loader truck that had two long arms attached to its left side. The arms lowered down to the ground, the logs were rolled onto the arms, and the driver could pull a lever causing the arms to lift, pitching the log onto the truck. After he cut the trees, Daddy loaded the truck while we were snaking the logs up to the pile. Then Daddy and I hauled them to the sawmill.

In mid-August of 1969, Daddy and I had hauled a load of oak logs to the sawmill from a tract of timber off Huckaby Bridge Road outside of Hartselle. We had unloaded the right half of the load and needed to pull the truck forward so we could unload the other half of the logs. As I pulled forward, the left rear wheels dropped into a depression in the ground causing the half-loaded truck to flip over with me in it.

It was a few seconds before I climbed out from the passenger-door window which was now the top of the truck. When I popped my head out the window, I saw Daddy running toward the truck. When he saw me, he stopped running and put his hands on his knees for a moment with a sigh of relief. He hurried over and helped me crawl out. He wrapped his powerful arms around me with a powerful hug and said he loved me. Being a teenager, I was embarrassed.

Our little sawmill operation was nothing like modern sawmills. Sawmilling is almost entirely automated nowadays. We were low-tech. Our sawmill was situated under an open shed about twenty-five feet wide and seventy-five feet long. Uncle Stanley used our homemade forklift converted from an old GMC ton-and-a-half truck to feed logs onto skids situated at one end of the shed. The logs waited on the skids until the log turner was ready to roll one onto the six-wheel carriage that ran along tracks. The log turner rolled the log onto the carriage with his cant hook—a wood handle with a moveable hook attached near the end of it. The longer the handle, the more leverage a worker had. The sawyer and the log turner secured the log with hooks attached to the carriage.

The log was then ready to be sawed. The sawyer pulled a long metal lever jutting from the front of the carriage to determine how much the log moved toward him which determined the desired width of wood to be sliced from the log. With his left hand, the sawyer operated the wooden handle that controlled the motion of the carriage. When the sawyer pulled the wooden handle, the carriage carried the log headfirst in the forty-inch diameter circular head saw spinning toward it. The head saw bit into the log, peeling off a slab of bark on the first cut and rough-edged planks on subsequent cuts.

When the sawyer was ready for the log to be turned, he would signal the log turner with his right hand as he pushed the wooden handle forward to bring the carriage backward. When the carriage returned, the sawyer and log turner removed the hooks from the half-moon shaped log while the sawyer unhooked the front one. The log turner then twisted the log until the flat side of the log was resting against the carriage. The log turner held the half-moon shaped log in place while the sawyer secured the log to the carriage with the front hook. The log turner then finished securing the log by sinking the two rear hooks into it.

The first cut into the half-moon shaped log sliced off another slab. Subsequent cuts sliced a few more planks and the process repeated, until the sawyer determined that the log was the desired thickness. He pushed a lever on the ground with his foot as the carriage returned causing the log, now flat on two sides, to fall flat on the carriage. It was once again secured with the hooks. Several more cuts were made until the log, now with three flat sides and one slab left, was turned a final time.

The edger operator took the rough-edged planks as they fell off the head saw and fed them into his edger, a machine with two saws inside. The edger trimmed the rough edges off the plank and fed it to off-bearers. The slabs and lumber were sent down rollers to the off-bearers, who loaded it on trucks or stacked it for later removal. It was a six-person operation.

In the summertime, Uncle Stanley's sons and I made up most of the crew. When I first started working at the sawmill, I usually worked as an off bearer. I didn't care for the job because it put me at the opposite end of the sawmill shed from my hero and we didn't get to interact except at lunch or on breaks. By the time I was a teenager, I convinced Daddy that I was big enough to turn logs. He never stopped teaching, and I learned something new from him every day we were together.

On the morning of Wednesday, August 27, we ate breakfast, got in the truck, and headed to the sawmill. I knew my time with him was running out since school started the following week. On the way to the sawmill, we stopped by the store and gassed up the truck. While I stood beside him while the pump was running, it occurred to me how much I would miss him when school started.

I fought back a strong urge to hug him. I was nearly fifteen and didn't want him thinking I was a kid. What if someone I knew drove by and saw me hugging my daddy? When we got back in the truck on the way to the sawmill, that same urge to hug him lingered until after we got to the sawmill and started sawing.

We sawed all morning until lunch time. As we sat on the ground talking while we ate our sausage and biscuits, Daddy told us that he had a dream the night before and Grandma visited him. She had died the previous year of breast cancer. Leldon Ball was a powerful man, but he was also a mama's boy. They stayed close until she died. It hurt to feel him grieve as she helplessly withered away. He said he had a dream the night before and she seemed so real it seemed like he was awake while stood at the foot of his bed while they talked. He said it was good to see her again, but I thought it sounded creepy to be visited by someone dead, regardless how much he loved her when she was alive.

After lunch, we went back to work, and I rolled the first log on the carriage. The huge white oak log was a monster, bigger than a ninety-pound teenager could handle alone. Daddy grabbed a hook and we strained together, struggling until it rolled onto the carriage. While he made the first couple of cuts, I sat on the middle skid and rested with our longest-handled cant hook beside me. I knew that the first turn on a log was the hardest and that white oak log was about as big as our sawmill could handle. It was going to be tough to turn.

While I was resting on the skid, Daddy shouted at me as I was struck on the back of my head by a flying board and knocked to the ground. When I got up, I saw Daddy lying in the sawdust with blood oozing from his ear. I walked across the carriage tracks to the water faucet and stuck my face under the water and then back to my daddy, but he hadn't moved.

When Daddy had made a cut into the log and brought the carriage back while I sat on the skid, the freshly cut board fell onto the spinning head saw.

Seeing the danger, he instinctively turned to me, instead of moving out of danger. As he shouted to get my attention, the spinning head saw picked up the board and hurtled it toward us. The board ripped through the air, striking him full force on the left side of his head, killing him instantly. The board continued its destructive path toward the back of the shed, brushing the back of my head as it passed.

When we are in danger, we do not think as we would under normal circumstances. Think is probably not even the right word for it. Under normal circumstances, we make decisions; but when we are in extreme danger, we don't make decisions, we have reactions. Our reactions never lie. They reveal what we fear most. They reveal who we really are, instead of who we wish we were, or who we want people to think we are.

When he saw danger, Daddy was more concerned for me than himself, and he paid for it with his life. His reaction proved that he loved me more than he loved himself. I can't be certain, but if he had gotten out of the way, it is likely he would have lived and I would have died. My life has been lived thinking each breath, every day has been a precious gift. It would be ungrateful to squander such an expensive gift. There have been many times when Daddy has awakened from his special resting place within my memory as I have started down a wrong path or struggled with a moral decision. He has helped me prioritize. He has never been far away. I regret fighting off the urge to get one last hug that morning.

A huge crowd showed up at Peck Funeral Home for visitation to pay their respects to Leldon Ball. The following day there seemed to be an endless line of cars in the procession to Bethel Baptist Church for the funeral. Our family sat in the section reserved in the center aisle near the front of the packed church as a few songs were sung and the preacher spoke. I don't remember the songs or the words the preacher spoke, but I vividly remember something else.

When the preacher finished, the funeral directors began to prepare for the final viewing. While we waited, a deputy walked down the aisle from the doors in the back of the church and told my stepmother that some colored people had gathered outside and wanted to pay their last respects. He asked if she would be offended if they came inside for the final viewing.

Claudine seemed to be stunned by the question as she told the deputy they had as much right to be inside as anyone and welcomed them.

About forty blacks had been excluded from entering the church because of the foolish customs of the time. When they filed past my daddy's casket, many with tears streaming down their cheeks, I noticed one looked like the man whose car Daddy had repaired on the side of the road a year or so before. Their presence made a lasting impression on me because I knew they had stood outside in the hot August sun for the duration of the service to say goodbye to a man who was a friend to all who crossed his path. They had endured the indignity to say goodbye to Leldon Ball because they knew what I knew about the man in the casket. They recognized greatness.

He would not have had an impressive resume. He didn't meet many of the standards that people usually use to measure greatness. He didn't have much money, education, or fame. But those are not the standard for greatness. That standard was set by Jesus when he responded to his disciples who were disputing among themselves which was the greatest. He took a pan, filled it with water, and began to wash their feet as he taught that those who serve others are the greatest in God's kingdoms. Leldon Ball washed lots of feet but scrubbed mine.

Fifty years that have passed since his departure, and I've been told by some who knew my daddy that I remind them of him. I hope so, because Leldon Ball was a great man.

CHAPTER 4

Surrender

With Daddy gone, it seemed like God abandoned our family. Grandpa Ball just gave up. He was still struggling with the loss of Grandma Ball the previous year. Losing his youngest son sent him further into a downward spiral until he went to the hospital and decided it was his time to go.

His real name was Zackey Mackery Ball, but everybody called him Mack. Daddy taught me how to live, but grandpa taught me a lot about how to think. I thought he was a genius. I still do. Though he only completed second grade, his wit and wisdom more than compensated for the lack of formal education. He was a sharecropper until he started logging and sawmilling. By the time that I met him, he was semi-retired and working part-time as a timber estimator for a wood products company.

Nearly thirty years after Grandpa died, I visited the owner of that company while campaigning. He reminded me how Grandpa would nonchalantly stroll through a tract of timber, telling stories and engaging in chitchat without writing anything down. After the stroll, he was always amazed that Grandpa could tell him how many board feet of pine or hardwood would come out of each section with amazing accuracy. The owner of that company thought Grandpa was a genius, too. He made a generous contribution to my campaign, probably with the hope that some of the genius might have travelled down the bloodline. Sorry to disappoint.

During the good times before Daddy died, I usually found Grandpa sitting in the shade of the three big water oak trees in the yard between our houses. I've been told that Grandpa was once a powerful preacher, but by the time I met him he was more of a philosopher who hardly ever went to church. I'm not sure why he lost interest in church, but he never lost interest in the Word. He spent his lifetime reading the Bible and pondering over it. He had much of it memorized. He loved to discuss it, explain it, and contemplate over it. He savored it like a connoisseur of fine wine.

He spent hours sitting under the shade trees with his Bible, the newspaper, or a magazine beside his rocking chair, although I seldom saw him reading anything. Soon after I'd arrived in Alabama, I noticed that he spent an inordinate amount of time just sitting in his chair. He called it studying. He studied a lot. Mulling things over. Thinking things through. Trying to derive meaning. Studying everything, especially the Bible. He was a creative thinker who relished the Bible and could extract deep meaning from every word.

He was delighted when I asked him to teach me about the Bible. He began with the first five verses of the Gospel of John: "In the beginning was the Word, and the Word was with God, and the Word was God. The same was in the beginning with God. All things were made by him; and without him was not anything made that was made. In him was life, and the life was the light of men. The light shineth in darkness, and the darkness comprehended it not."

We spent hours and days discussing that one passage of scripture, and I was fascinated by how much information he could glean from so few words. He taught me that God, the Word, and Truth are interchangeable because they are the same. When we search for truth, what we are truly searching for is God. And vice versa.

Grandpa was full of insight and wit. "A man with a watch always knows what time it is, but a man with two watches is never sure" and "A woman can throw more out the back door with a teaspoon than a man can shovel in the front door with a scoop" are two examples of his sayings that immediately come to mind. Some of my friends jokingly refer to some of the things I say as "Ballisms." I should probably attribute most of those nuggets to Grandpa Ball, but since he gave them to me, they're mine now.

Other old men from the neighborhood often dropped by and joined him under the shade trees. I listened intently as they shared stories and discussed news events. But no matter where the conversation started, it always eventually gravitated to the Bible. Once they got on the Bible that's where the conversation stayed. They dissected it, analyzed it, and debated it. It would go on for hours, sometimes lasting until bedtime. Back then, children were not supposed to interrupt when adults were talking. Sometimes I wanted to join in, but I wouldn't dare interrupt.

I remember a Jehovah's Witness randomly came by once and struck up a conversation about the Bible with Grandpa. It ended a couple of hours later with the hapless visitor fleeing, his mind tied in knots by scripture-based logic and reason. He seemed to have a way of doing that with most theology. He just couldn't seem to settle into any singular dogma. He loved to explore them, but they all eventually led him into a blind alley, and he'd wind up right back where he started with me at the first verse of John's Gospel: "In the beginning was the Word. . ." It is an endless loop, like an old 8-track tape. All the roads seem to start there. The question of every doctrine seemed to be which route it takes before it winds up back where it started.

When Grandma died, Grandpa's light began to dim. After Daddy died, his light flickered out. His cause of death was never determined, but I knew he died from a broken heart. I knew it because I had one, too. But Grandpa was sixty-five years old and I'd just turned fifteen. What he loved most was on the other side; so, in December 1969 he just willed himself to death. I guess that the Lord decided that Grandpa had done what he was supposed to do and could come on home. Grandpa had run his race, but I was barely in the starting blocks.

Uncle Stanley kept the sawmill, but I don't think his heart was in it without his brother. Stanley and Leldon were not just brothers and business partners, they were best friends. Uncle Stanley just didn't seem to be whole after Daddy died.

My stepmother Claudine never remarried. The idea of her loving any man other than my daddy was as absurd to her as it was to the rest of us. My sister Linda got married and left home a couple of months after Daddy died; and Claudine was left with me, my nine-year-old half-sister, Angie, and my four-year-old half-brother, Randy. She went to work on an assembly line at an auto parts manufacturing plant in Decatur. Claudine's mother moved in the house to help her take care of Angie and Randy. I didn't feel like I belonged anywhere. With Daddy gone, I was a rudderless vessel, adrift and alone.

There are interesting theories about how we struggle through psychological trauma and stages of grief. A psychologist might describe what I experienced during the weeks that followed my father's death as post-traumatic stress disorder or a severe depression. Since I'm not a psychologist, I don't know how to classify it, and the sorrow and despair that engulfed me are beyond description. It is a miserable darkness filled with helplessness and hopelessness from which there seems to be no escape.

It is understandable to those who have suffered in such a spiritual condition how suicide presents itself as a reasonable option. I was alone in my room in that condition desperately searching for another option when a glimmer of hope emerged. I started talking to it and hurling confrontational questions at it.

If you're there, why are you cruel? Why did you take away the person I loved and depended upon more than anyone else? What do you get out of all this suffering? Is it something I've done to make you hate me? How can you be good and allow such bad things to happen? Are you real or just something desperate people believe in to make them feel better? The last thing I needed was another false hope.

Power struggles create confrontation. I was trying to engage in a power struggle with something I didn't understand.

It led me to recall I once didn't believe Leldon Ball existed, and he turned out to be real. What if this glimmer of hope that I'm trying to communicate with is my father, too? The thought caused the bitterness, resentment, and self-pity that had threatened to overrun my soul to recede. I began to think of the glimmer of hope as I would my real father. I tried to negotiate.

Back then, I didn't know much about negotiation. My "demands" were reasonable. I wanted to be like most other people with a "normal" life, a good job, a home, and a family who I can love and will love me in return. I wasn't asking for anything that had not been given to almost everyone else I knew. I could not understand why I seemed to keep getting a raw deal.

I didn't realize the futility of negotiating from a position of weakness. Either Grandpa forgot to tell me that God only accepts unconditional surrender, or he told me and I forgot. The response was a silence that flooded my mind with doubt. I was unaware God always listens, but seldom, if ever, responds overtly and immediately to demands.

Most of the Lord's work is done discreetly, like a background computer app. But the work continues, nonetheless, according to His purpose. We are usually oblivious to it, although we can see its effects if we know what to look for and how to look for it. My struggles were part of a process of preparation for a life of service that would require empathy for those who suffer and simultaneous indignation toward those who cause the suffering.

But first, I was at a crossroads and had to make a choice. I had to decide if I was going to believe in a Creator who had divine plans or if I was going to do it alone. There was no preacher or Bible scholar to share a passage of scripture with me and walk me through it. Although I was physically alone in my room, I believe there was something else that guided me through a decision.

There was more desperation than faith that compelled me to pray, "Lord, if you are there and listening, I've told you what I want; but if you've got something else for me, please let me know and I'll do that. I give up. I don't want to fight you because I can't win. Do with me what you will, just let me know."

At the time I didn't know if my prayer had been heard or answered, but surrendering to that glimmer of hope gave me immediate relief from the pain. I didn't get immediate answers, but I didn't have anything else to believe in. Surrender wasn't a very tough choice for me because I didn't have to give up anything but resentment, bitterness, and self-pity.

During the fifty years that have transpired since that surrender, that glimmer of hope has continually expanded my awareness of it as I have witnessed it work in a manner that is usually subtle, sometimes overpowering, but always uniquely creative and never completely predictable. It has continued to reassure me that it heard the desperate prayer of fifteen-year-old Mike Ball and accepted that surrender, but not on my terms. My request for a normal life was denied. It's just as well; a normal life would have been boring.

CHAPTER 5

Daddy's Guitar

When Daddy died, Claudine gave me his guitar. In the years that followed, it went wherever I did. Despite being badly mistreated, it remained a faithful friend that comforted and entertained me through difficult teenage years, an enlistment in the Marine Corps, and a stint in Birmingham as an Alabama State Trooper. By the time I transferred home to Hartselle in 1982, the Gibson was in dreadful disrepair.

The once-beautiful natural spruce top had been scratched and banged. It was bucked up, and string tension had almost separated the bridge from it, rendering it almost unplayable because the strings were so far from the fretboard. When I did pick it up, the mellow Gibson tone that had captivated me as a child had departed. It was like a corpse with no soul.

I was barely making ends meet as young trooper with a family during difficult economic times, struggling to pay a home mortgage with a 15 percent prime interest rate (and that was with good credit). That old beat-up guitar became worthless clutter to me, so I decided to sell it. I didn't understand its true value was not its function but what it represented. But Hack Ward knew its worth.

During my teenage vagabond years, my closest friends were my music friends. I often stayed with their families, and they treated me like family. Steve Ward was one of those music friends, and his father Hack became the the role model and mentor that I had been missing. He might have as much influence on my tutelage as my daddy. Although they've both passed on, I've never stopped seeking their approval and shunning their scorn. Neither man made criticisms or gave compliments casually, but they didn't need to; I could see it in their eyes. The standards they lived by have become the standards that I've aspired to follow.

They were different from each other in some superficial ways, but very

The old Gibson still makes a sweet sound.

similar in the ways that matter most. Daddy was more tender on the outside and tough on the inside, while Hack was more tough on the outside and tender on the inside. But they both had a knack for being appropriately tough or tender, depending on the circumstance. Both epitomized manhood as it should be. In some ways, the bond that Hack and I had was even closer than that of a father and son. Hack was my mentor. Fathering and mentoring are two very different things, and one of the greatest differences is choice. A man can choose to be a father, but a boy doesn't choose to be a son. The relationship between a mentor and a protégé is one of mutual consent.

During my teenage years, I lived in a room over a storage building behind Hack's house. Hack was a roofer, and he gave me the opportunity to work for him carrying shingles. When he first offered me the job, it was doubtful whether I could do it. I was no stranger to serious physical labor, but when he hired me, I barely weighed a hundred pounds and wasn't strong enough to carry an eighty-pound bundle of shingles up a ladder. I couldn't keep up at first because I had to break up the bundles and make extra trips up the ladder. But Hack helped me and gave me encouragement, confident that I was putting forth my best effort. Hack respected grit and determination, and as long as he saw an honest effort, he was patient. I was soon running up the ladder with two bundles at a time.

I'm sure there are those who believe that a young boy performing strenuous physical labor is cruel, but that wasn't the case at all. Although working alongside these men was physically exhausting, it was spiritually uplifting. Both men were great teachers who taught me not only how to work but how to be a man. Recognizing the intrinsic value of work is an integral part of manhood as they knew it. They were hard-working men who respected others willing to do the same, with little use for those who considered themselves above it. To them, manual labor was honorable, a standard that seems archaic by today's standards.

I managed to graduate high school, but college for someone in my situation seemed to be a bridge way too far. Hack and I discussed my options for the future. Although I worked for him, he encouraged me to explore whatever opportunities might arise, as long as I was "bettering myself." He minimized risks by assuring me that if I tried something that didn't work out,

I always had a home and a job with him. A veteran of the Korean War, Hack suggested that a military enlistment might be a good step. As I considered which branch of service that I should enlist in, several friends suggested that I avoid the Marine Corps because it was too tough and I was too little. That's probably the main reason I joined. I needed to prove myself to me.

In February 1973, I entered boot camp at Parris Island with self-doubt and trepidation. However, the following May, I graduated boot camp with a meritorious promotion and newly discovered self-confidence. There's something about earning the title "Marine" that puts swagger in your step. The Marine Corps satisfied my need to be part of something bigger than myself. It seemed to be a perfect fit for an undersized misfit like me about to enter manhood and needing to sow some wild oats. Although I went on quite a few deployments with fighter squadrons from the Marine Corps Air Station in Beaufort, South Carolina, I "swooped" home to Hartselle frequently.

As the end of my four-year enlistment approached, I knew that a military career was not for me. I had been a good Marine, earning the rank of Sergeant and a good conduct medal, but I couldn't seem to get over my homesickness. I yearned for a normal life, with a family and a home of my own. I didn't want to be a nomad; I wanted roots. I wanted to go home, work with Hack in his roofing business, and play music in his band on weekends.

A few weeks before my enlistment ended, I read in the local newspaper that the courts had ruled the height and weight restrictions for the Alabama State Troopers unconstitutional. On a whim, I decided to apply, and without any preparation, I took the written examination. I'm still not exactly sure why I took the test, since I didn't really have a desire for a career in law enforcement, but most likely I did it for the same reason that I joined the Marines: to see if I could cut it. Had I not gained the confidence one gets from being a Marine, I wouldn't have had the self-confidence necessary for me to even consider the possibility of becoming a state trooper. But Marines tend to believe they can do anything.

I was content roofing and playing music with Hack and had forgotten about taking the test until several months later when I was notified that I had one of the top scores. After passing the physical examination and background checks, I was scheduled to report to the Alabama State Trooper Academy in Selma on July 5, 1978. As that day approached, I began to doubt whether a law enforcement career was something that I wanted to do. I had met my wife soon after getting out of the Marines and had gotten married only a few months earlier. I was just beginning to settle down and was reluctant to spend four months away from my new bride at the trooper academy and, after that, move to another part of the state.

At 5'4" and 120 pounds I didn't exactly fit the image of a stereotypical Alabama State Trooper. I began to doubt. Maybe I wasn't suited to be a trooper, and this wouldn't be a career that suited me. I wasn't the type. I didn't much care for cops, anyway. But the truth was that I was afraid I couldn't do it. Hack wouldn't have any of my doubt. He reminded me of what I had already been through and how I struggled to get those bundles of shingles up the ladder when I first started working with him. He insisted that I shouldn't pass up a good career opportunity, and if I didn't at least give it a try I would always regret it. I had doubts, but Hack did not. My desire to live up to Hack's expectations supplied the motivation, and his assurance that I could do it supplied the confidence. And his guarantee that I was always welcome to come back minimized my fear of failure. He didn't let me chicken out. He kicked me out of the nest, and I flew the coop. As usual, Hack was right.

The Alabama State Troopers has evolved a great deal in the years since tarnishing themselves on Bloody Sunday at Edmund Pettus Bridge. During the 1970s it was not known to be an organization accepting of people who were. . .different. From its inception in 1935 until 1972 the Alabama Department of Public Safety had refused to hire a single black trooper and only then when they were forced to do so by the legendary U.S. District Judge Frank Johnson. Judge Johnson eventually ordered that at least one black trooper be hired for each white trooper hired until the force was 25 percent black.

In a lesser-known ruling, handed down in 1976, Judge Johnson ruled that minimum height and weight restrictions of the state troopers were unconstitutionally discriminatory against women and should be abolished. In the face of the litigation, the Department of Public Safety didn't hire another trooper class until July 1978. Although one of Judge Johnson's rulings worked against me because of skin tone, the other cracked the door open for me. I doubt that a white male was the intended beneficiary of the litigation, but it worked out that way. I was hired to be a trooper, an unintended consequence of the removal of unreasonably discriminatory and arbitrary barriers to opportunity based on a superficial, politically motivated policy. Regardless of the intention of the litigants, I am grateful to Judge Johnson for both rulings; one provided the opportunity for me to serve, while the other did the same for many of my future friends.

Being fresh out of the Marines, the trooper academy was a breeze and soon after I reported for duty at the Birmingham State Trooper Post as the smallest Alabama State Trooper ever, it became apparent that what I lacked in physical stature could be compensated for by wits, guile, and determination. After a successful four-year stint as a state trooper in Birmingham, I was able to transfer home to Hartselle and built a house next door to Hack. That was when I decided to sell my daddy's old beat-up guitar.

When I told Hack that I'd decided to sell the guitar, hoping he might help me find someone who might be interested in buying it, he was obviously displeased. He reminded me that it was my daddy's guitar and selling it would be a mistake that I would regret. But I thought I knew better. I was no longer Hack's apprentice, eager to learn from my mentor. I had been successful as a Marine and was now a veteran state trooper, respected in the local community. My self-doubt had been replaced by something much worse: hubris. I ignored Hack's advice and decided to sell Daddy's guitar. Selling it was disrespectful to both Hack and Daddy. I should have known better, but I believed the money was more important, like many others who have sold their soul for some quick cash.

I found a buyer willing to pay $150 for that old messed up guitar that had become worthless to me. Soon after I sold it, the money was gone, and I realized Hack was right, as usual. Even though I had other guitars that sounded much better and were easier to play, regret swept over me. I'd betrayed an old friend for $150, selling out the memory of the man who'd given his life for me. I'd sold part of my soul and it sold cheap.

For months, I grieved over it and tried not to think about it, but my mind's eye kept conjuring up the memory of my daddy letting me sit in the middle of the bed and strum it while his big hands gently placed the fingers of my left hand on the fretboard in the proper position as he showed me my first chords. In my mind, I could hear the chords ringing from that beautiful guitar as we sang simple old gospel tunes together. Remembering our time together revived the love that I had for it and deepened my regret.

When I got a little older and Daddy let me play it whenever I wanted, he warned me over and over to take care of it and I'd dishonored him over and over by neglecting it, and finally selling it. I'd let it get wet, wound the strings too tight, and just generally banged it around. Instead of fixing it or at least keeping it close, I sold my birthright. It really wasn't even mine to sell—it was his. I expressed my regrets to Hack and apologized for ignoring him. I'd dishonored him, too. I wished I'd have listened, but what's done is done. Usually.

About a year after I sold the guitar, I got a phone call from James Gipson, a sweet old gentleman I'd picked with many times. He said that he had traded for an old Gibson that might have belonged to my daddy and asked if I was interested in buying it. Someone had tried to fix it, but it was still in disrepair. It didn't have that sweet Gibson tone like it did when my daddy strummed it, but I didn't care how it sounded or whether it was playable as long as we were together.

I asked Mr. Gipson how much he wanted for it. I would have taken a second mortgage on my house regardless of the exorbitant interest rates at the time. He could have gotten much more but he only set the ransom at $150, a paltry sum for a second chance. Hack was pleased, because it isn't often that we get such a clear opportunity to undo what we've done wrong. He didn't seem very surprised that I had gotten the guitar back. I suspect that he could have been behind Mr. Gipson's call.

For the next twenty years or so, the old guitar wasn't played much. It just rested on the couch most of the time to keep the dogs from jumping on it. But it was out in the open where I could see it and know it was always there. Sometimes I'd pick it up and try to play it, but it was still in bad shape. I thought that its playing days were over until October 2013, when I got the urge to get it fixed. My favorite guitar aficionado, Doyle Bradley, knew someone who might be able to restore it and gave me the number for Chris Bozung in Fairview, Tennessee, a master luthier and maker of top-notch, high-end CB guitars. When I called him, I knew he was the doctor I could trust to heal my loved one.

The following Saturday morning, Leldon (I named the guitar after my daddy) and I made the 120-mile trek to Fairview and met Chris in the work-shop attached to his house. I asked him to do what he could to make it play and sound as good as possible and he assured me that he could bring it back to life. He had a kind, humble manner, but he also had the confidence of a master craftsman. I drove back home and soon forgot about it, distracted by my preparation for the upcoming legislative session and an obsession with helping others get healing for their loved ones by passing Carly's Law.

About five months later, I was struggling through the most difficult period of the Carly's Law saga and was almost ready to give up, when Chris Bozung called and told me that the guitar was ready. He apologized for the time it had taken due to a life-threatening medical issue. From the tone of his voice I knew that he was pleased with his work, making me eager to pick it up. A true craftsman's satisfaction is derived from a search for perfection. Satisfaction increases the closer they get. The feeling of satisfaction is as much a reward as the money. Of course, the money is how we express our gratitude for their talent and effort. It allows them to continue their quest for perfection. I couldn't wait to get to Fairview for the reunion.

When I put the address in my GPS for the two-hour drive to Bozung's workshop, it took me on a different route than before. As I approached from the opposite direction, I noticed a log yard and a sawmill obscured by a big metal building across the street from Bozung's workshop. The sawmill was buzzing away. I don't know how I hadn't noticed the sawmill months before when I delivered the guitar. It goes to show how different things appear when we approach them from different perspectives.

The smell of fresh-cut white oak dust wafting into my nostrils reminded me of the last day that I saw my daddy alive. I sensed the presence of my daddy in my car as we pulled into the workshop driveway, grateful for the six years that I was given to be by his side in this world. I stayed in the car and savored the moment, knowing it had been a long time since I had felt so close to him. The realization came over me that he has never been very far away; it was me that had wandered away. My urge to hug him returned to me. I'd have done it this time, but I didn't know where to hug. He was with the Lord and the Lord was everywhere.

When I went inside, the master craftsman was glad to see me as he laid the guitar case on a worktable. He stepped back to watch as I opened the case and saw that the formerly warped, battered, and scarred guitar had been transformed by his hands into a thing of beauty. I stroked my fingers across the strings, and the sweet tone that flowed into the ears of a nine-year-old urchin had returned. I lifted the wooden masterpiece from its resting place and held it close to my belly and laid the fingers of my left hand on the fretboard while the pick in the fingers of my right summoned sweet tones from the depths of the belly of my old friend.

It played and sounded even better than I remembered. The sight, touch, and smell of the beautiful wood warmed my heart while the mellow tone emanating from it soothed my ears. My delight gave the luthier delight. Nothing brings fulfillment like knowing that you've been given a unique talent and you have developed it and applied it in a way that helps someone else.

It was an uplifting spiritual experience, impeccably timed by the Greatest Craftsman of all. This all happened at a time that I was spiritually broken over what appeared to be the imminent failure of Carly's Law. As I was getting ready to leave, Bozung asked me, "Aren't you that legislator that's trying to pass that marijuana oil bill in Alabama?"

"Yes, I am," I replied.

He told me that a loved one suffered from seizures and he had been praying that we'd be successful, and Tennessee as well. "Don't ever give up," he told me. I was reminded of the scripture "The effectual, fervent prayer of a righteous man availeth much" and that there were many people like him praying for the suffering who would be helped with the passage of Carly's Law. That kind of prayer has a cumulative effect.

In January 2016, Hack's oldest son, Steve Ward, told me that his dad had been diagnosed with cancer and was only expected to live a few more weeks. Fifteen years had passed since I had moved away from Hartselle and I had only seen Hack a couple of times since, but I thought about him often. I still do. I put my guitar case in the car and headed to Hartselle. When I walked in his front door, Hack was pleased to see me. He smiled as he sat on his couch looking at the guitar case in my hand and said, "Whatcha got there?"

I opened the case and handed him the beautiful Gibson. He held it in his lap and beamed as he strummed a few chords on it. He grinned at me and said, "I tried to tell you not to sell it. You were lucky to get it back."

"I sure was," I replied with a smile, knowing full well that it wasn't luck. He had arranged for me to get the guitar back. If there was any luck involved, it was that I was lucky to have a friend like Hack. He had been an instrument in the Unseen Hands, and I am grateful that those hands converged Hack's journey and mine. I knew the same hands would soon carry him home.

We shared memories for a couple of hours, and it was obvious that his health was in rapid decline. The once powerful specimen of manhood was humbled by the wisdom that he had accumulated over his long life and not broken by the physical infirmity that was sapping his mortality from him. He didn't mention his declining health and I didn't want to risk being disrespectful by bringing it up.

Hack was not one to show fear and he was not someone who talked about his own problems. He usually seemed more concerned about others. If he was afraid, I couldn't tell it. Although the physical strength of the man that had taken me under his wing nearly fifty years before was almost gone, his spiritual strength had grown exponentially, the result of a long life of helping many others like me who had crossed his path.

As I was about to leave, Hack said that he wanted to get our old band together one more time in a week or so. I looked forward to picking with him one more time.

I put Daddy's guitar back in its case and said goodbye. As I started out the door, Hack said, "I've been following what you've been doing over the years. When I see you on the news explaining what's going on and trying to do the right things, I remember where you come from. I want to make sure you know that I am proud of you. You're a good man."

I replied that if I've turned out to be a good man, it was because he showed me what one looked like. I hurried out to the car and left. I didn't want him to see me cry. He had never said anything like that before, but he had ways of letting me know. There is nothing I can accomplish that would be more satisfying than to be the kind of person who could make Hack and Daddy proud.

A couple of weeks later, we got the old band together one more time—Hack's oldest son Steve on lead guitar, his youngest son Tim on the drums, our friend Glenn Wood on guitar, and me playing my daddy's guitar. Hack's health had declined even more since our visit. Hack sat in a chair and could barely play his bass for a couple of songs before he got too tired and had to stop and rest. The place was packed with his friends.

As I was leaving, Hack hugged me and said, "I love you, Mike. Goodbye." We both knew it was for good. A few days later when I got the word that he had died, there was peace in my heart. Parting with a loved one is heartbreaking, but much less traumatic when we can have a proper goodbye. A great movie should have a great ending, and so should a great relationship. But I'm not the Producer. I have often regretted that my father's sudden death deprived us of a proper goodbye. However, I have since learned to recognize that genuine love never dies. It is rejuvenated and resurrected by the hands of the Master luthier.

CHAPTER 6

The Littlest Trooper

A career in law enforcement was not my ambition at the end of my Marine Corps enlistment in January 1977. Roofing work and playing some music with Hack was about as far as my ambition went. Since roofers don't work much during cold weather, I decided to file for unemployment compensation until spring. But at the employment office, a recruiting poster for the Alabama State Troopers featuring a woman and a black man caught my eye, reminding me of a newspaper article I had seen about the removal of height and weight as criteria for qualifying to be hired as troopers. I wasn't part of the police culture and didn't even know anyone in law enforcement. At 5'4" and a whopping 120 pounds, I didn't exactly fit the profile. Alabama State Troopers were expected to be white, male, and big; but that recruiting poster suggested they might have relaxed the profile. On a whim, I halfheartedly turned in an application, mostly to help me qualify for unemployment compensation until roofing picked up.

The Alabama Department of Public Safety was established in 1935, but it was 1972 before the first black patrolmen were hired. Even then, it was only after being forced to do so by a federal court order. In a 1976 lawsuit, the federal court ruled that the arbitrary 5'9" height and 160-pound weight restriction was unnecessarily discriminatory against female trooper applicants. The ruling opened the door for me to become the littlest state trooper in Alabama history in July 1978, the year before they hired the first woman trooper, Clara Ziegler.

Alabama had been ground zero for the civil rights movement during the previous decade and the political battle associated with it had put the Department of Public Safety in the middle of a no-win situation. News footage of state troopers clubbing civil rights marchers at the Edmund

Pettus Bridge placed an indelible image in the collective mind of the rest of the nation and put them under a legal microscope.

The subsequent examination eventually led to a court order by Judge Frank Johnson Jr. mandating the Troopers hire blacks at a rate equal to or higher than whites until they reached a ratio consistent with the state population. As a result, the Alabama State Trooper Academy Class 78A, comprised of twenty-eight black and seventeen white candidates, represented a significant step toward correcting a past wrong. There wasn't much attention given to those who had been denied opportunities for other reasons. When it comes to discrimination, size doesn't matter, at least not in the public eye, but those who have a need to look down their nose at someone else can always find a reason.

There were skeptics when I reported to the Birmingham Post, fresh from from the trooper academy in my miniature uniform with my Smokey Bear hat draped over my head and the huge .357 Colt nestled in

Trooper
Mike Ball

the holster riding on my left hip, and I was one of them. However, my own skepticism was camouflaged by the swagger that Marines have been known to display.

One of the first people that I met in my new assignment was another Marine. Captain Robert Miller's swagger was still with him, even though it had been many years since he was discharged. When I walked down the hallway past his office, his booming voice thundered through the open door, "What in the hell is that? Get your ass in here."

"I can't believe those idiots in Montgomery are sending a runt for me to turn into a state trooper," he declared. That's probably a misquote. Although I believe the rest of the quote is accurate, "idiots" was not his exact terminology.

It was followed by a cuss-filled rant that would have made a Marine Corps drill instructor blush. Even so, there was something about him that put me at ease. I knew who was in charge, and it wasn't the first time that I'd gotten a butt-chewing for no good reason. Despite the apparent display of bluster, I was amused by his unorthodox method of sizing me up. There is something to be said for laying the cards out on the table for all to see.

His wry grin and the twinkle in his eye put me at ease and threatened to reveal his true persona when he asked, "What in hell makes you think you've got what it takes to be a trooper?"

"I don't know," I responded, "but I've got what it takes to be a pretty good Marine and a roofer. I doubt this will be tougher than that, but it won't take long before we will know."

The tough old Captain's belly laugh signaled that he approved of my response. By today's standards of political correctness, some might judge Captain Miller with disdain, but it is unfair to pass judgment on others without putting forth the effort to understand their perspective and the entire context surrounding their comments. Of course, it's much easier and more self-satisfying to shame, blame, and put a derogatory label on those who make us uncomfortable in any way, but all we gain from it is a false sense of superiority.

Despite his crusty deportment, Captain Miller was no bully. Cussing was just his preferred method of communication. I never sensed an ounce of meanness in it, and he didn't cuss around ladies, children, or strangers. He cussed when he was at ease with men he liked. He must have really liked me.

He was a lot like Hack and my daddy, although their language was less colorful; they were throwbacks to the generation that survived the Great Depression and two world wars. He was a Marine who had served in the Pacific during World War II, making the cycle from Private to Sergeant and back again several times. It shouldn't be surprising that Bear Bryant was one of his closest friends and he served many years as the beloved coach's trooper escort. From what I gather Coach Bryant was also cut from the mold of men who had the wisdom to distinguish trivial slights from what really matters.

It is important to note that those who bring out our best aren't always nice to us. Good mentors are straightforward and blunt, but without malice or contempt. They acquired their wisdom through their own struggles, and it motivates them to try to share their life lessons with younger people with similar obstacles. They admire underdogs and can't resist helping, but without coddling.

Fearing that it might be perceived as a weakness, they struggle to keep their tender hearts hidden, but their empathy is what distinguishes them from bullies whose predatory egos feed on a steady diet of bending and breaking those they perceive as weak. Great mentors help the weak learn to be strong.

Being a roofer and a Marine wasn't enough to guarantee that I'd be a successful trooper. Compared to the Parris Island, the physical demands of the trooper academy had been a breeze. During the seventeen weeks between July 5 and October 25, 1978, I had been fed the basic information that a state trooper needed to know about things such as state and federal law, how to do the paperwork, pursuit driving, firearms, first aid, investigation, and use of force.

Academy training helped me understand the letter of the law and department policy, but it was learning to implement the department motto, "Courtesy, Service, Protection," that integrated the lessons my daddy taught me into my state trooper persona. The troopers assigned to me as training officers, Bill Bailey, Ray Wilemon, and George Bassett, taught me that law enforcement was about much more than making arrests. It was about treating people respectfully, serving justice by protecting the innocent, and trying to save lives by promoting safety.

It wasn't long before I was all alone working the graveyard shift from 11 p.m. to 7 a.m. covering five counties. With only four troopers working the entire state of Alabama after 11 p.m. and an obsolete radio system that didn't integrate well with local agencies, available backup was nothing more than a fantasy. There's no way that I'd have done it if I hadn't been fresh out of the Marine Corps and unaware of my mortality.

During one of those long, lonely shifts, I stopped a drunk driver who claimed to be one of Captain Miller's fishing buddies. After thoroughly frisking him and making sure to ask if he had a weapon, I helped him into the back seat of my patrol car and started to the Jefferson County Jail. On the way to jail he told me I was going to catch hell from Captain Miller for arresting him. I decided to find out.

"Maybe you should give Captain Miller a call when we get to the jail. If he tells me to let you go before you're booked in, I'd probably do it," I offered.

By the time we got to the jail, my intoxicated prisoner was convinced that calling his fishing buddy at 3 a.m. was just the thing to do. At my request, the jailer permitted him to use the telephone before I booked him in. I dialed Captain Miller's home number and handed the receiver to his "friend" and stepped back.

I listened from a few feet away as the man explained his plight to my boss. In just a few moments, Captain Miller was wide awake and in rare form. I should probably be ashamed to confess how I enjoyed seeing the surprise on the face of my hapless victim as he held the telephone receiver an arm's length away from his ear while the captain had an early morning conniption.

After a few minutes, the captain's "friend" handed the receiver to me saying, "I don't think he's going to help me. He wants to talk to you."

I fought back an urge to snicker while feigning innocence as I humbly accepted my well-deserved butt chewing. I've heard lots of cussing and even done it more than a little bit myself, but Captain Miller's exposition of salty language that morning was the pinnacle of perfection. My position as one of his favorite troopers was obviously safe.

People can be apprehensive and easily agitated when they're stopped by police, especially if they've had a bit too much alcohol or other issues. A friendly smile and a calm demeanor can usually de-escalate the tension that naturally rises when someone sees flashing blue lights in their rearview mirror. It's also a useful way to make a few quick preliminary assessments. A friendly countenance conveys to most people a signal that they are not likely to be treated harshly or unfairly. Getting a ticket or being arrested is bad enough; there's no reason to add to it by being harsh or uncaring. Motorists usually said "thank you" to me as I handed them a ticket.

You never know how being nice can pay off. There's one time it sure did, after I stopped a swerving automobile and discovered the driver had consumed too much alcohol. After inviting him out of his car, I frisked him and helped him take a seat in the back of my patrol car. I seldom handcuffed folks during routine arrests, since reaching for the handcuffs was more likely to garner resistance than just sitting in the back seat. I figured that if I frisked them thoroughly, there wasn't much harm they could do in the back seat with the cage up and no rear door handles.

After a thirty-minute ride to the Jefferson County Jail filled with friendly chitchat, we pulled into the sallyport and exited the patrol car. As we walked toward the elevator that would take us to the jail on the ninth floor, I stopped at the gun locker and pulled my Smith and Wesson Model 19 revolver from its holster, prompting my friendly prisoner to ask, "Do you want me to put mine in there, too?"

"Good idea," I responded, while doing my best to hide the butt-puckering cringe I felt before asking, "Where is it?"

"In my back pocket," he said.

I took the small .25 automatic from his back pocket and asked, "Why didn't you tell me when I frisked you?"

"You didn't ask," he replied.

It's been said that the Lord looks out for fools and drunks. I don't know if that's always the case, but it was certainly true for this fool and that drunk that night. It's just another one of the countless times the grim reaper could have easily taken me if it had been my time. Law enforcement is serious work, but taking the duty seriously and taking oneself too seriously are two very different things. I am grateful that divine providence has allowed me to look back at it and laugh.

In addition to the "regular" patrol work, my first few years as a trooper seemed to be filled with natural disasters, civil disturbances, swat team operations, street fights, and manhunts. Wherever there was trouble, I had a knack for getting in the middle of it. But there is one incident that I have relived over and over in my mind.

On June 9, 1979, a line of several hundred Alabama State Troopers in full riot gear stood in the center of Lee Street in Decatur. Their comportment that day was a clear display of the progress the Alabama Department of Public Safety had made during the nearly fifteen years that had passed since the fiasco on the Edmund Pettus Bridge. It would have been easy to spot the littlest trooper standing in the middle of the blue line, wearing a riot helmet with "Atom Ant" emblazoned across the back.

On one side of the blue line was a loud group of demonstrators supporting Tommy Lee Hines, a mentally retarded black man who had been charged with rape and robbery a year earlier. On the other side of the line was a much smaller but equally loud group of demonstrators dressed in the white robes of the Ku Klux Klan.

The spiritual atmosphere was polluted by the contempt that had accumulated in Decatur, exacerbated by the arrest of Tommy Lee Hines during the previous year. As the stench emitted by torrents of hatred flowing between the opposing forces permeated my spiritual senses, it occurred to me that each side had been feeding the other. I aware of the dynamics of intrinsic mimetic desires, collective passions, or scapegoating and how that interaction has shaped history, and that day I could certainly feel it in the air.

There appears to be no way to know for certain whether he was the perpetrator or not, but those who really knew Tommy Lee Hines had plenty of good reasons to question the veracity of accusation and, after that, the fairness of the process. It was apparent to them that investigators had taken advantage of Hines's lack of cognitive ability and used him as a convenient scapegoat to blame for someone else's crime. Those who knew him best did not believe he had the mental capacity to perform the actions the assailant had been reported to have done during the commission of the crime.

Unfortunately, the authorities charged with investigating the crime knew little about Tommy Lee Hines before May 23, 1978, when a woman reported that a black man had peered into the window of the Morgan County Press Building. A series of sexual assaults had recently occurred in the area, prompting the police to sweep the vicinity looking for the man who looked in the window, hoping to make a connection with the perpetrator of the sexual assaults.

An officer located Tommy Lee Hines at a manufacturing company across the street filling out a job application. He was taken to the Morgan County Press Building where he was identified as the man who had peeked in the window earlier. He also fit the very general physical description of the perpetrator of the serious crimes that the police were rightfully focused upon.

They had been busy collecting evidence, interviewing victims and witnesses, and searching for a suspect who would be the missing piece of the puzzle they were trying to put together. It all went sideways because the responding officer didn't seem to have known enough about his suspect when he began interrogating him about the sexual assaults. Tommy Lee Hines perfectly matched the profile of the black man who peered in the window at the Morgan County Press Association but not the man who had committed the sexual assaults that had occurred at another time and place.

There is a great deal of misunderstanding about profiling. It is not evidence and shouldn't be considered as such; but if properly used in its proper context, it is an investigative tool that should be as useful in shifting suspicion away from the innocent as it is in moving it toward the guilty. Had Tommy Lee Hines been properly profiled before he was interrogated about the sexual assaults, it would have turned out very differently.

Instead, Hines was hastily arrested and charged with a crime he probably didn't commit, and those who recognized that Tommy Lee Hines did not match the psychological profile of the rapist police had sought were stunned and outraged. A rally was held the following week with about five hundred supporters in attendance.

Unfortunately, when passions burn hot, justice usually turns cold. Although it brought a great deal of attention to his plight, it may have done Tommy Lee Hines more harm than good by provoking the headstrong Morgan County district attorney to dig in deeper. Lawyers and politicians tend to be adversarial and competitive, focusing more on procedure, personality, and politics than truth. That's why it is important the truth be foremost in the minds of police throughout the entire course of an investigation. The truth doesn't always reveal itself immediately.

Seeking truth forces us to be receptive to new evidence even when it makes us rethink our previously drawn conclusions. Truth-seeking humbles us by forcing us to recognize how little we know. It is unfortunate that the further a case progresses through the justice system, the dominance of procedure over truth increases. It is much less humbling to be proven wrong before an arrest is made.

Newton's third law of gravity, "For every action, there is an equal and opposite reaction," might be more applicable to human behavior than physics. The outrage expressed by the protesters convinced of Tommy Lee Hines's innocence didn't just encourage an equal and opposite reaction by law enforcement; it was not long before the ensuing media circus presented an opportunity for right-wing political extremists to generate interest in their movement. Soon after the demonstrations proclaiming Tommy Lee Hines's innocence began, white-hooded Klan members began counter-demonstrating.

The hostility between the opposing forces had been escalating for an entire year when gunfire erupted between some of Hines's supporters and Klan members on the streets of Decatur on May 26, 1979. On a hot summer day a few short weeks after the shoot-out, wearing full riot gear in the middle of a storm of hatred and contempt, I pondered the question, "How can we resist evil without allowing it to turn us evil?"

The question is simple, but the answer is not. Searching for the answer to that question and struggling to hone it to perfection in practice has been the catalyst that has forced my faith to grow from that day to this.

In 1982, after four very active years in Birmingham as a state trooper, I was grateful to get the opportunity to transfer home to Morgan County. By then, it was apparent that size didn't matter as much as folks might think, at least not as far as law enforcement is concerned.

Other than an occasional drunk that might look at me and get the mistaken impression that he could fight his way out of a trip to jail and a few wisecracks about things such as police uniforms in children's sizes, it hardly ever came up. Nothing silences skeptics like performance.

Barbara Estes was former high school classmates from Hartselle and a radio dispatcher at the Decatur State Trooper Post. After I transferred home, she made a cross-stitch for me that I've kept on the wall ever since: an old Texas Rangers' motto that says, "A little man can whip a big man every time, if the little man is in the right and he keeps a' coming."

Being an undersized trooper came in handy in early 1984 when I was summoned from routine patrol to an underground cave on Burningtree Mountain where two spelunking teenagers were surprised by a sudden rainstorm that flooded water into the cave that they were exploring. One of the teenagers managed to escape and summon help for his friend who was trapped deep underground in a narrow crevice with water rushing in on him.

From left, Trooper Mike Ball, Sgt. Mickey Carwile, Trooper Dale Adams, and Chief Deputy Paul Cain.

When I arrived, fellow trooper Dale Adams and Morgan County Chief Deputy Paul Cain were standing beside a large hole in the ground with a rope that led deep underground where Army Reserve Sergeant Mickey Carwile had located the stranded caver. Trooper Adams and Chief Cain were both too large to squeeze through the narrow openings to get to the spot where the slimmer Sergeant Carwile was unsuccessfully attempting to pull the stranded caver out.

I stripped down to my pants and undershirt in the freezing rain and lowered myself into the hole with freezing water gushing over me. Being a little guy, I was able to get even closer to the trapped teenager than Sgt. Carwile and together we pulled him through the narrow opening by the rope tied under his armpits, while icy water continued to pour onto us from above. The teenager, Sgt. Carwile, and I were freezing, drenched, and elated when we emerged from that miserable crater together.

Anyhow, I wasn't the littlest trooper in Alabama very long. Others even smaller than me were soon hired, like Agatha Windsor. She was one of the first women troopers in Alabama and was assigned to the Decatur Post, where the Tommy Lee Hines debacle had occurred. In addition to her gender and diminutive stature, she was also black. Even though Agatha typified the stereotypical trooper of the day even less than I did, she was a consummate professional.

Working a shift with Agatha was a joyful experience. She was smart, brave, and had a great sense of humor, but her faith was what really made her a special friend to me. It enlivened her and her attitude projected it.

We had a good laugh upon learning that some of the local teenagers who she'd ticketed referred to her as "the Black Widow," a clear reference to the bite she was capable of. She was tough when it was necessary, but her true nature was to be warm, friendly, caring, and helpful to others. Agatha changed some hearts and minds by the way she faced her skeptics. She did not let them define who she was by confronting them on their level. She knew how to control the battlefield by controlling herself. Her temperament was the embodiment of her faith.

One incident reminds me of her faith and temperament. We were standing together with other law enforcement officers in the back of a packed courtroom when one of her cases was called. It was an older man, visibly angry that she had given him a speeding ticket. He did not dispute the charge but told the judge that he didn't think that a white man should have to pay a ticket she wrote, referring to Agatha with a derogatory racial epithet. His words inflamed me, and I started down the aisle toward the front of the courtroom. Agatha caught me about halfway to the front and grabbed me by my arm. She said, "I'm okay. That doesn't hurt me. He doesn't know any better. Let the judge take care of it." We returned to our place in the back of the courtroom and she was right. The judge handled it in an appropriate manner, but the Lord's response was better.

A few weeks later, the same man was seriously injured in a traffic accident in which his car was struck by another that had run a stop sign. As fate would have it, the driver of the other car was a young black man and Trooper Agatha Windsor was dispatched to the scene. As you might expect, she conducted the investigation as if she had never seen the man before, in a manner indicative of a polished professional; but she also did something that you would probably not expect. Agatha became an instrument in the hands of the Lord who loved the bitter old man. She allowed herself to be part of a plan to melt his crusty old heart and change his narrow stubborn mind.

I would have loved to have seen the look on his face when he realized that the black woman who had been the object of his scorn in open court was the same state trooper investigating his wreck. He must have been surprised at her calm, friendly tone as she proficiently conducted the investigation; but I don't think it was her professionalism that melted his brittle heart. I believe that it was the genuine compassion that she had for the bitter old man suffering from the injuries he had received in the wreck. He was admitted to the hospital and Agatha made several visits. They even struck up a friendship.

A few years later, after Agatha transferred to Montgomery on her successful path up the ranks, I was eating lunch in a restaurant in Falkville, the tiny town where the old man lived, when the waitress asked me about Agatha. She said he ate regularly at the restaurant and wasn't shy about sharing his admiration for Trooper Agatha Windsor. The waitress said that the old man was her biggest fan. She made a profound impression on him, and he believed she was the best trooper that ever wore a badge. I don't know if he was right about that, but it is possible. What I do know is that Agatha was a true believer who put her faith into practice.

Caring for those who hate us is counterintuitive to our human nature, but its effects can be remarkable. Our natural impulse is to strike out with hurt and anger at those who say and do hurtful things, but hating those who hate us turns us into what they are. If our actions are nothing more than in-kind reaction to evil, hatred controls us and we become part of it.

Fighting off the contempt that would control us and resisting the temptation to seek immediate vengeance demonstrates that our faith is in the Lord and not in ourselves. It is not easy to do and we all sometimes fail; however, continued effort can produce remarkable results.

In his autobiography, Dr. Martin Luther King recounts his own struggle to control his anger. He could have easily justified his animosity after being threatened, attacked, jailed by local authorities, harassed by the feds, criticized by religious leaders, and even condemned by some other civil rights activists who favored more aggressive and violent means of resistance. He knew that if he did not control his anger, the anger would control him. By learning to control his own anger, he was given the grace necessary to mitigate the anger of more militant factions that would have undermined the civil rights movement with violence.

Dr. King knew that his battle was not against any of those individuals, but against what the Bible refers to as "principalities, powers, rulers of the darkness of this world, and spiritual wickedness in high places." His battle was the same one we face daily, just on a different scale.

An eternal battle rages between good and evil that continually forces us to choose the side we are fighting on by the spiritual weapons we use. Bullies use bitterness, resentment, and brute force, like Goliath. But believers use truth and grace in tandem, like David used his sling and the stone, with the stone being truth and the sling being grace. By an experienced user, grace is the delivery device that gives truth power and meaning.

One of my favorite examples of such a practitioner of the spiritual power of truth and grace in tandem is James Meredith. After serving nine years in the Air Force, he applied for admission to the segregated University of

Mississippi in 1961 but was denied admission because of his race. Believing it to be his divine calling, he re-applied and was again denied. After prevailing in the federal courts, Meredith became the first black to be enrolled at Ole Miss. He kept his composure in the face of harassment, isolation, and other indignities until graduation.

Unlike some of the other civil rights efforts of that period, his were not part of any coordinated effort or any organization but the result of one man's commitment to doing the next right thing. In 1966, Meredith again demonstrated the power of his faith when he decided to embark on a solo 220-mile march from Memphis, Tennessee, to Jackson, Mississippi. His faith and courage inspired many thousands to peaceably resist those who would deny an entire race their opportunity to live as equal citizens under the law.

Resisting evil is that simple. Being in the right isn't about choosing sides. It is doing the right thing, the right way, at the right time, for the right reason. Getting all of that right without divine guidance is more than can be expected from mere humans. But with divine guidance, it is not only possible, it is likely. It all begins with having the wisdom to know we need it.

CHAPTER 7

Justice Denied

I was ten days away from trading my trooper uniform for a coat and tie as an agent of the Alabama Bureau of Investigation on June 5, 1986, when I was dispatched to a wreck at the intersection of Vaughn Bridge Road and Forrest Chapel Road in rural Morgan County. The final wreck I would investigate as a highway patrolman would alter the course of my life and ultimately draw me into the political arena.

When I arrived on the scene of the crash, emergency responders were already preparing to transport the injured to the Hartselle Hospital. A Flint police officer was standing beside a belligerent man sitting on the ground beside his wrecked car, angrily cursing the woman who had driven the car that he said had struck him. Investigation later revealed that he had been fleeing a burglary less than a mile away when he barreled through the stop sign and broadsided the woman who was now the object of his contempt.

It was a hot summer day in Alabama, and I could feel the coolness of three unopened cans of Stroh's Light beer on the driver's side floorboard of his car and three more unopened cans in a twenty-four-pack carton on the passenger side floorboard. It was subsequently learned that several leftover cans in the pack of Stroh's Light beer had been among the items taken in the burglary. In the trunk of the man's car were other items taken from the burglary including several rolls of coins labeled with the name and address of the burglary victim, a VCR, some video cassettes, a radiotelephone labeled with the phone number of the burglary victim, and a 35mm camera in a case. In the glove box of the angry man's car was a gold band ring in a blue jewelry box. All the items were later identified as having been taken in the burglary that day.

After I finished working the scene, I went to the hospital where the woman and her five-week-old infant son were undergoing treatment for severe injuries. The baby died in the emergency room and the injuries sustained by the mother plague her to this day. The burglar that ran the stop sign and caused the crash continued to cuss his victim in the emergency room, separated from her only by a curtain. When the injured woman's husband heard it, he started going after the man who had just killed his baby.

While stopping the grief-stricken father from taking justice in his own hands, I assured him that a thorough investigation would be done and promised justice would be served according to the facts and the law. At my words, I saw his anger turn into anguish as his attention shifted from scorn for the man who had caused this tragedy to compassion for his suffering wife and grief for their dead son.

The thief was charged with murder and first-degree burglary a few days later. The Morgan County district attorney recused himself from the case because he had represented the accused in a previous case. The burglar was a career criminal with over fifteen prior felony convictions and was quite adept at manipulating the legal system to his benefit. Johnny Wayne Campbell was as much or even more of a lawyer than most of the attorneys that had been appointed to represent him. I can't blame the district attorney for avoiding him; the Morgan County circuit judges did the same thing, and a supernumerary judge from another county was brought in to handle the case.

The Alabama Attorney General's Office assigned Geri Grant to prosecute the case, and she executed her duty superbly. After a solid presentation of compelling evidence, she summed it up with a favorite scripture of mine: "The wicked flee when no man pursues: but the righteous are bold as a lion," Proverbs 28:1.

The jury was clearly convinced and convicted the man of murder and first-degree burglary. His extensive criminal history mandated that visiting judge sentence him to life without parole. The Alabama Court of Criminal Appeals unanimously upheld the conviction, but on September 21, 1990, the Alabama Supreme Court overturned the verdict, citing insufficient evidence to prove the burglar was in immediate flight from his crime at the time of the collision, when he blew through the stop sign and killed the baby.

Patrick Jordan Smith in his father's arms.

The decision was not only shocking to the victim and her family, but it stunned me, too. It made no sense. It seemed obvious to the jury and anyone else with common sense that the circumstances were there to prove immediate flight beyond a reasonable doubt. The proximity of the crash to the burglary, the direction of travel, and the stolen items found in his car were all circumstances that pointed toward flight from the burglary. The decision downplayed testimony that he busted through the stop sign at a greater speed than the woman with the right of way, which is certainly evidence of immediate flight.

I believe the still-cool cans from a twenty-four-pack of Stroh's Lite beer, stolen from the refrigerator during the burglary and found in the burglar's car in the middle of a hot summer day, were an important link establishing immediate flight and likely a key factor in leading the jury to its verdict. Either the Alabama Supreme Court made an arbitrary decision to overturn the jury without proper consideration of the totality of the circumstances, or there was something else I couldn't see.

Under our system of governance, the law is what the Supreme Court says it is, whether we like it or not. As an agent of the Alabama Bureau of Investigation actively working criminal cases, I couldn't enforce the law without understanding it. I was under the impression that the jury's duty was to determine the facts and the judge's duty was to decide the law, but the ruling seemed to belie that concept.

The reasoning used by the Supreme Court that either legally or morally justified ignoring the totality of the evidence and that disregarded the jury's verdict eluded me. I could not fathom how evidence which seemed to fit so tightly when taken in its entirety by the jury and almost everyone else familiar with the case could have been overlooked by the learned justices of the Alabama Supreme Court. But amateurs often see what experts can't, especially if the experts are lawyers. Being mostly adversarial thinkers, lawyers tend to get bogged down in details that can dilute, distort, or camouflage the truth. They can hide a forest with trees, and Supreme Court Justices are lawyers.

The broken promise to the father of little Patrick Jordan Smith morally obligated me to at least provide the victim's family a reasonable explanation for why it was broken. The prosecutor from the Attorney General's Office, Geri Grant, seemed to be as flummoxed by the ruling as I was. The most plausible explanation I could find for the ruling came from a lady who worked for one of the Supreme Court Justices. She suggested that the Justices of the Supreme Court probably overrode the jury's verdict because they considered two mandatory sentences of life without parole to be too harsh for a traffic fatality, which had the ring of truth. Whether a judicial activist mindset triggered their personal bias to override the law or they simply failed to consider the facts of the case properly when they disregarded the jury's verdict, it still looked like a miscarriage of justice to me.

I've never found a reasonable explanation for Campbell's immediate release and probably never will, but I've learned a lot by trying to unload the weight of that moral obligation from my shoulders. One of those lessons is that the promise I expressed that day wasn't mine alone. The promise that justice is served according to the facts and the law is a collective promise that all who serve within our criminal justice system are duty-bound to uphold. Without commitment to it at every step in the process, from the first police officer on the scene to the highest court in the land, the promise is impossible to fulfill.

Law enforcement is more than just a game of cops and robbers. The fundamental purpose of the law is to provide structure in a civilized society and to protect the innocent and weak from oppressive bullies. This case seemed to fit that mold perfectly. A callous criminal had devastated an innocent family. The injured mother was the epitome of sweetness, a kindergarten teacher who was loved and admired by all who knew her. What is the point of even having law if it doesn't work in a case such as this?

In theory, Lady Justice wears a blindfold; but the reality is that she peeks more often than we care to admit. She peeks when the system is corrupted, and nothing corrupts the justice system more than politics. Judges are not only lawyers—whether they are elected or appointed, judges are also politicians, and the resultant adversarial mindset from this double whammy adds difficulty to their duty to keep the judicial system from being corrupted. The more a judge can constrain their personal bias and resist the urge to peek through the blindfold, the more ethical that judge is.

Before the emergence of Reagan-era Republicans, statewide elections to the Alabama Supreme Court had mostly been low-key political groups within the Alabama Democratic Party. By the time the fateful decision was made to reverse this case in 1990, the political winds had begun to shift in favor of Republicans across the South and were already intensifying. Politics is like weather, perpetually causing subtle changes to the landscape, but dramatic changes are usually the result of the tumultuous and chaotic storms that periodically sweep through and turn weak deteriorating structures into debris.

Although my personal political sympathies gravitated toward Reagan- and Bush-era Republicans, I was more of a political pragmatist than an ideologue. That ruling piqued my interest in the effect of political forces on the judicial process and was a major factor that swept me into the world of politics.

I began to participate in partisan political campaigns during my off-duty time, particularly in those of judicial candidates who I believed were more inclined to rule according to what the law says than what they wanted it to say. My goal was to find judges who would turn off their political switches and see themselves more as referees than political players.

When political activism and criminal justice are co-mingled, both are corrupted, as are those who allow it to happen. I was careful to avoid mixing criminal investigation with political activity not only because it was morally wrong, but also because it was strictly prohibited by department policy and state law. One statute that particularly concerned me plainly stated, "Any person who attempts to use his or her official authority or position for the purpose of influencing the vote or political action of any person shall be guilty, upon conviction, of a Class C felony."

My efforts to atone for the broken promise to that family by exercising my rights as a citizen would be futile if I broke the law I was sworn to uphold. Mixing political activity and official duty is like mixing vinegar and bleach: Separately, they are stable, but when combined, they become toxic. I was wary to keep politics out of my investigations and my investigations out of my politics. Years later, I would be shocked to witness the degree to which law enforcement authority can be abused by the politically ambitious and how the justice system works to keep it hidden.

One of my favorite quotes, made by one of my least favorite philosophers, hung on the wall of my office at the Alabama Bureau of Investigation throughout my tenure. It simply stated, "Whoever fights monsters should see to it that in the process he does not become a monster. And if you gaze long enough into an abyss, the abyss will gaze back into you." As a state trooper, criminal investigator, and legislator, I've gazed into the abyss way too many times.

Of all the evil I've witnessed, the most stunning is that which is done by those who think they are doing good. It is easy to believe that fighting a villain automatically makes us a hero, but when self-righteousness creeps in, the tables are turned. By doing the right thing the wrong way, would-be heroes become villains and the villains they are fighting become their victims.

The adoration of heroes and scapegoating of villains is the driving force in the world of adversarial politics. That driving force also interferes with our ability to discern truth. Unfortunately, the same thing causes the truth to get lost within our adversarial judicial process. We are all human, capable of heroic or villainous acts in varying proportion, whose motives only God knows and only God can perfectly judge.

However, our judicial system relies on imperfect human judges, susceptible to having their decisions corrupted by the arrogance of power and often fueled by pride, prejudice, and political expediency. A major reason I was drawn into the political world was my belief that arrogance of power fueled the judicial activist attitude behind the Alabama Supreme Court decision that denied justice to little Patrick Jordan Smith.

I became convinced of the necessity to replace activist judges with more conservative judges who might be more likely to follow the law and the facts more objectively. Political changes already underway in Alabama promised to do that, and I wanted to be part of it.

PART 2

Politics

CHAPTER 8

Delusional Heroes

In July1986, I became an agent with the Alabama Bureau of Investigation (ABI), the investigative division of the Alabama State Troopers. I usually described it as a state version of the FBI but with a Southern accent, fewer resources, and less bureaucracy. Most of the casework was initiated by requests from other law enforcement agencies, either because a potential conflict of interest called for an independent investigation or because an agency might lack resources or expertise to tackle certain types of difficult or complex cases. There seemed to always be plenty to do, including background investigations, criminal intelligence, security details, hostage negotiation, and special inquiry investigations of public officials. If that wasn't enough, we also initiated our own investigations.

Criminal investigation has probably been fictionalized much more than most professions because each case is a little drama where the protagonist detective tries to uncover a hidden truth that brings a crisis, potential crisis, or dilemma to a successful conclusion. It is a humbling occupation that stretches the faculties, requiring a creative thinker who is patient, persistent, and dedicated to due process and the truth.

Danny Thornton was a Morgan County sheriff's investigator who didn't seem to be humbled by it at all. I first met him a few weeks after I joined ABI while working on my first murder case. I was called to a scene where an unidentified, badly mutilated, decomposing body had been discovered in a ditch along the side of a rural road. The sheriff recognized that this case was suitable for ABI to investigate and could bolster his under-staffed investigative division that barely managed its regular flood of domestic crimes, thefts, and smoking-gun cases.

Thinking is the most important part of investigative work, and an investigator's mind is his most valuable tool. They are puzzle masters who collect the pieces and fit them together until the truth emerges. Whodunit murder cases with an unidentified body are among the most difficult puzzles to solve, and they often remain unsolved without a "lucky" break, usually the result of a major effort by investigators who put their full attention to finding it.

Calling on the ABI not only gave the case a better opportunity to be solved, but it was also politically advantageous for the elected sheriff to shift blame if the case couldn't be solved. If we solve it, the sheriff gets the good press because the ABI was a low-profile organization and usually yielded its camera time to the originating agency, unlike our federal counterparts. We were an intentionally non-political organization.

With great effort and lots of help from the Huntsville Police Department in neighboring Madison County over the following weeks, we identified the victim as a drug addict with a lengthy criminal record who had been murdered and mutilated by a drug dealer with a violent temper and little patience for delinquent payments for his product.

Investigator Thornton did not seem pleased that ABI had been assigned the case and was largely absent from our effort, ostensibly pursuing his own avenues of investigation which seemed to amount to nothing. I tried to keep him up to date with the leads as we developed them, but he didn't seem interested in a cooperative effort and instead closely guarded the few leads he came up with, claiming he needed to protect his sources. Had the sheriff not called us, I have no doubt that the "secret agent" would have never solved the case.

I wouldn't have been able to solve it by myself either, but one of the first lessons I learned as an investigator was that sharing information is how we gain information. By sharing the information with veteran Huntsville Police Detectives Howard Turner, Bud Parker, and Wayne Sharp, they held my hand and we put it together.

Less than a year after working that case, a Decatur police officer reported to ABI that Thornton had approached him about forming a vigilante squad to assassinate people who he deemed to have evaded justice. It seemed the errant detective had watched too many Clint Eastwood and Charles Bronson vigilante movies and had gotten carried away by Don Pendleton's *Executioner* action book series.

The officer told us that Thornton was plotting to approach the loved ones of crime victims with an offer to knock off the prime suspect for a fee. The report seemed too outlandish to be true at first. Thornton tried to come across as a tough guy, but I thought of him more as a "wannabe," a harmless blowhard—all hat and no cattle.

I didn't doubt the credibility of the police officer making the report, but I doubted that Thornton would have been serious about a bizarre vigilante murder-for-hire scheme. My initial thought was that Thornton had probably taken his Walter Mitty-like fantasies a bit too far, but we decided to initiate an investigation and play it out, just to be safe. We invited our friends from the FBI to join us with their manpower, surveillance equipment, and expertise. The police officer who Thornton had approached posed as a willing triggerman and played along with Thornton's elaborate scheme to bring his hero fantasy to life.

Thornton identified prime suspects from several unsolved case files and located victims' loved ones who might be willing and able to pay for some extrajudicial retribution. We recorded several conversations of Thornton bloviating to his "triggerman" about details of his bellicose scheme. He loved to hear himself talk and brought his closest friend on board, a Morgan County jailer that had previously served with him as a police officer in Burleson, Texas. As far as I could tell, the hapless jailer's role in the scheme was minimal, mostly serving as the self-aggrandizing hero's fawning sidekick who had completely bought into the counterfeit paladin's fantasy come to life. Narcissists need fawning admirers.

While under surveillance, the leader of the hapless hit squad reached out to several family members of the crime victims offering speedy "justice" for a fee. Had he gone through with the harebrained scheme, any "justice" dispensed to the guilty would have been overwhelmingly negated by the execution of the suspects who have since been proven innocent of the crimes that the self-righteous avenger had decided to adjudicate. We approached one of the people our avenger had previously contacted, a man whose daughter was harassed by his former son-in-law. The former son-in-law had been charged with reckless endangerment of his infant child and false imprisonment of his ex-wife. They asked the man to play along with the aspiring avenger who had offered to eliminate his problem expeditiously for $5,000.

The concerned father accepted Thornton's offer while under surveillance and the wannabe widow-maker arranged to receive the payment in cash while watching *The Untouchables* inside a movie theater in a Decatur mall. When he left the theater with the $5,000 payment to commit the murder, the wannabe "untouchable" was touched by state and federal authorities.

Like almost every other public official that goes bad, Danny Thornton was corrupted by ego more than greed. His overblown self-image caused him to identify with the wrong heroes, fictional characters known for meting out their own justice like "Dirty Harry" Callahan and "The Executioner" Mack Bolan. When we begin to believe we are either worthy or qualified to be the ultimate arbiter of justice, it is a warning sign that we are trespassing into God's territory, and that is dangerous ground for mortals.

On April 23, 1999, I was called to a mobile home in rural Lawrence County where a severely mentally ill man was holed up, threatening to kill his three-year-old son with a sword. I arrived at the scene ahead of the SWAT team and spoke to the man's mother who lived nearby. She told me that her son had been suffering from mental illness for many years, but his condition had grown progressively worse since he had recently begun obsessively reading the Bible. The whole family had grown terrified of him, and the child's mother had fled several days before.

She allowed me to set up my hostage negotiation equipment in her dining room about fifty yards from the mobile home where the endangered child was being held, and soon I was on the phone establishing rapport with the man and further assessing the situation. Almost every hostage negotiation or crisis intervention begins with an attempt to deescalate the emotional level with persistently soothing language. Fruitful negotiation cannot even begin until emotions are brought down.

When our conversation began, I was pleasantly surprised to discover he didn't seem to be the raging madman I was expecting. He was soft spoken, polite, and lucid. The nonconfrontational tone of our conversation gave me hope that this situation would be easily resolved. That hope quickly dissipated as our dialogue continued and I began to comprehend his delusion.

Negotiation is the attempt to resolve a conflict between opposing desires. For the hostage negotiator, the release of the hostage unharmed is nonnegotiable, but almost always negotiable for the hostage-taker, regardless of suicidal ideation. However, in this case, the safe release of the man's young son was nonnegotiable for him, too. Bible study from his delusional perspective led him to believe that he was the "Chosen One."

My initial hope that we might find some common ground that would lead to the release of his son was dashed when we agreed to pray together about it. The magnitude of the gulf between our drastically differing perspective became clear when I began my prayer with "Dear Lord," and he stopped me. What he did then was more pronouncement than a prayer, along the lines of "I am the Lord of Hosts, and my will must be done."

His debilitation had tricked him into believing he was the "Chosen One" depicted in the book of Revelation, destined to open the seventh seal and initiate the apocalypse. But first, he had decided it was necessary to prove himself worthy by presenting his son as a blood sacrifice to complete what Abraham started. He was convinced that the blood sacrifice of his son was necessary for him to open the seals and keep the word that he had given in the Bible. The sudden realization that this sick man really believed that he was God and that nothing I could say would convince him otherwise was unnerving. If there's one thing I know, it is that you can't negotiate with God. Without forceful intervention, the little boy was going to die.

I could see no hope for a peaceful resolution. As far as I could tell, a forceful resolution was the child's only chance to survive the ordeal. I began stalling until the SWAT team could arrive and extract the child. My attempt to bring him to reality and dissuade him from sacrificing his son ended and I began to play along with his delusion, pretending to agree and giving the impression that I wanted to help him fulfill his destiny.

It was a moral dilemma that demanded a choice between conflicting values. Deceit and lying are wrong, but so is failing to prevent the death of an innocent child. If those are the only options, it is not a difficult choice. A good hostage negotiator is reluctant to be dishonest, but when a life is on the line, we rationalize our deception by calling it "a series of tactical statements." Under normal circumstances, I am not very effective at the art of deception, but when an innocent life is on the line, I am an unabashed liar.

He was anxious to get on with it, but I suggested that such a momentous occasion required media coverage and that television crews were on the way. While he eagerly anticipated the arrival of the television crews, I was antsy for the arrival of the SWAT team. At one point, he became irritated and impatient that the camera crews were taking so long and stepped out his front door holding his son with one arm and waving his sword with the other, ready to get on with it. I believe he was about to kill his son then but I managed to convince him to wait a little while longer. The SWAT team was on the scene and was trying to move into position to make a rescue attempt when he saw them moving up and escaped back inside the mobile home with his son. I deeply regretted the missed opportunity to rescue the child while they were out in the open and I was distressed by the prospect that he would do it inside, so I continued to encourage his desire for the drama of a public display.

With the sniper in place and the SWAT team in position for rescue near the front door, I got the man back on the phone and told him that the camera crews were ready. My attempt to coax him back outside failed as his earlier glimpse of the men in the black uniforms had spooked him. Hoping to get him in position for the sniper, I tried get him near the front window to show me he was okay, but he wasn't amenable to it.

As we talked about how he planned to make the sacrifice, I was completely flummoxed about how to separate the child from his father enough to give the SWAT team the best opportunity possible for a successful rescue. It is written that the effective, fervent prayer of a righteous man avails much. I doubt that I've ever measured very high on the righteous scale, but on the fervent side of the scale I was off the chart as I prayed the shortest but most effective prayer for those in desperation: "Now what?" It is uncanny how often a good idea pops into an open heart and mind within moments after it is uttered.

"What is your son wearing?" I asked.

"Blue jeans and a T-shirt," he replied.

"What about shoes?" I asked.

"He's barefoot," came the answer.

"Don't you think he should be dressed better than that for something as important as this? People will think that you don't care about him. He should at least have some shoes on," I suggested.

He told his son to go put his shoes on and I heard the patter of his bare feet over the phone as he scampered to the other end of the mobile home. Back then, telephones had cords attached to the wall, so I knew they were at separate ends of the trailer. I hit the mute button on my phone and urged the tact team commander to go. He gave the green light, and the entry team immediately broke through a door near the middle of the mobile home between with the child in a bedroom to their left and his father in the living room to their right.

As the team entered, the man attacked them with his sword, resulting in his immediate death from multiple gunshot wounds. I partially regret how it ended. My conscience has compelled me to relive it many times to consider whether I could have done something differently to avoid the loss of a human life. It has forced me to acknowledge some things I could have done better, but it has also helped me recognize the moral reasoning behind the decisions made that day that put my colleagues in a position that forced them to take a human life.

Despite the man's mental illness, it is troubling that a human being can find a rationale to morally justify the murder of a child, but, throughout history, the worst atrocities have been committed by those who believe themselves to be most virtuous. One of the most frightening movie villains of all time to me is Mildred Ratched, the psychiatric nurse in the 1975 award-winning movie *One Flew Over the Cuckoo's Nest*. Nurse Ratched had no idea how much harm she did to those she thought she was protecting. She probably even saw herself as a hero. But her lack of compassion was more harmful to her patients than their mental illness was. What's worse is that she was oblivious to it and always would be. The only cure for self-righteousness is self-exposure. The evil that we should detest and fear the most is our own that we hide from ourselves. Being honest with ourselves is risky and requires sound moral reasoning. But I believe it is the best antidote to dangerous thinking that can lead into a personal drama where we are always the hero, surrounded by inferiors who must be either protected or vanquished.

DEMOCRATIC PARTY
OF ALABAMA

*This was the ballot symbol of Alabama's Democratic Party
until after the Voting Rights Act in the mid 1960s.*

CHAPTER 9

The Rooster Ruled the Roost

From 1904 until 1996, the symbol of the Alabama Democratic Party was a proud little rooster, and it seemed to fit the party that had ruled the roost in Alabama since the Civil War. Until 1966, the rooster appeared at the top of voters' ballots in Alabama with a banner proclaiming "White Supremacy" above the proud rooster's head and "For the Right" emblazoned beneath his feet. The defiant little rooster was an apt symbol of a political party that held power in Montgomery for over a century by promoting Jim Crow and segregation, using racial fear to win elections and maintain power. The passage of the Civil Rights Act of 1964 set the course for the proud little rooster's ultimate demise. In 1966, the banner proclaiming the contemptible party slogan was axed. Another thirty years would pass before the cocky little rooster finally got the axe.

I recognize the necessity for political parties in our system of governance to serve as a mechanism to keep other political parties from getting out of control. However, partisanship is neither noble nor ethical. It promotes hypocrisy and is driven largely by fear. When a political party becomes too powerful, it can operate as a shadow government by causing public officials to be more accountable to their political party than to the people they are constitutionally elected to represent.

Fortunately, competing factions within the party usually provide a limitation on the ability of a political party to subvert the power of the constitutionally designated government. For a political party to become large enough to be successful at the polls, it must be able to manage divergent factions within its ranks. Smaller parties obviously have fewer factions and are much easier to manage.

A faction is usually a nebulous group of people with common political purpose. A political party is also a group of people with common political purpose, but with official membership and some semblance of organizational structure with a legally recognized governing body. The internal struggles between factions roiled from within throughout the history of the party symbolized by the defiant little rooster.

Alabama was a one-party state with the Democratic Party firmly in control from Reconstruction until the emergence of the Alabama Republican Party in the mid-1980s. But those who truly understand Alabama politics recognize that the two-party system is more conducive to national politics and that state politics revolves around the more loosely organized right, moderate, and left factions. Each of the major factions are comprised of many other special interests and factions that usually make the political scene appear more like a kaleidoscope than a picture.

Prior to the civil rights movement, the little rooster was cock of the walk while the populist right, left, and moderate factions struggled with one another for power within the Alabama Democratic Party. The Republican Party was almost non-existent, and many of the relatively few blacks registered to vote supported Republicans.

The moderate faction tends to be more conservative, at least in a conventional sense. They could be considered the "establishment," since they do most of the actual governance. The left and right factions are naturally at odds with the establishment. Black voters tend to gravitate toward the left faction and rural white voters toward the right faction. Both are often driven by populist appeal and viewed by whoever holds power with apprehension and suspicion.

Despite their insistence to the contrary, populist appeal is more dependent upon public sentiment than political philosophy, which is why they are susceptible to demagoguery and politicians with charismatic personalities who will feed them the red meat they are hungry for. Unfortunately, the politicians who have the most populist appeal are usually more effective at campaigning than governing.

Big Jim Folsom epitomized the progressive populism that flourished during the years following the Great Depression and World War II. He rose to prominence in Alabama politics by using the same template as Louisiana's singing Governor Jimmie Davis and Texas Governor Pappy O'Daniel, whose

"Light Crust Doughboys" were an integral part of his campaign. Folsom swept across Alabama with his "Strawberry Pickers," drawing crowds and stirring them up with toe-tapping country music.

While the band played, Folsom glad-handed and back-patted the crowd before getting on the stage. After a few minutes of banter with the band, he would turn to the crowd and promise pensions for old folks, fair wages for teachers, paved roads, and repeal of the poll tax. A political campaign needs a boogeyman and the ambiguous "Big Mules" in Montgomery fit the bill for Folsom. "Big Mules" is the moniker given to whichever groups or interests are perceived to hold the most power. They are the establishment and easiest to incite passion against.

Folsom would wave around a mop until the crowd was ready to fill up the "suds" bucket with coins and dollars bills symbolizing the suds needed to help him wash out the self-interested politicians and their cronies at the capitol. The formula played on the scapegoating mechanism, fostered by that fear and contempt that is naturally harbored toward whoever holds power. It was the centerpiece of populist appeal then, just as it is now. Folsom played it well, but George Wallace mastered it.

George Wallace recognized Folsom's populist appeal and was riding his bandwagon, until he recognized that the dismantling of the existing "Jim Crow" system throughout the South had created an even more powerful boogeyman than the nebulous "Big Mules."

Skillful politicians know how to build a base of support by playing "hero" and tapping into the power of fear that unites people against whatever "villain" serves them best as a scapegoat that symbolizes that fear. This fearmongering has been a universally practiced political tactic among politicians of every political stripe throughout history, but George Wallace knew how to do it as effectively as anyone I've seen, at least until Donald Trump came along.

When Wallace said, "There ain't a dime's worth of difference between the Republicans and Democrats," he was right. Or at least, he was right in the context of the similar nature, purpose, and use of fear as the tie that binds political parties together. Although he made a third party run for President of the United States in 1968, he never completely severed his ties to the Alabama Democratic Party. Until he announced his retirement from politics in 1986, the Alabama Republican Party would remain unable to establish much of a beachhead.

In what has been characterized as one of the ugliest political campaigns in U.S. history, Wallace came dangerously close to being defeated in the 1970 gubernatorial primary. The race pitted George Wallace, the masterful self-promoter with populist appeal, against Albert Brewer, a dutiful public servant with a knack for governance who ascended to the governor's office in 1968 after Wallace's wife, Lurleen, died from cancer.

Lurleen Wallace had been decisively elected two years earlier without a runoff in a primary field of ten candidates that included two former governors after a legislative effort failed in 1965 that would have allowed her husband to run for a second consecutive term. George Wallace saw to it that every state senator who voted against removing the term limit was defeated in the1966 election which got his wife elected governor. During her brief term as governor, she seemed much different than the stereotypical Southern politician of the day. So did Lieutenant Governor Brewer, who followed her in office. He tried his best to avoid conflict with the politically ambitious and powerful George Wallace.

Albert Brewer was from Decatur, a few miles up the road from Hartselle, where I grew up. He was much like my daddy in many ways. They were about the same age with similar values, attitudes, and demeanors. Although one was a simple working man with only a sixth-grade education and the other was a refined, well-educated attorney with a much higher social standing, they had a personal connection and my daddy considered him a friend.

Albert Brewer served in the Alabama House of Representatives for twelve years from 1954 to 1966. In 1962 he was only thirty-four years old when he was elected Speaker of the House, making him the youngest Speaker in Alabama history. In 1966, he was easily elected lieutenant governor. Although he worked well with Wallace and gave tacit approval to segregation out of political necessity of the day, Albert Brewer was no race-baiting demagogue. He was a genuinely reform-minded individual who preferred to change the system from the inside out instead of outside in.

Brewer was one of the first high-ranking state officials to propose the formation of the Ethics Commission, constitutional reform, and expanded funding for education. His entire political career was based on trying to improve the political process; however, he was shackled by the political circumstances of the time. Unfortunately, Brewer became an obstacle in the path of an ambitious, charismatic, self-promoting politician with a gigantic ego. As an influential politician, he probably wasn't lacking in the ego area either. Nonetheless, Albert Brewer epitomized statesmanship. All statesmen must be politicians, but all politicians are not statesmen.

I am reminded of another Albert who is a marked contrast from Brewer: Representative Albert Hall was first elected to the legislature in 1978 and had already served twenty-four years by the time that I was elected in 2002. He was chairman of our Madison County Legislative Delegation. We hit it off from the start, both being working-class people with a strong distaste for phonies. His manner might have appeared crusty and crude to some, but Albert was a crafty politician with a brilliant mind. He didn't have a college degree, but if universities awarded degrees for street smarts, Albert Hall would have been a PhD.

Party label didn't seem to mean much to Albert, except as a means to an end. Shortly before his sudden death in 2006, he told me that if Republicans ever got to fifty-two members, one short of a majority, he would make fifty-three. If he would have ever switched parties, you can be assured it would have been for purely political reasons. He would have only switched to leverage his position to his greatest advantage. You wouldn't have heard Albert repeating the mantra common to party-switchers, "I didn't leave the party, the party left me." He would have probably said something like, "I represent my people, and my people are tired of them Democrats, so I am, too." And he would be telling the truth.

Albert Hall was no hypocrite and gave no pretension of statesmanship, but he was a politician who effectively represented his constituents in rural Madison and Jackson Counties. Despite his obvious flaws, I liked Albert for several reasons; one of which was that he didn't lie to himself. There was something else that I liked about him that he tried to keep secret, but I knew, and he knew that I knew. Albert Hall had a tender heart. He probably thought it was a weakness that would make him vulnerable to his adversaries, because he was tough as nails in the face of them. He was a friend to those he saw as needy and vulnerable, but to those who he perceived as haughty and looked down their noses at common folk, he was a formidable foe.

About midway during my first session, after I got my first bill out of committee, I didn't know how to get it on the House calendar for final passage. I asked Albert what to do. Without batting an eye, Albert said the best way to get a bill on the calendar is to go to the Speaker's office and perform a sexual favor for him. He used more graphic language, but you get the idea. I was surprised as I responded, "If that's what it takes to get a bill passed, I don't want to even think what you must have done to have gotten on the Rules Committee." He had a big laugh and told me that I'd just have to figure it out.

To my surprise the next week, my bill magically appeared at the top of the House calendar. While I presented my bill to the full house, Albert had fun sharing with other legislators the advice he had given to me about getting a bill on the calendar for a vote. Albert shouted from his seat while I was at the podium, "Tell 'em how you got that bill on the calendar!" In today's world, some might want to file a sexual harassment complaint and demand an apology.

But that was a different time, and my feelings weren't hurt, so I ignored his crass behavior and called for the vote. After the bill unanimously passed, I said from the podium, "Thank you, Mr. Speaker, and members of the House, and I would especially like to thank my dear friend and mentor, Representative Albert Hall, who was gracious enough to do whatever was necessary to get this bill on the calendar. I don't know what he had to do, but I am grateful for whatever it was he did. He is a true friend." Albert led the chorus of laughs that erupted on the House floor.

A couple of years later, I was in Albert's office seeking his sage advice and grumbling about the unfairly rigged political system. After he heard enough whining, Albert gave me a serious piece of helpful advice: "Your problem, Ball, is that you've come down here trying to be a statesman. We've had them here before. They don't last very long, and they don't get much done. You can have the best ideas in the world, but if you think you're too good to be a politician, you're wasting your time, because if you can't play the game, you ain't gonna get nothing done for the people that sent you here."

Albert was right. I've learned that successful statesmanship is always tempered by political reality. Albert's advice was always simple and straightforward. About ethics he once told me, "Ball, ain't nobody down here that matters gets bought off by a meal from a lobbyist. If you ain't strong enough to eat their steak and drink their whiskey and vote against 'em the next day, then you ain't strong enough to make no difference anyhow."

Albert Hall may have been crude, but he was a very effective, crafty politician who knew the angles. He served his constituents well and would never be mistaken for a hypocritical goody two shoes. Albert Hall might not have been a statesman, but he taught me a lot about being one. A statesman is an effective politician who keeps their eyes on what's important. Albert Hall was probably more of a statesman than he realized. His lack of polish kept it hidden, like his compassion.

True statesmanship requires humility, discernment, and introspection. It is a continual moral balancing act that forces one to regularly reconcile the dictates of one's personal conscience with the will of the people they represent. Seldom are the dilemmas as clear and linear as the dualist political forces that paint them. There are few "this-or-that" solutions, where one thing is entirely right and the other totally wrong. Much of the time, choices require discernment to distinguish the lesser evil from all the bad options available.

Politicians campaign and statesmen govern. One makes noise, the other makes a difference. Self-righteous demagogues proudly proclaim the dictates of their conscience with certitude that stirs emotions while statesmen take a humbler approach that make them appear less effective and more conformist. Firebrands are hardly ever effective at either reform or governance. Statesmen work the system from the inside out which requires a cooperative approach, rather than an adversarial one. True governance is hard work and requires complex, nuanced, and creative thinking to develop and institute policy that reconciles the many conflicts within the collective conscience of the people they represent.

Statesmen avoid intimidating tactics and prefer the art of persuasion to develop and implement public policy, while incendiary politicians attempt to overcome opposition with the political force created by the passions of their supporters. Even when a demagogue enjoys a policy victory, it is often undermined by the fermenting resentment and contempt their tactics create. Statesmen are inside-out reformers who know how to humble themselves so they can be flexible enough to bend, yet tough enough to stiffen up when necessary.

Albert Brewer was more statesman than politician and George Wallace was better suited for political campaigning than effective governance. Wallace was detached from the intricacies of governance after the death of his wife and gave Brewer a free hand to govern. Many political watchers didn't expect Wallace to run for governor in 1970 but focus on running for President of the United States in 1972.

However, Wallace recognized that holding the position of governor could be helpful to his anticipated presidential run and threw his hat in the ring to the surprise of many political pundits and Governor Brewer. In a crowded field of contenders that included several wannabes, has-beens, and never-wases, Brewer surprisingly emerged from the pack of candidates in the Democratic primary with a narrow 42 to 41 percent lead over Wallace in second place.

George Wallace's fight for his political life at what was thought to be the pinnacle of his popularity in Alabama turned the ensuing Democratic primary runoff into what is considered by many historians to be one of the dirtiest political campaigns in U.S. history.

Albert Brewer built a strong coalition of support that included Republicans with the endorsement of Richard Nixon, working class whites from the Tennessee Valley, and more educated voters. He was also the first viable Alabama gubernatorial candidate since Reconstruction to openly solicit black votes, which guaranteed to bring out the race-baiting. Although Wallace was one of a long line of politicians who stoked the fires of racial fear to energize voters, there is another important element of his popular appeal that is easily overlooked by those who only view politics through the prism of race.

George Wallace was a master of class warfare before he was a race-baiter. He appealed to the large mass of common folk who resented being looked down upon by the haughty academics, media elites, powerful "Big Mules," and the greedy Republicans. Wallace knew how to appeal to voters who believed they were being frowned upon by those that considered themselves their "betters." The coalition that supported Brewer in the primary was a perfect foil for Wallace in the runoff.

Knowing that a defeat by Brewer might end Wallace's entire political career as well as his presidential aspirations, his campaign pulled out all stops. In a campaign marred by vulgarity, racism, and cruel personal smears on Brewer and his family, Wallace narrowly prevailed. Albert Brewer never regained an appetite for electoral politics, although he ran for governor again in 1978 when Wallace was again term limited. Brewer finished third in the Democratic primary and spent the remainder of his life as a former statesman-turned-academic.

Despite his success in gubernatorial elections, George Wallace wasn't the only powerful Alabama Democrat on Goat Hill during the sixties, seventies, and eighties. Dr. Paul Hubbert, the executive secretary of the Alabama Education Association, was just as influential and maybe even more powerful but with a much lower public profile. George Wallace was a fiery populist with a powerful, charismatic personality whose main agenda was self-promotion, while Dr. Hubbert's soft-spoken, underwhelming personality was the opposite. Instead of charisma, Dr. Hubbert's power was derived from organizational skills and intellect. He had a broad view of the political battlefield, focusing on specific policy goals. George Wallace focused on political ambition and self-promotion, but Dr. Hubbert was not as concerned about making a name for himself as he was promoting the organization that he controlled, the Alabama Education Association.

Before 1969 the AEA represented white teachers, and another organization, the Alabama State Teachers Association, represented black teachers. Shortly before the run-up to the Wallace-Brewer race, the organizations merged, and Dr. Paul Hubbert became executive secretary with former ASTA President Joe Reed as associate executive secretary. Together, they became the driving force in Alabama legislative politics for decades. Dr. Hubbert's discipline steadily grew his political capital, allowing him spend it wisely to promote his organization and expand its influence.

During most of the seventies and eighties, Hubbert was probably more politically powerful than George Wallace, but it was not obvious to the casual political observer. Although Dr. Hubbert and his organization supported

Brewer against Wallace in 1970, eventually they became a classic example of the strange bedfellows that politics is known to produce, uneasy allies of political convenience. When they did conflict in legislative battles, Dr. Hubbert often prevailed.

There were other powerful players in Alabama politics in the seventies and early eighties, but George Wallace and Dr. Paul Hubbert were clearly on top of the heap. After his close call with Brewer, Wallace remained invincible statewide at the ballot box, while Dr. Hubbert's superiority was on the legislative front because of his political organization that optimized large grassroots support and a steady stream of funding from membership dues.

By 1978, term limited and humbled by the effects of a would-be assassin's bullet, it was widely believed that Wallace's political career was over. Many believed his successor would be Bill Baxley, a rising star in Alabama politics, who in 1970 at only twenty-nine was elected Alabama attorney general.

As attorney general while Wallace was governor from 1971 to 1979, Baxley was careful not to cross swords with the political icon. The ambitious young Baxley aggressively pursued polluters and corrupt public officials, but he was most noted for his tenacity in pursuing justice for the four little girls murdered in the 16th Street Baptist Church bombing in Birmingham in 1963.

Shortly after Baxley's election as Alabama attorney general, pursuing the murders became his passion and he became engaged in a lengthy struggle to obtain information previously withheld from local officials by orders of FBI director J. Edgar Hoover. Baxley was eventually able to collect enough evidence to obtain the murder conviction of Klansman Robert Chambliss in connection with the terrorist bombing.

While he was pursuing the case, Baxley received a letter from Klan leader Ed Field stating, "We would like to congratulate you, you are now an honorary nigger. We hope that you are proud of yourself now, you WHITE NIGGER. We hope you are soon blessed with the same condition that the nigger lover Kennedy contracted, which is dead. . ."

The letter prompted the following reply from Baxley on his official state letterhead:

February 28, 1976
"Dr." Edward R. Fields
National States Rights Party
P. O. Box 1211
Marietta, Georgia 30061
Dear "Dr." Fields:

    My response to your letter of February 19, 1976, is—kiss my ass.
Sincerely,
BILL BAXLEY
Attorney General

In 1978, Baxley was widely regarded as the favorite among another crowded and colorful Democratic primary field of thirteen that included Albert Brewer, Lieutenant Governor Jere Beasley, the former governor "Big Jim" Folsom, former Alabama First Lady Cornelia Wallace (Folsom's niece and recently divorced from Governor Wallace), perennial candidate and political clown Shorty Price, and Fob James, a former all-American halfback from Auburn who had become a successful businessman.

Fob James had only recently left the Republican Party to run for governor as a Democrat, and to the surprise of many, the political newcomer led the field promising "a new beginning." Baxley finished second and forced a runoff, but the former football star won decisively. He immediately began attempting to make good on his promise of a new beginning.

Governor James had limited success in his attempts at reform, instituting well-needed reforms in education, mental health, and prisons while making modest selective spending cuts. His efforts were likely boosted by getting on Dr. Paul Hubbert's good side, favoring K–12 over higher education on spending issues. Governor James's progress in racially integrating Alabama's state government has been largely overlooked, but he appointed Alabama's first black state Supreme Court Justice Oscar Adams and had more blacks serving in his administration than any previous administration.

However, many of James's reform proposals caused the conservative faction to shudder and fell short, including a gasoline tax increase, constitutional reform, and the removal of the income tax deduction for social security taxes paid. It is also probably worth mentioning that James also expanded Medicaid during his first term.

In 1982, James surprised Alabamians by keeping his 1978 campaign promise not to run for another term. George Wallace, paralyzed from a would-be assassin's bullet, emerged from the political graveyard to announce his run for a fourth gubernatorial term. Having humbly apologized for his past ambitious political opportunism and grandstanding, the repentant Wallace narrowly won the primary by about the same margin he defeated Brewer. However, he received over 90 percent of the black vote as he handily defeated the Republican in the general election.

Bill Baxley was elected lieutenant governor that year, biding his time for Wallace's inevitable retirement. Waiting with Baxley in the wings was the term-limited, tough-on-crime Attorney General Charlie Graddick. Graddick was a former Republican district attorney in Mobile but switched parties out of political expediency to run for attorney general. A Republican had not won a statewide election in Alabama since Reconstruction.

George Wallace announced his retirement in 1986, setting the stage for a showdown between Democratic loyalist Bill Baxley and the Democratic pretender Charlie Graddick. After a rough-and-tumble runoff campaign, Graddick eked out a victory by encouraging Republicans to vote for him in the Democratic primary, contrary to party rules.

The unanimously Democratic Alabama Supreme Court ordered their party to either award the nomination to Baxley or hold a new election, giving party leaders the green light to award the nomination to their favorite, Bill Baxley. The ruling of the Alabama Supreme Court and the actions of the Alabama Democratic Party were widely perceived as an affront to the Alabama voters who summarily ended Baxley's political career, handily sweeping Republican Guy Hunt, a little-known preacher and Amway salesman from tiny Holly Pond in Cullman County, into the Governor's office.

The adverse political effect of the 1986 election fiasco upon the Alabama Democratic Party was exacerbated in that only three years earlier they had handpicked the legislature. Although the Constitution of Alabama, adopted in 1901, requires the legislature to reapportion itself every ten years after the federal census, districts had still not been redrawn sixty years later when

U.S. District Judge Frank Johnson ordered it in 1962. After another twenty years of legal wrangling, the federal court imposed new legislative district lines in April 1983 and ordered new elections to be held in the fall.

After the Alabama Legislature had shirked its constitutional duty for seventy years, the Alabama Democratic Party Executive Committee selected their nominees instead of holding a primary. Some of their incumbents were replaced by nominees more to the liking of Dr. Hubbert despite having only served one year of the four-year term to which they had been elected. In a one-party state, it was tantamount to being handpicked.

There were many other factors contributing to the decline of the Democratic Party and the steady rise of the Republican Party in Alabama. The role of national politics, particularly the presidency of Ronald Reagan, can't be overlooked as a major contributing factor to the political shift moving Alabama toward the Republican Party. President Reagan's cheerful and optimistic countenance made it possible for vast numbers of middle-class voters who didn't care for demagoguery to have a champion who seemed to care about them but wasn't such a jerk about it. Reagan replaced Wallace in the minds of many as a champion who would stand up for common folks against those who thought themselves to be their betters.

President Reagan's conservative principles and optimistic outlook coupled with the blunders of the Alabama Democrats and the retirement of George Wallace created a prime opportunity for the Alabama Republican Party to broaden its base by rebranding itself from the party of the well-to-do to the party that stands for the common people who are looked down upon by the haughty academics, media elites, powerful liberal special interests, and self-serving Democrats.

The table was set for an en masse shift by the socioeconomic demographic that had consistently supported George Wallace to the Alabama Republican Party. For the next thirty-five years after the election of Guy Hunt, Alabama Republicans would win almost every gubernatorial race, but they were a long way from controlling the legislature. The Alabama Democratic Party still dominated state politics, but their ultimate decline seemed obvious to me. Regardless, I was fascinated at how they managed to hold back the rising tide of Republicans for over two decades.

CHAPTER 10

Longshot Legislator

When the Alabama Supreme Court inexplicably ruled in 1990 to overturn the murder conviction for the crash that I investigated two years earlier, I had already begun to identify myself as a Republican. It only added to my growing perception of the bizarre twists in recent history of Alabama politics that the Democratic Party's dominance had made them arrogant, and time for a change had arrived. In addition, President Reagan's soothing leadership style and hopeful optimism during the previous decade, followed by more of the same from President Bush, provided me with a marked contrast to the cocky politicians in the political party that controlled the state government in Montgomery since Reconstruction.

Many politicos considered the 1986 election of Guy Hunt, the first Republican to hold statewide office since Reconstruction, to be a fluke, and Democrats were eager to challenge the Republican farmer, Amway salesman, and primitive Baptist preacher who had stumbled into the Governor's Mansion. In 1990, they produced a strong primary field that included the powerful executive secretary of the Alabama Education Association, Dr. Paul Hubbert; Attorney General Don Siegelman; former governor Fob James; the reliable congressman from the Tennessee Valley, Ronnie Flippo; and the colorful state senator from Walker County, Charles Bishop, who would one day gain national notoriety by punching a colleague on the floor of the Alabama Senate.

Dr. Paul Hubbert prevailed in the spirited primary to face Attorney General Siegelman in the runoff. Siegelman came up short in the runoff, as his political prowess was no match for the powerful organization at Dr. Hubbert's beck and call. The upstart "hayseed" living in the Governor's Mansion was widely anticipated to be straightway evicted by the professional, seasoned, erudite, Democratic loyalist, but the voters didn't cooperate. It would take an ethics conviction to remove the Republican rube and restore the Democratic regime.

The Democratic Lieutenant Governor Jim Folsom Jr. assumed the office of governor in 1993 and was a highly popular governor like his father "Big Jim" once was.

Affectionately referred to as "Little Jim," his major achievement in the governor's office was attracting the Mercedes-Benz automobile manufacturing plant to Tuscaloosa, giving birth to Alabama's now successful automobile industry. The generous package of economic incentives used by Governor Folsom to lure the German automaker to Alabama ruffled the feathers of Dr. Paul Hubbert, who protected Alabama taxpayer money earmarked for K–12 education as if it belonged to him.

The powerful lobbyist challenged the popular governor in the 1994 Democratic primary but was handily repulsed. It would be the last time Dr. Hubbert would try to run for public office, but as vice-chair of the Alabama Democratic Party, he would remain a powerful force in the legislative process and Alabama for some time to come. From then on, he would mostly wield his power from behind the scenes.

Polling in September showed that Folsom had a 20 percent lead over the Republican nominee, former Democratic Governor Fob James, who had switched parties. As the election neared, James had steadily closed the gap, but only two days before the election, polls showed that he still trailed Folsom by 7 percent. Hubbert's less-than-enthusiastic support for Folsom in the general election campaign—perhaps in part because James had a record of support for K–12 education—was a major factor in Folsom's narrow defeat, making Fob James the only Alabama governor to be elected as both a Republican and a Democrat.

The challenge Alabama Republicans faced to flip the state Supreme Court was probably even more daunting in 1994 than winning their third consecutive gubernatorial race. Alabama's reputation within the business community as "tort hell" prompted the Business Council of Alabama to retain the services of political guru Karl Rove to flip the partisan makeup of the Alabama Supreme Court during the election cycle in which five of the nine justices were up for election.

The political warfare between powerful business interests and the trial lawyers for the Court caused campaign spending to skyrocket. Although the four Republican candidates for associate justice were defeated by the trial lawyer-backed Democrats, the court races were far more competitive than they had ever been. The race for chief justice was another story. Republican Perry Hooper narrowly defeated the incumbent Democrat Sonny Hornsby, but the incumbent refused to vacate and continued to hold the office for nearly a year while the lawyers litigated the election.

It was even more difficult to find credible Republican candidates at the local level. I gave some thought to a run for Morgan County Sheriff in 1990, but the administrative duties surrounding the office and the jail seemed like drudgery to me. When Steve Crabbe, a retired FBI agent, expressed an interest in running, my longtime friend became the first Republican elected official in Morgan County history.

My personal political perspective became even more partisan after the 1994 election cycle. Some of my closest colleagues in ABI were assigned to Governor Fob James's security detail and another was assigned to Chief Justice Perry Hooper when that election was finally upheld in federal court. I maintained contact with my former colleagues after they left the major crimes unit, frequently helping them with security details, and became familiar with the incumbent Republicans and their staff.

In 1997, Michael Ciamarra, the senior policy advisor for Governor James, suggested I consider running for the legislative seat held by State Representative Paul Parker, who was a dependable ally of Dr. Hubbert and no friend of Republicans or Governor James's administration. Republican strength had been steadily growing in the district and it seemed like a winnable longshot.

At first, I did not embrace the idea of running for the legislature, even if the district had been reliably Republican in federal and statewide races for several election cycles. Politics was like an interesting hobby, but criminal investigation was my career and about four years remained before I would be eligible for state retirement. Although it was legal and the legislature is supposed to be part-time, serving in the legislature while trying to fulfill the duties of an active ABI agent seemed like it would create too many opportunities for conflicts of interest.

Instead of running, I searched for credible Republicans to run. One person I approached about running for the House 9 seat was a friend of many years, Hugh Henry. His easygoing manner and broad perspective would have made him a good candidate and great legislator. He was not even a bit interested but instead suggested that I do it. His wife JoAnn chimed in agreement but was more direct, as she shot down my litany of excuses not to run. She was not shy about pointing out my hypocrisy in trying to get others to do what I believed needed to be done. She threw down the gauntlet and made an offer I couldn't refuse: If I would run, she would manage my campaign. I accepted.

My first legislative campaign in 1998 was strictly an amateur operation. We had no paid consultant and didn't know what we were doing, but JoAnn's ideas and energy made it a credible campaign on a shoestring budget. She worked tirelessly, designing brochures and printing them. The idea to use eye-catching round white yard signs with baseball stitches to boost "Mike Ball" name recognition was all hers.

The Henrys and their family were my strongest supporters, including their oldest son Ed and his wife Wendy, who had recently completed an Air Force enlistment. Ed Henry's first foray into political campaigning had more to do with family loyalty and friendship than political ideology. Since his

early teen years, he has had the air of a wise guy: intelligent, quick-witted, and cocky in a usually likeable and funny way.

Several years before, Hugh and JoAnn had saved a

My first campaign sign in 1998.

nest egg from their family carpet installation business to send their brilliant but immature son to Auburn University. Soon after Ed went off to college, he gave his inner party animal a free rein. I was disconcerted to return to my office from lunch one day to find nineteen-year-old Ed Henry sitting with his head hung down at the Alabama Bureau of Investigation in Decatur.

"What are you doing here?" I asked.

"They brought me in," he nonchalantly replied, pointing at our narcotics agents' office. He didn't seem to recognize the gravity of the situation—at first.

While Ed waited outside my office, I spoke to my colleagues in the narcotics division. He had been busted with a small amount of marijuana, and they were planning to offer him a deal to allow him to escape the charge if he helped them go after a dealer. I didn't care much for giving him a deal; all I could think about was his father and mother laying carpet and saving their hard-earned dollars to give him an opportunity for a college education.

Maybe my admiration for his parents and the sacrifice they made for him triggered a subconscious memory of the sacrifice made for me many years before, or maybe I just thought he looked too smug sitting in the lobby, but something unleashed my inner Marine Corps sergeant. I went back out to the lobby and angrily ordered him into my office

I don't remember specifically everything that was said, but we definitely had a come-to-Jesus meeting, despite the salty language that I used in my description of where he was heading and of how he disrespected those who loved him most. Unexpected tears from his eyes caused my anger to subside, and the tone of the conversation changed. We began to talk about taking an alternative path.

"It doesn't have to be that way—you have a choice," I told him.

"I do?," he asked.

We had a long talk in my office that day about choices, consequences, respect, and living for something greater than we are. Ed made a life-changing decision that day in my office about the direction of his life. I gave him some instructions that would help him change course and start becoming a man. First, he should stay away from Auburn. Second, he should come home and show his parents respect and gratitude by spending some time working alongside them. Finally, he needed to figure out what he would have to do to get the criminal case behind him.

I shook Ed's hand as he left my office that day, wondering if our conversation would make a difference. Walking across the lobby together, I told him, "I'm going to keep an eye on you."

Ed took the advice to heart and immediately began making better choices in his life. He came home and laid carpet with his folks for a while before joining the Air Force, where he trained to become a medical technician. He is happily married to a wonderful wife and has two sweet daughters. He didn't go back to Auburn for another twenty years.

There are some things about Ed that will never change. He is still creative and mischievous with a knack for getting himself into trouble. Admired by some and hated by others, at least he isn't boring. I wonder what the odds would have been that day against both of us someday serving together as members of the Alabama House of Representatives.

While running for office in 1998, my twenty-one-year marriage ran out of gas. Public service can take its toll on a family. It didn't die all at once; it happened gradually over time, like boiling a frog. By the time that I realized how seriously ill it was, the time for a cure had passed. If a couple doesn't pull together, they pull apart, and that's what gradually happened.

For much of my legislative campaign, I didn't want to talk to anyone. Unless a life is at stake, I'm usually not very good at putting on a fake smile. It just takes too much energy for me to display a pleasant demeanor when my insides are in turmoil. Until I experienced it I didn't know how painful divorce is. It hurts far worse than losing a political campaign. Suffering through the death of a marriage is much like the death of a loved one.

During the run-up to the 1998 general election, my Democratic opponent Ron Grantland and I had breakfast often. His wife was the principal of the local elementary school, and he was the chosen successor of Paul Parker, who had opted not to run for a fifth turn in deference to his wife Susan's run for state auditor. My opponent had the solid support of Dr. Hubbert's powerful political machine.

We may have been rivals in a very close race and leaned in different political directions, but friendship is more important than our respective roles as surrogates for the powerful special interests struggling for political dominance. I spoke freely with him about my impending divorce several times. To my knowledge, the divorce was never brought up by him or anyone else on the campaign trail. That kind of class is a rarity in partisan politics.

I lost the race by a razor-thin margin. Although it was disappointing for JoAnn and all the others who worked to help me with the campaign, I was relieved that it was finally over. I thought the loss meant that I wasn't supposed to be a legislator, but it really meant "not yet and not here." It wasn't a defeat; it was a delay.

Hartselle had been home to me from the time I arrived from California in 1963 as a nine-year-old refugee until my divorce and the election loss in 1998. Living in a small town often feels like being on display. I've always been approachable and I usually enjoy pleasant conversation, but when it became tedious, it was time to get away. The opportunity for a fresh start presented itself when budgetary constraints forced the closure of the nearby ABI office and I transferred to the Huntsville office. In 2001, I moved twenty-five miles to Madison in the bustling Huntsville metropolitan area across the Tennessee River.

The Huntsville-Madison metro area is a more cosmopolitan city with a rapidly growing population. The Redstone Arsenal serves as the hub of a thriving economic engine. The defense, aerospace, technology, and research jobs attract people to the area from all over the nation. Living in Madison was convenient and refreshing, but my new-found anonymity didn't last very long.

I understand why some people would like city life. Life is simpler when we mind our own business and avoid getting sucked into the drama that gravitates around personal relationships in small towns. To my surprise, the Madison-Huntsville metro area wasn't a place I could become a recluse, and that's fine because I enjoy people when not trying to recover from emotional wounds.

Within a few months in my new hometown, I had remarried and was making new friends almost every day. My itch to run for public office had been thoroughly scratched, but the same concerns that niggled my craw and sucked me into politics remained. I saw systemic flaws in all three branches of state government in Montgomery and was under the impression that the best remedy would be to replace the Democratic cabal that held power, putting in independent-minded Republicans who would be more responsive to the will of the people. I began circulating in political circles again, getting to know elected officials and potential candidates that I could support.

I had about $7,000 left over from my 1998 legislative campaign, and was getting rid of it, donating to charity, judicial candidates of both parties, and other friends running for political office that I thought could make a difference. One of those was a young trooper from Mobile County that I met during a training session at the state police academy. Spencer Collier was planning to run for the legislature in 2002 and would eventually become a central figure in a series of interwoven scandals that would rock the Alabama Capitol and force me to recognize that the link between power, politics, and corruption would remain regardless of which political party had control.

By February 2002, when the Alabama Republican Party held its annual winter meeting in Huntsville, only a small amount remained in my campaign account. I expected it would soon be all gone, and I could close it. Qualifying for the 2002 election had begun and I was disappointed to hear that Jim Haney, the state representative in my new district, didn't plan to run for re-election. I encouraged Representative Haney not to retire, but his declining health and advancing age made the decision for him. Being a fervent foe of Dr. Paul Hubbert in the legislature, Haney was expecting a strong primary challenge in the solidly Republican district and didn't have the stomach left for the inevitable re-election fight with the candidate supported by Hubbert's powerful machine.

Haney had not publicly announced his decision, but he was looking for a candidate the business community could support for his legislative seat. I asked him at the meeting to let me know when he found someone so I could get rid of my leftover campaign funds and close the account. He asked me about running for the seat, but I wasn't interested. Dale Strong, a Madison County commissioner, was privy to the conversation and egged on the idea of me running for the legislative seat. Those who know Commissioner Strong would agree that he is like the energizer bunny—he keeps going and going.

I told Haney, "I guess I could run if we can't find anyone else, but I'd rather not," thinking it might shut Dale up.

Haney said, "You would?"

"I would, if you can't find anyone else, but I'd rather not," I repeated.

That seemed to satisfy Commissioner Strong, and I expected it to be the end of it. But the next day, Haney announced his retirement and that he found someone he would support. At first, I regretted the commitment, and I hoped Haney and Commissioner Strong could find someone more suitable. I didn't mention it again; but after a few days of prayer and contemplation, I filed qualifying papers. I had just enough money left in my campaign account to pay the qualifying fee and had lived in the district just long enough to meet the one-year residency requirement.

When qualifying for the primary ended, two others had qualified to run in the June 4th Republican primary. One, a former two-term mayor of Madison, was a colorful character and somewhat unpredictable. He had a relatively small but dependable base of support. Fortunately for me, he had an even larger base of opposition.

My other primary opponent previously served on the Huntsville City Council and had the full support of Dr. Hubbert's political machine, but he had also made enemies from his time on the Huntsville City Council. For the first few months of the campaign, my opponents ran against each other and seemed to ignore me. They obviously didn't think I had much chance, and it seemed they were right.

While they were occupied feuding with each other, I added the adversaries they had accumulated during their political careers to my coalition of support that included new church friends, music friends, my wife's friends, and my law enforcement friends. The support of Representative Haney and Commissioner Strong and my previous political activity, including the 1998 legislative race in another county, guaranteed solid support from the local Republican faithful and the pro-business, anti-Hubbert political factions as well.

I stayed out of my opponent's line of fire and focused on building my name identification in the district where I had lived less than a year. Once again operating on a shoestring budget, I used several of JoAnn Henry's ideas from 1998 in the 2002 campaign, especially the baseball-shaped yard signs. When the round "Mike Ball" yard signs went up, my name ID shot up in no time. I even kept the same campaign theme: No promises, just honest and effective service.

Politicians almost always make campaign promises, and they usually lead to a moral dilemma. Seldom do candidates making the promises know as much as they pretend. They say what sounds good to get votes. If elected, they should quickly discover that it looks different from the inside looking out than the outside looking in. Promises create moral dilemmas for thinking people.

Sound decision-making requires being open to information and evidence as it becomes available. The closer to the time for a decision, the more likely that new information will develop. What if the thing promised isn't the best policy? Which is the more moral thing to do: Finding the best policy or keeping a promise that shouldn't have been made in the first place? It is a lose-lose situation and that's why I avoid making campaign promises.

Politicians who are full of promises are often just as full of themselves. They don't need to listen and learn because they already know everything. Once in office they often spend more time stubbornly fighting over their conflicting promises than making a cooperative effort to find meaningful solutions. Or they are lying.

Either way, promises are problematic. My entire 2002 campaign revolved around getting voters to know me and avoiding promises that couldn't be kept. It was once again an entirely amateur operation. I wrote my own campaign materials and carefully tried to give the people in my district enough information for them to know what to expect of me. My only promise was to be honest, work hard, and be as effective as possible.

I narrowly led the primary but was forced into a runoff with the candidate who was strongly supported by Dr. Hubbert and the Alabama Education Association. A runoff with only three weeks to get the message out intensified the advantage of polling, direct mail, boots on the ground, professional consultants, and funding over an amateur campaign. With that operation behind a legislative race, all a candidate needed to worry about was making personal contact with as many voters as possible.

There were very few primary runoff races in Alabama during that cycle and a very low turnout was expected. Whichever candidate got their voters to come out would be the winner. During the three weeks leading up to the June 25th runoff, my opposition telephoned all the voters in the district, compiling a database of their identified supporters. In the evening before the election, a company would automatically call their identified supporters from the database and remind them to vote.

It is probably one of the most effective methods of turning out votes in a low-key down-ballot race. Like the race in 1998, it had run clean without negativity. A very close race was anticipated, and I expected the get-out-the-vote phone calls would be a major advantage for the other side, maybe even enough to put them over the top.

However, I was astonished when the returns on election night reflected a huge win for us, 60 percent to 40 percent. The compliments I received about the upset by an upstart were flattering, but a few days later, I learned something that put the win in a better perspective.

Rex Cheatham was the AEA representative for the Huntsville area and had played an integral role in my opponent's campaign. I had known him since he was elected to the Morgan County Board of Education many years ago. Although our politics differed greatly, our faith did not. It was no surprise when Rex graciously offered congratulations soon after the election, but he took it farther than simple courtesy when he added that he knew without a doubt on election night the Lord had chosen me.

Almost everyone thinks the Lord is on their side, and they are right. God is always constant, and we are always variable. Rex was a Baptist deacon and church folks are notorious for attempting to flip the script, erroneously imagining they can bend the Lord's will in their direction instead of the other way around. Bewildered by his comment, I asked Rex what made him say that. He replied that the night before the runoff, the out-of-state company they had contracted to do their get-out-the-vote calls was moments away from getting underway when a storm came through and knocked out the phone system. That explained his comment and the margin-of-victory. We always win when the winds blow in our favor. But the wind doesn't shift for our benefit—we must let it move us.

Like the feather in the movie *Forrest Gump,* there's no use resisting that wind. It's easier to ride the breeze than to fight the storm. It blew in my favor and put me in public office, but if I resist it, it can just as easily blow against me. Since my election in 2002, I have prayed for the discernment to know when the wind is about to shift and it is time to leave so that a storm won't be necessary. I wanted to leave someday with a gentle breeze at my back.

CHAPTER 11

The Road to Hell

If the road to hell is paved with good intentions, then most politicians are doomed, since politics is mostly a mixture of good intentions and oversized egos. No matter how noble the cause, powerful egos eventually corrupt the best intentions.

Effective governance within a free society is a complex balancing act. The founders of our system of governance recognized that when political power is concentrated and mixed with imperious human nature, people invariably become intoxicated by it and abuse it. Individuals with outsized egos usually crave power most and are best suited to pursue power but they are also least suited to wield it. Like other addicts, they are almost never willing or able to limit their own use of it. They more they get, the more they want.

Although these people with good intentions and large egos cannot be relied upon to restrain themselves from overexercising their authority, they are perfectly suited to resist others like them. This is the underlying principle that has led us to this clunky arrangement of responsibilities and powers divided among branches within the federal, state, and local layers of government.

If everyone understands who has what responsibility and stays in their place with a cooperative mindset toward others, it can be an effective way to promote the common good of a free society. However, when egos inevitably clash and feelings get hurt, the cooperative spirit gives way to an adversarial one, and the ensuing power struggle makes it difficult to accomplish anything.

If we recognize that the primary purpose of politics is to provide an arena where ego conflicts can be at least temporarily resolved without physical violence, it is not surprising that the institution is often repulsive to decent, civilized people. It is also not surprising that many others are drawn into the competitive spectacle of politics like they would be to a sports contest or to gladiators in the colosseum, if they lived many centuries ago.

Political warfare is fraught with intimidation and manipulation, the primary spiritual weapons of narcissistic bullies throughout history. It should be no surprise that psychopaths like Republican Ted Bundy or Democrat John Wayne Gacy took to politics like a duck to water. I'm not trying to imply that all politicians are psychopaths, although some certainly are. What I am saying is that people with outsized egos who derive stimulation and satisfaction from controlling and torturing others can find the political arena to be to a target-rich environment where they can murder reputations and inflict psychological suffering upon their prey. People who really enjoy politics most likely do not understand it as much as they think they do, unless they are a narcissist—or even worse, a psychopath.

Regardless of how ugly it might seem, the lack of civility is not necessarily a symptom of a broken political system. It is the barometer that points toward an overall decline in civility within the society, and the political arena provides an outlet where internal tensions can play out. If politicians are rude, obnoxious, and full of hypocrisy, it is likely because they reflect the society they represent. Politics gets ugly, but it is a much better method of settling power disputes than the alternative, which is physical violence, bloodshed in the streets, or even civil war.

Despite the failure of participating political combatants to recognize or acknowledge it, the primary source of political energy is not faith in their own purported political philosophies, issues, and policies. It is fear, not faith, that provides the cohesion to hold political movements together. When people are afraid, they flock together with those who have similar fears and separate themselves from those whose fears differ from or even contradict their own. Narcissistic political opportunists are aware of this and capitalize on it, convincing people to put faith in them to face whatever has stoked their fear.

Political operatives use hero worship and symbolism in conjunction with the vilification of adversaries to stoke fear and gain support for whatever cause or candidate they are promoting. It is important to recognize that much of this behavior is subconscious; many, if not a vast majority, of the participants are reasonably sincere. They sincerely believe that politics provides a framework for their concept of good and evil instead of just disagreements in matters of public policy. When that happens, it is no longer politics; it is religion—and politics as religion is idolatry.

When politics becomes religion, it loses its value as a venue where meaningful public policy discussions and negotiation can occur. Politics and religion are not just entirely separate matters, but they are the antithesis of one another. Religion is faith-based. It is about believing in something greater than ourselves. It is spiritual. Politics is worldly, and it is fear-based. It is about self-preservation. Faith brings people together and fear sets us against one another. However, fear does unite those who have the same fears in common, making them instinctively flock together like sheep. Faith makes us free to think for ourselves and follow our own path. The founders of our system of governance called it "pursuit of happiness."

The conflict between fear and faith is invisible to us most of the time because we have been fighting it so long that it is mostly done subconsciously. Yet, it rages on within each of us, often with politics and religion as surrogates. I recognize fear as an integral component of our natural, instinctive system of self-preservation. It can drive us in search of faith, but until we find it, those who thrive on intimidation and manipulation can control us by our fear. The supernatural love we seek can quench the fear that often leads to hero worship and idolatry.

My own internal struggle led me into the Alabama Legislature like a blind man following his seeing-eye dog. As a career law enforcement officer with a faith-based perspective, I recognized that truth and justice were often corrupted by politics. Like many before me and many who follow, I wanted to fight corruption. The problem is that corruption means different things to different people depending on the value system they follow.

In adversarial politics where the ends justify the means, corruption is a double standard. It is a relative term used to decry the opposition when they appear to take an unfair advantage of their position. We usually view the behavior of those we consider to be our adversaries in the worst possible context, while we perform moral calisthenics to rationalize and justify our own behavior and that of our allies. Pride magnifies the corruption of others while it camouflages our own. It makes us self-righteous.

Few people realize that the most lethal form of moral corruption is self-righteousness. It is the most dangerous because the worse we have it, the more invisible it is to us (but not necessarily to others). Hypocrites infected with this insidious moral disease often pride themselves as anti-corruption crusaders, but all they usually do is substitute someone else's corruption with their own.

For those who wonder if it is even possible to serve in a position of power and authority without being ensnared in a web of hypocrisy, I would respond that it is possible—but difficult. A group of law enforcement officers must have had that concern when they approached one of the greatest corruption fighters in history, John the Baptist, with their dilemma. For many years, his response has served as my template for ethical public service.

Roman soldiers were peace officers with law enforcement responsibilities, assigned to monitor John the Baptist and the crowd that gathered to hear him proclaim the message that had driven him out of the wilderness. Their purpose was twofold: to maintain order and to monitor the speaker for signs of sedition. The message John brought from the wilderness was intended to be neither seditious nor political; it was entirely spiritual. And something special about it compelled those who heard it to seek a better way.

Although they were agents of the supreme civil authority, the Roman soldiers were intrigued by the moral authority that compelled John the Baptist and pointed in a different direction. It made them wonder if it was possible to reconcile their duty to the Roman government with a moral obligation to a higher spiritual authority. They asked the eccentric character from the wilderness, "What shall we do?"

John the Baptist foreshadowed Christianity with an answer that provided the peacekeepers with what I believe to be the universal template for resisting corruption: "Do violence to no man, neither accuse any falsely; and be content with your wages," Luke 3:14 KJV.

The first precept, "Do violence to no man," seems simple enough. However, what seems simple at first glance becomes complex when we consider the spiritual context of John the Baptist's response. In a spiritual context, physical force is not a necessary ingredient of violence, although it is often the result. Violence is any excessive or unnecessary force driven by contempt and intended to harm. Violence is oppression. Bullying is a form of violence that doesn't always entail physical force.

Although everyone has a moral obligation to resist violence, peace officers are legally obliged to do so. They are authorized by law to utilize additional levels of physical force to subdue it. However, it is important to remember that being morally justified and legally justified are two different things. Roman soldiers were given broad discretion in the amount of force they were legally authorized to use, and those with a violent disposition took full advantage of it.

When the level of force used exceeds the amount necessary to protect society from oppressors, moral authority is lost, and the protectors become themselves oppressors. Legal authority is political; moral authority is spiritual. The legal authority the soldiers were given by the Roman government to fulfil their civil duty as protectors permitted them to violently exceed their moral authority to refrain from inflicting their personal contempt on fellow human beings.

Making false accusations is usually less physically harmful than violence and is therefore a more socially acceptable and widely practiced form of moral corruption. Humans learn at an early age to play the blame game until scapegoating becomes the centerpiece of their social behavior. Whenever something bad happens, we instinctively search for someone or something to blame and hold accountable.

There is nothing inherently wrong with honestly trying to figure out what went wrong and to take steps to remedy the situation. However, a moral problem arises when we begin to manipulate the blame to avoid culpability and redirect it toward a target of opportunity or contempt. The more egocentrically motivated the accuser, the less concern for either the innocence or the suffering inflicted upon the target. A psychopathic accuser might even enjoy seeing the scapegoat suffer.

Law enforcement duties require making legal accusations. To ensure the veracity of their allegations and avoid manipulating the outcome of their investigations, officials must be humble enough to exercise restraint and circumspection.

Making false accusations is the most common form of corruption. It is also the most easily overlooked and politically acceptable. But the invisible suffering of its victims and the lengths the accusers will go to conceal their errors, even from themselves, make it particularly insidious.

"Be content with your wages" was a warning against what has been most often prosecuted as "corruption": using a public position in an unauthorized manner for personal monetary enrichment.

Upon my election to the legislature, John the Baptist's warning and my experience with public corruption cases made me cognizant that there was great room for improvement in our state Ethics Law. From the time I was elected as a minority member in 2002, ethics and transparency were among my top legislative priorities. However, there was little opportunity for progress until 2010, when a major power shift occurred that replaced the old guard with a fresh Republican supermajority.

If the road to hell is paved with good intentions, then it is littered with ethics laws scattered along the right of way with the devil filling in the details. When the Republican supermajority took over the Alabama Legislature 2010, ethics reform was a major plank in our "Handshake with Alabama" platform that all the Republican legislative candidates signed and that helped propel us into power in 2010. Democrats ran on a similar platform in 2006, but for us in 2010, it was a serious commitment that we intended to keep.

Soon after sweeping into power, we rushed through comprehensive ethics reform. Unfortunately, in our haste to make good on our promise, we were too naive to recognize the necessity of ensuring that those conducting the ethics investigations would be insulated from corruption by the accompanying politics. We didn't eliminate corruption like we promised. We just moved it around.

Unfortunately, wherever there is politics, there will be corruption. But John the Baptist told us how to contain it. If we would heed his words, our good intentions would take us to a much better destination.

CHAPTER 12

The Handshake
with Alabama

I've had it both ways, and it is much better to be riding in the train than standing on the tracks. After eight years of standing in the tracks with the minority, the 2010 elections brought a political tsunami in Alabama that swept the Democratic train away, leaving many powerful members of the old guard, especially Dr. Paul Hubbert, the leader of the Alabama Education Association, and many of his political allies, standing on the tracks in the aftermath.

The engineer of the new Republican train was the presumptive Speaker Mike Hubbard, who had orchestrated the train swap from his position as minority leader in the Alabama House of Representatives and chairman of the Alabama Republican Party. As a loyal partisan, as well as his political ally and friend, I had a first-class seat on the train.

Although the old political guru had been unceremoniously tossed off, Dr. Hubbert still had friends on the legislative train. Some of those friends were also Governor-elect Robert Bentley's close friends in the legislature, eager to derail Mike Hubbard's election as Speaker of the House. By the time the caucus meeting was held, the opposition coalition within the caucus had begun to fade into the shadows and Hubbard easily had the votes to be elected speaker.

Although Mike Hubbard's speakership was not derailed, the opposition coalition was not completely without influence or success. Their support helped elect Representative Mickey Hammon as House majority leader over Representative Greg Canfield from Birmingham and me. I was deeply disappointed at the time to be rejected by my colleagues. From my lofty perch in the future, it is now apparent that divine providence was working in favor of both Canfield and me by leading us in a less partisan direction. What felt bad to us was not bad for us.

During the next legislative session, Canfield conceived and passed his "Rolling Reserve Act," which has since proven to be a key component of setting Alabama on a path toward fiscal responsibility. Soon after passing the act, Governor Bentley tapped Canfield to head up Alabama's economic development efforts. Since then, he served as a pillar of stability for his fellow Alabamians during a time when others were crumbling. His nonpartisan leadership has been integral to promoting a healthy business climate and has resulted in attracting companies from across the world.

Other than promising not to take a salary until Alabama reached full employment, Governor Bentley made few promises during the 2010 election. For the most part, he managed to stumble into the governor's office by avoiding the political imbroglios that entangled his opposition. While his opponents pounded each other, he accurately presented himself as a grandfatherly doctor with a desire to help people and without an agenda.

The newly elected governor might not have an agenda, but that was not the case for the recently empowered Republican supermajority. Emulating the strategy Newt Gingrich used in 1994 with his "Contract with America," we made a lot of hay with our "Handshake with Alabama" during the 2010 election. The agenda was almost identical to the unfulfilled promises the Democrats had made in their 2006 "Compact with Alabama." The biggest difference was that we meant it and were eager to prove it—probably a bit too eager.

The "Handshake with Alabama" was full of political "red meat" issues that included a small business health insurance tax credit, Canfield's rolling reserve budgeting to control spending and prevent budget shortages, illegal immigration legislation, and an anti-Obamacare bill prohibiting any person, employer, or health care provider from being compelled to participate in any health care system. But the part of the "Handshake with Alabama" that probably captured the most attention and had the greatest impact on the outcome of the election was the promise to end corruption in Montgomery.

Although the promise was sincere, and we made a valiant attempt to keep it by passing each of the bills in the "Handshake," we did not end corruption in Montgomery. We only rearranged it. The worst form of corruption is self-righteousness, and it is most infectious to those who believe themselves immune. Those in greatest danger are often most oblivious to it.

In 2010 it was easy to generate political fodder by having the public mind associate Democrats and our archenemy, Dr. Paul Hubbert, with the corruption prosecutions surrounding the community colleges. The arrest of eleven lobbyists and legislators on federal corruption charges the month before the 2010 November general election added to our political momentum that fed the monumental power shift in Alabama politics.

The federal charges were associated with the gambling legislation that was introduced in the Alabama Senate during the 2010 session. The legislation died in the House without a vote when news of the federal investigation broke. All the legislators who were charged in October 2010 were eventually acquitted, as well as most of the others. However, the gambling issue and the arrests associated with it contributed to the perception that corruption was running rampant in Alabama, and it was heavily propagandized in our favor during the 2010 election cycle.

We often sow the seeds of our own doom along with the seeds of our success. When basking in the glow of success, pride can make us full of ourselves and cause us to sow seeds of bitterness and resentment in the hearts of others. Swollen pride of the victorious exacerbates the wounded pride of the defeated. Gloating attracts adversaries like flies to garbage.

In Alabama, legislators assume office immediately upon election; however, other constitutional offices, including the governor, assume office in January following the November general election. This gave outgoing Governor Bob Riley an opportunity to call the new legislature into special session to pass sweeping ethics reform before he left public office forever.

For those who appreciate increased transparency in the political process and reining in spending by special interests on public officials, the hastily called special session was a resounding success. However, the reforms rushed through the legislative process in only seven legislative days were fraught with unintended consequences. Since most of us had never worn a bullseye, many of us, including me, were blind to the inherent dangers associated with the politicization of the enforcement of the Ethics Law, or any law for that matter.

We passed several long-overdue reforms during the special session. We made it easier to identify the source of campaign funds by eliminating the PAC-to-PAC transfers, placed restrictions on legislators working as lobbyists, mandated ethics training for public officials and lobbyists, and imposed reasonable limits on the wining and dining of public officials by lobbyists and their principals. We also passed legislation that empowered the Ethics Commission with subpoena power and protected them from the possibility of retaliatory budget cuts.

In addition, I introduced and passed a bill that restricted the ability of certain powerful legislators to appropriate money in an agency's budget for an unspecified purpose so they could later secretly direct it wherever they chose. Alabama politicians of every stripe had been speaking out against this "pass-through pork" for decades; however, this was the first bill addressing that issue that wasn't dead on arrival when introduced.

But it was probably the legislation designed to sabotage Dr. Hubbert's political machine that compelled Governor Riley to hurriedly call the special session after the new Republican supermajority legislature took office in November but before Bentley was inaugurated in January. Bills that eliminated automatic payroll deduction of state employees' dues to be used for political purposes and restricted state employees from also serving in the legislature were anathema to Dr. Hubbert and those politically allied with him.

There was concern that a coalition of surviving Democrats and Dr. Hubbert's Republican sympathizers might dig in and derail those bills with Governor Bentley's help if we waited until after he took office. After all, as a legislator Governor Bentley had voted against the Republican caucus on behalf of his loyal friend who had played a major role in helping him get elected. The entire reform package passed during the special session.

In retrospect, I believe it would have been more prudent to have been more deliberative and to have waited until the regular session. We could have still passed everything that we wanted to, including the bills designed to dismantle Dr. Hubbert's political machine. To the surprise of many, Governor Bentley jilted Dr. Hubbert and threw him under the school bus driven by the newly empowered Republican majority. Many of those who had helped him get elected felt betrayed and disappointed, but it shouldn't have been entirely unexpected, especially for Dr. Hubbert—he knew how he had convinced the pliable Representative Bentley to throw the Republican House caucus, headed by Mike Hubbard, under the bus while he and the Democrats drove it.

Governor Bentley didn't betray all his friends. He helped those who had been his close friends in the legislature by giving plum appointments within his administration. It was a win-win solution to the problem of his friends who were renegade Republican legislators that we expected would undermine the caucus agenda. By making these appointments and systematically moving these "rebels" out of the legislature, Bentley telegraphed that he had no intention to undermine the majority agenda, including the "Handshake with Alabama." Bentley wasn't the engineer of the train that ran over his former ally, Dr. Paul Hubbert, but he was certainly on board, blowing the whistle.

One of the legislators Governor Bentley appointed to serve in his administration was Representative Spencer Collier, a Republican legislator from Mobile County who supported him in the Republican primary over the Gulf Coast's favorite son, Bradley Byrne. When Governor Bentley appointed Collier director of the Alabama Department of Homeland Security, I wasn't sure that his personality, temperament, or background was well suited for an executive position at that level, but I understood the Governor's desire to reward Collier's loyalty. I just hoped he would at least have an assistant director who could compensate for his lack of executive experience and temper his often stubborn and sometimes volatile temper.

I met Spencer Collier at the Department of Public Safety 2001 in-service training at the Trooper Academy in Selma. He was a twenty-eight-year-old trooper, still wet behind the ears, and I was a seasoned veteran nearing the end of my career with a penchant for taking younger folks under my wing. One of our colleagues introduced me to Jack Collier, as he was then called, knowing that Jack was planning to run for state representative in Mobile County the following year. Since I'd narrowly lost my run for the legislative seat in Morgan County in 1998, I was glad to share some insight with him over the next couple of days.

Only a few months earlier, I'd moved from my hometown to a different district in another county and was enjoying a period of relative anonymity. Content with my personal and professional life, I had no intention of running for office again. I'd been emptying the remnants of my campaign account and was happy to contribute to his campaign. I probably wouldn't have done it had I known that I'd have my own dark horse campaign in a new hometown. Spencer and I were both elected to the legislature in the 2002 general election, same as Robert Bentley. After his election, Collier was reassigned from being a trooper in the Highway Patrol Division to serving as a spokesperson for the department in the Public Information Unit.

Soon after we were elected, it was apparent that, although our political philosophies were similar, our personalities and approaches to the legislative process were decidedly different. Collier was more confrontational and assertive, and I preferred a more conciliatory and collaborative approach to lawmaking. One evening early in our first term, we were at a reception in Montgomery continuing a discussion that we had begun earlier in the day about the Republican minority caucus leadership and political strategy. He advocated a hardline approach, like a hammer, and I preferred a subtler, more methodical strategy, like a screwdriver. Unlike me, Spencer was more predisposed toward force than persuasion, which might explain why he rose from his seat when the discussion became heated, pointed to the door, and said, "Let's take it outside!"

I was surprised that he wanted to fight over a discussion about political strategy. Fighting had not occurred to me, but I'm not one to cower. I got up and said, "Okay, if that's what you want," as I started walking for the door. Fortunately, Collier came to his senses and decided that a fight might not be a good idea and toned himself down. I don't think that we ever had any sort of confrontation after that, and I'm glad he changed his mind. A former collegiate football player, Collier was bigger, younger, and stronger than me and would have probably given me a good thrashing. It would have certainly been a public embarrassment for both of us, but in my mind, it would've still been better than cowering. I can't run from a bully.

Governor Bentley's personality was a marked contrast with his volatile friend who he placed in charge of Alabama's consolidated state law enforcement function. His desire to avoid confrontation and seek the path of least resistance also made him susceptible to being manipulated or intimidated by allies and adversaries alike and often led him to widely vacillating positions. It's difficult for those who have not personally experienced it to imagine how a person could discuss an issue with Governor Bentley and hear only a few hours later that he had changed his mind completely.

Despite this tendency, I don't believe he was intentionally dishonest or deceptive. He was just easily swayed by strong personalities. Grandpa Ball used to say that a man with a watch can always tell what time it is, but a man with two watches is never sure. Governor Bentley was like a man with two watches.

I doubt anyone bore the brunt of the governor's tendency to vacillate and choose the path of least resistance any worse than Dr. Hubbert's formerly dominant—but still powerful—organization, the Alabama Education Association. After guiding Bentley into the governor's office, they were almost entirely shut out. Dr. Bentley joined in the Republican "Handshake with Alabama" with one hand while giving Dr. Hubbert a thumb in the eye with the other. I have little doubt that in his prime, the brilliant political tactician Dr. Hubbert would have seen it all coming and outmaneuvered everyone to find a way to make the most out of it. But his advancing age and declining health, coupled with being repeatedly steamrolled by the Speaker Hubbard and the Republican supermajority during the 2011 session, finally took the fight out of him.

In October 2011, Dr. Hubbert knew that his long, valiant struggle to overcome the frailties of an ailing body and remain a powerful force in the political arena was over. It's a remarkable testimony to his perseverance that he'd survived against the odds for as long as he did. He had undergone a liver transplant in 1989 and, the following year, was almost elected governor. As one of the longest surviving liver transplant patients in the world at the time of his retirement, he underwent frequent dialysis due to kidney failure associated with his ongoing treatment. Dr. Hubbert realized that it was in the best interest of the powerful association that he dearly loved to hand over the reins to his chosen successor, the far less shrewd Dr. Henry Mabry.

Dr. Mabry was the Ray Perkins of Alabama politics. For those who do not follow Alabama football with religious fervor, Ray Perkins was Coach Bear Bryant's chosen successor at Alabama. Dr. Mabry was doomed to failure because he was unable to recognize that the success of his predecessor could not be replicated under the new paradigm.

The rise of the Republican supermajority in the legislature led by Speaker Mike Hubbard resulted in changes implemented by his "Handshake with Alabama" that significantly weakened the power of the Alabama Education Association and certain other powerful interest groups. Some of the powerful interests were able to adapt to the power shift very well, but others, especially the powerful teachers' organization, could not. Systemic changes being made, such as taking away the ability to use payroll deductions for political campaigns, were viewed by some as a stake into the heart of the AEA.

The Republican supermajority's agenda might have been a "Handshake with Alabama" to some, but for others, it was a cold slap. Dr. Mabry still had a pile of money to use while legal challenges delayed the implementation of the reforms. Plans were in the works for a major push during the 2014 election cycle to remove or weaken the powerful Speaker Mike Hubbard, which would require the traditionally Democratic AEA to secretly shake some Republican hands.

Unfortunately for Speaker Mike Hubbard, the ethics reforms that were rushed through the legislative process by the well-meaning but misguided Republican supermajority with the intention of curbing traditionally Democratic power brokers backfired terribly. We had inadvertently executed an extensive power shift from the legislative branch of state government, controlled by two bodies containing 140 bipartisan officials elected from all over the state, to the Attorney General's Office, controlled by a single politically ambitious statewide elected official.

During the remainder of my political career, the extent of that dangerous power shift would continually unfold itself to me. It seemed that no matter what I did to sound the alarm, nobody listened. Maybe nobody cares. But I care. And when you finish reading the rest of this book, I hope you will, too.

PART 3

Corruption and Cannabis

CHAPTER 13

Unholy Alliances

After orchestrating the 2010 election sweep as the chairman of the Alabama Republican Party, Mike Hubbard focused his attention on the Speaker's chair and opted not to run for another term as party chair. Despite overwhelming success at the ballot box, all was not well within the bowels of the Alabama Republican Party.

Party loyalists, regardless of political stripe, tend to be more opinionated, strong willed, and combative than the general populace. Without a common enemy to band together against, they will divide into factions and squabble among themselves. This tendency usually makes strong partisans better suited for resistance than governing.

Politics is a never-ending struggle between the "ins" and the "outs," and the 2010 Alabama general election kicked Democrats out and put Republicans in. Mike Hubbard was positioned in the center of power at the state level. Unfortunately for him, that also meant he was in the center of the bullseye for those who felt left out and wanted in, creating a sizeable number of adversaries pointing their arrows at him from many different directions.

For those wanting to exercise influence with lasting impact from within a political system, I would suggest the outer edge of the inner circle as a more optimal position than the center of power. It's close enough to power to influence decisions but far enough to minimize many of the dangers of holding power. Adversaries usually aim at the center of the bullseye, not the outer edge of the inner circle. You still might take an occasional hit, but at least it won't be intentional. The best shooters hit the bullseye or very close to it most of the time and the worst ones miss the target completely.

The internal power struggle within the state GOP in the aftermath of the 2010 election sweep seemed even more intense than the struggle with the Democrats had been. At the February 2011 meeting of the Alabama Republican Party, one of Hubbard's intraparty rivals, former State Senator Bill Armistead, was elected to replace him as chairman. Mike Hubbard might have risen to power in the legislature, but his influence in the Alabama Republican Party had waned considerably.

Chairman Armistead was a staunch hardliner who would later serve as campaign chairman for Judge Roy Moore's ill-fated 2017 run for U.S. Senate. Hubbard was aligned with the more pragmatic business-oriented wing of the party. Not only were they aligned with differing party factions, but personal animosity seemed to add to their rivalry—although both made occasional attempts to appear friendly.

Persistent rumors from Hubbard's rivals about party spending during the 2010 election prompted Chairman Armistead to call for a complete audit of the party finances. When the audit was finished, Armistead refused to release it under the claim that he didn't want to harm Speaker Hubbard. However, his refusal to release the audit had the opposite effect by helping to fuel the rumors of impropriety throughout 2012, despite the Speaker's persistent requests that it be released. Years later, when it was eventually released, there were no surprises in the audit.

It was no secret that while Hubbard was party chair, his company Craftmaster Printing contracted a high volume of printing with the party, and it was no surprise when a report generated by the audit indicated Hubbard's company had received about $800,000 in direct and indirect payments from the state party for printing. Although the company had done a huge volume of the printing work for Republicans during the 2010 election cycle, I saw no evidence of impropriety associated with it. The service was excellent and the pricing competitive.

Politics creates strange bedfellows, and some of the most unlikely of them were allied to knock Mike Hubbard off his pedestal. Although wounded, Dr. Paul Hubbert and Dr. Henry Mabry were not politically dead, and they were not about to allow the Alabama Education Association to continue to bleed power without a fight. Although left wing by most conservative standards, they were looking to help fund any credible legislative candidate willing to oppose Speaker Hubbard or those aligned with him.

But in 2010, public support from the Alabama Education Association was thought to have been the kiss of death for an Alabama Republican. The state party had even passed a resolution discouraging Republican candidates from accepting AEA contributions. The AEA leaders needed someone whose animosity for Mike Hubbard exceeded ideological qualms a political activist from the right might have about secretly funneling AEA money to Republican candidates. John Rice was perfect for the task.

During the 1980s, Rice served a term in the Alabama State Senate as a George Wallace populist-style Democrat. While serving in the legislature, his volatile personality earned him the nickname "Hand Grenade." In recent years, he had been involved with the populist tea party movement and his antiestablishment fervor seemed to only be exceeded by his disgust for Mike Hubbard.

Rice founded the "Alabama Foundation for Limited Government," a federal nonprofit which was used as a shell to funnel large amounts of AEA money to his state political action committee "Stop Common Core," which in turn funded Republican candidates willing to challenge Speaker Hubbard and his allies.

"Common core" is one of the many education reform fads that have come and gone over the years. It was apparently conceived with noble intentions, one of which was teaching students to think more conceptually, with less emphasis on rote memorization than more traditional methods. It was originally intended to be driven from the state level as a nonpolitical effort to rationalize American education into a twenty-first century model. Notable early supporters included Republican Governors Jeb Bush and Chris Christie, and the reform was already adopted by several states before it began to draw major opposition, mostly rallying around concerns about nationalizing education.

When President Obama embraced common core, Republican opposition began to rise until it eventually went through the roof. When it became a partisan issue, the common core movement lost any potential it might have had to transform education in a positive way. It became a rallying cry among tea party-style activists, one of which was John Rice. The Alabama Education Association shrewdly took no official position on common core, but its leadership recognized its value to them as a political wedge between the business and tea party wings of the Alabama Republican Party.

John Rice provided a secret conduit for AEA money to flow to the candidates of their choice under the auspice of his "Stop Common Core" PAC. At least some of those candidates were used as what Vladimir Lenin is said to have referred to as "useful idiots": political jargon for those who are unwittingly manipulated into aiding a political cause they would not otherwise support.

Jesse "Big Daddy" Unruh was Speaker of the California Assembly from 1961 to 1969 and has been credited with coining the phrase "Money is the mother's milk of politics." If money is the mother's milk of politics, propaganda is the baby that it feeds.

Politics and propaganda are almost synonymous with one another. Neither can exist without the other. To be truly effective, propaganda needs at least some element of truth it can bend to suit whoever or whatever cause it promotes. Political campaigns are nothing but propaganda machines, and political consultants are propagandists. The degree of truth contained in propaganda is always debatable, but the primary purpose of propaganda is to sway public opinion. A propagandist only presents that portion of truth that serves its purpose while ignoring, obscuring, or even suppressing whatever does not work.

After Mike Hubbard became Speaker, the propaganda machine that helped him rise to power began to fade, while the one designed to turn public opinion against him began gaining momentum. A persistent din of accusations became a steady source of irritation for the Speaker. The allegations emanating from the droning cacophony of dissent continued to intensify throughout 2012, making it clear to Speaker Hubbard and his allies that opposition was preparing an all-out effort during the 2014 election cycle to topple him. At the center of that effort would be a crafty Republican consultant and young attorney named Baron Coleman.

Before the 2014 election cycle began, Coleman had been a practicing law partner with State Representative Joe Hubbard, one of the few bright spots for the Alabama Democratic Party during the 2010 Republican wave. He had been the blue dot in the middle of a red tsunami, the only

Democrat to defeat an incumbent Republican for a seat in the Alabama House of Representatives.

A brash young attorney with a brilliant mind, Hubbard had an impressive pedigree among the attributes working in his favor. His great-grandfather was Dr. Leonidas Hill, who in 1902 became the first American doctor to successfully perform open-heart surgery. His grandfather, J. Lister Hill, represented Alabama in the U.S. House of Representatives from 1923 until 1939 before a thirty-year stint in the U.S. Senate that lasted until 1969.

An Indiana native, Baron Coleman didn't have an impressive Alabama pedigree like his law partner, but he had plenty of chutzpah and a brilliant mind. The law practice established by the two bright young attorneys would probably have been highly successful had they not been bitten by political bugs that led them in different directions. Joe Hubbard would be the 2014 Democratic nominee for Alabama attorney general while Coleman would form a new firm, Spot On Strategies, to provide consulting services at a few dozen legislative races in conjunction with the forces aligned to unseat Speaker Mike Hubbard. Many of the services would be funded by AEA through the conduit provided by John Rice.

In 2011, Attorney General Luther Strange hired Matt Hart to serve in the Public Corruption and White-Collar Crime Division. From media reports and talk among those in my political and law enforcement circle, it seemed Luther had made a good choice, expecting the package of ethics reforms we had just passed to be professionally and impartially enforced. I was completely unaware of Hart's methods and the degree to which he utilized propaganda as part of his prosecutorial strategy.

In 2012, Baron Coleman began collaborating with Hart to target Speaker Hubbard, bringing the audit report to the attention of Hart, who became chief of the Alabama Attorney General's Special Prosecutions Unit. The surreptitious, illicit information pipeline between the crafty political operative and the zealous prosecutor was mutually beneficial to the political and prosecutorial propaganda efforts aligned against the beleaguered Speaker and his allies throughout the 2014 election cycle and beyond.

By December 2012, a subpoena was issued from the Attorney General's Office for the Alabama Republican Party audit report covering Mike

Hubbard's tenure as party chairman. The following month Attorney General Strange recused himself, ostensibly because he had used Mike Hubbard's Craftmaster Printing. Van Davis, a retired district attorney from St. Clair County, was appointed to convene a special grand jury in Lee County to investigate Coleman's allegations, but Matt Hart was ever present. Throughout much of the Lee County investigation and prosecution directed against the Speaker, Davis was distracted by a struggle against cancer that he would eventually lose.

Speaker Hubbard had been wanting the Republican Party audit report released, so I figured he would get his wish. Davis enjoyed an excellent reputation and I expected him to get the truth of the matter in the open and take appropriate action, regardless of how it fell. Aware of the propaganda machine churning innuendo and gossip against the Speaker leading up to the 2014 election cycle, I didn't give the allegations much credibility at the time.

My first indication that something might be hinky with the investigation was around late 2013 when my longtime friend, Representative Ed Henry, told me that Baron Coleman's former law partner, Representative Joe Hubbard, had given him information that he surmised could have only come from the Lee County grand jury investigation.

Ed and I had been friends for many years, and I didn't doubt the veracity of his recollection. Though we often disagree and walk very separate paths, I've always tried to be a worthy mentor to him. He has never lied to me, and I don't believe he ever will.

While Ed believed that the information Joe Hubbard shared with him must have been intentionally leaked by authorities through Coleman, I was skeptical. Baron Coleman and Joe Hubbard were both smart as whips and it seemed possible to me that they could have gotten lucky by gleaning useful bits of scuttlebutt and patching them together to form an accurate picture. It seemed that Ed was jumping to a conclusion. As a former investigator, I am conditioned to resist quick conclusions.

Finding the truth is like putting together a huge jigsaw puzzle. It requires patience to collect the pieces, figure out where they fit, and finally how they all fit together to form a big picture of the whole truth. If we force a piece into the wrong place, the picture is distorted. Until the puzzle is finished, we're just guessing. An experienced investigator's mind is trained to search for missing pieces, put them in their proper place, and continually contemplate how they all fit into a larger pattern. Unresolved issues can gnaw within an investigator's mind, like mice chewing on electrical wires until they create a spark.

Hubbard and Coleman keeping their ears to the ground and picking up tidbits of information about the case is one thing, but intentionally seeking information from someone within the official investigation to use in a political campaign would be an entirely different matter. Using an official position to influence political action is not just unethical—it is illegal under Alabama law.

My professional experience caused me to dismiss my friend's conclusion as amateurish speculation, but sometimes professionals are wrong and amateurs are right. This was one of those times. Ed reported the leak to Mike Hubbard's attorney, Mark White, who reported it to Matt Hart, the lead prosecutor for the Hubbard case. Unfortunately, Hart was the source of the leak, and he summoned Coleman to a meeting outside the Lee County Courthouse to discuss keeping their relationship from being exposed. The conversation was recorded by Coleman.

An excerpt from the conversation between Hart and Coleman indicates that Hart knew their collaboration was improper and even told the consultant that he would need to lie to the grand jury if questioned about their relationship. He also speaks about using the grand jury secrecy act to keep their relationship hidden:

HART: It isn't going to cause me heartache, it's going to cause you heartache; because the way it is, is, we are going to be back in front of that grand jury and we're going to be going into some shit that we don't want. And then that will be ultimately disclosed if this grand jury produces it.

COLEMAN: And I don't want to do. . .

HART: And I don't want to do that, um, and I don't want, um, you know, we're not making, you are a confidential source for us, that's what you are. I mean, you would be classified under the federal system as a confidential source, not an informant, but a confidential source. I don't want to document all of that. I don't want to document all of that, but if others reasonably believe that your name was raised by Mark White, your name was raised by Mark White. We're leaving all this shit out.

COLEMAN: Yeah. . .

HART: We're playing defense. I'm gonna do what I need to do in my job. . .

COLEMAN: Yeah. . .

HART: We've got to, we have procedures in our job.

COLEMAN: Right.

HART: So, if you leave someone with the impression that you have a connection with someone in the Attorney General's Office, one of the things you do to make that believable is leave them with an impression that is believable.

COLEMAN: Right.

HART: Well, if they repeat that, we're gonna have to be in here in front of this grand jury, saying, "Well, it may be believable, but it just isn't true."

COLEMAN: Right.

HART: And there's a way to do that, and it's going to be painful. It's going to be somewhat painful for me and I think it's going to be painful for you.

COLEMAN: Yeah.

HART: You know, and then we're gonna be under the grand jury secrecy thing and that really is gonna shut you down because once you go in there and we say, "Don't you speak about this;" it is a very broad prohibition, people argue about the constitutionality of it. But up until the time the case is adjudicated for sure. . .

COLEMAN: Uh-huh. . .

HART: . . .and, uh, the investigation is finished, and the case is, uh, completed, in the judicial system, we're on utterly solid ground shuttin' people up, and that will completely close you down on these things.

COLEMAN: Uh-huh, you're right. . .

HART: Or cause us huge problems, where if we get a report then, it just puts us in a whole different. . .

COLEMAN: Well. . .

HART: . . .universe, that I'm just telling you, I know what I'm talking about. . .

COLEMAN: I know, I know.

HART: You know your area. . .

COLEMAN: Yeah

HART: . . .and my area is a narrow little niche, and I know my spot. This will be a fucking mess.

The excerpt of the conversation recorded by Baron Coleman, obviously without Hart's knowledge, was not made public until March 3, 2016, when it was imbedded in an article written by AL.com reporter Chuck Dean. The news article did not give the context of the conversation and I didn't know the recording was made shortly after Ed Henry reported the leak until Baron Coleman told me in 2017.

The recording indicates that Matt Hart was aware that his relationship with Coleman was improper and that he was willing to bring Coleman before the grand jury and deny what the recording confirmed. It sounded like Hart would have been willing to suborn perjury and conceal his relationship with Coleman had it been necessary. The cagey political consultant agreed to keep quiet, aware of the political value of his information pipeline with Hart and the campaigns that hired his firm during the 2014 election cycle. Besides that, he didn't want Hart to squeeze him into committing perjury.

Coleman was sufficiently silenced, but Ed Henry was not. In January 2014, Hart used the investigation as a pretense to bring Representative Henry before the Lee County grand jury, but his ulterior motive seemed to be suppression. He needed to stop Henry from speaking publicly about his information pipeline with Baron Coleman, and that is exactly what he did. He placed the pesky legislator under oath, interrogated him about the "leak," and then invoked the grand jury secrecy act to silence him. The tactic worked, and Henry stopped speaking publicly about Hart and his relationship with Baron Coleman.

Matt Hart's abuse of his authority and position was not limited to secret collaboration with Coleman and taking official action to keep their illicit relationship concealed. He also conspired with one of Coleman's clients, Josh Pipkin, to ambush Pipkin's opponent in the upcoming June 3rd Republican primary. The ambush occurred on the very same day in front of the same Lee County grand jury that he used to silence Ed Henry.

Barry Moore was the House District 91 state representative. He was the owner and operator of a waste-hauling business in Enterprise when he was recruited by Mike Hubbard to run for the legislature. He defeated the incumbent, Representative Terry Spicer, a favorite of the Alabama Education Association, during the 2010 Republican sweep of the State House. The year after he was defeated by Moore, Spicer pled guilty to accepting bribes from a gambling lobbyist while serving in the legislature. As the 2014 election cycle approached, Moore was a prime target of the Alabama Education Association and the political coalition funded by them to bring down Speaker Hubbard.

The Enterprise city attorney Josh Pipkin was the coalition's choice to run against Moore in the Republican primary. He was one of Baron Coleman's clients and received over $50,000 from John Rice's Stop Common Core PAC. It is telling that Representative Moore, a diehard conservative, was and remains a staunch opponent of the Common Core Curriculum. Hypocrisy and politics are like Siamese twins.

Pipkin secretly recorded a conversation with Moore during the summer of 2013 in which they tried to discourage one another from running in 2014. In what appeared to be jostling between political rivals, Pipkin manipulated the discussion toward whether Speaker Hubbard planned to use his authority to block an upcoming economic development project in retaliation for upcoming campaign, and Moore took the bait. Trying to discourage a potential political opponent from running is one thing, but it appeared the city prosecutor from Enterprise was doing something more sinister. He was trying to entrap his legally naïve opponent into a committing a crime.

On January 24, 2014, over seven months later, Moore innocently appeared before the Lee County grand jury without any knowledge of what he would be questioned about. He had no idea when Matt Hart began questioning him about his phone call with Pipkin that he was in the middle of an orchestrated political ambush. It never occurred to Moore that Hart's interrogation was part of a conspiracy with Pipkin to create a crime, an unethical departure from investigating crime.

When Hart began springing questions at Moore about his conversation with Pipkin, Moore initially responded that he couldn't remember. When Hart pressed him further, Moore did something an experienced witness would not do: He answered while attempting to recall, while he was still unsure, and remembered some of it wrong. Hart then used the recording furnished by Pipkin, who was the Enterprise city attorney, Baron Coleman's client, and Moore's opponent in the upcoming Republican primary, to spring a "perjury" trap on the hapless waste hauler.

Hart began squeezing Moore with the threat of a perjury charge to pressure him into cooperating with the investigation of Speaker Hubbard. The problem was that Moore was already cooperating and had no knowledge of illegal activity. He was not part of a criminal conspiracy and was innocent, unless being a friend and political ally of Mike Hubbard was a crime. What Hart had done was tantamount to hunting over a baited field, and as far as trophy value is concerned, he had bagged Bambi.

On Monday, April 14, 2014, the Coffee County Republican Club invited the political rivals to speak at a meeting. Pipkin went after Moore about his association with Speaker Hubbard and the grand jury investigation in Lee County. It was reported that Pipkin told the group that he had been given permission by the Attorney General's Office to share the information. The following week, Barry Moore was indicted for two counts of perjury.

I was unaware of Matt Hart's illicit collaboration with Baron Coleman at the time, but even so, the indictment of Moore for perjury seemed hinky. Even from what little I could glean from the sketchy media accounts, it looked like an obvious political ambush. Even an investigator with rudimentary interview skills should know that getting details wrong while struggling to remember something is completely different than perjury. Moore's naivety about the criminal justice system and his association with Mike Hubbard made him an irresistible target for Hart. If you're a hammer, everything looks like a nail.

The recording Hart used in the ambush raised questions in my mind. How did the prosecution acquire it? Was it made under the direction of the prosecution or fed to them by the candidate? If the recording was made under the supervision of the prosecution, they would have been clearly engaging in a political activity, a huge no-no. If the recording had been furnished to the prosecution by candidate Pipkin, using it in a legal proceeding would also be problematic because of its political context. A recording furnished by an active political operative to an investigating authority should be taken with apprehension and caution, as if it were a volatile explosive or a venomous snake. But this one was exploited with reckless abandon.

Timing Moore's arrest at the end of April before the June 3rd primary election added to my growing suspicion that the prosecution was colluding with political operatives. If they weren't trying to influence the outcome of the election, they should have waited until after the primary. It was patently obvious to me that prosecutorial decisions were being made that gave maximum political benefit to the anti-Mike Hubbard coalition, and information flowing from the investigation was feeding the propaganda machine operating on behalf of the political forces aligned to bring Speaker Hubbard down.

Despite the ill-timed arrest and the leaks, Hart's support was not enough to drag Pipkin to victory. Barry Moore still managed to win decisively, 55 percent to 45 percent. However, the June 3rd Republican primary was not a total loss for Coleman and the anti-Hubbard coalition. The arrest of Barry Moore and the information that leaked from the investigation was heavily propagandized with some success.

Of the sixteen House races targeted by the coalition that hired Baron Coleman in the 2014 Republican primary, seven pro-Hubbard candidates were defeated. Coleman managed some very good candidates that might have been able to win some of them even without the information that he received from Hart. Political consultants are like jockeys in a horse race: The jockey doesn't matter much if a thoroughbred is running against a nag; but if the horses are closely matched, the ability of the jockey can be crucial in determining the winner, especially if the jockey has inside information unavailable to his competitors.

Coleman is a talented political consultant who knew how to play the inside information flowing between him and Hart. The mailers and television ads he produced to smear Speaker Hubbard's allies could be used with complete confidence that nothing from the investigation could exonerate Hubbard or his associates prior to the election and cause the ads to backfire.

Barry Moore miraculously survived the primary election, despite the perjury trap. But it would take more than an election win to free him from the legal trap that Matt Hart and his primary opponent had sprung on him. He still had felony charges hanging over his head and would have to face the duo again in court in front of a jury.

CHAPTER 14

Carly's Law

On Sunday morning, October 13, 2013, I was wading through my regular slew of emails, when I opened one titled "Health Issues." The first line of the message almost caused me to swipe it into the trash folder. It read, "I am asking for your support for Alabama Medical Marijuana."

Medical marijuana was a political nonstarter in Alabama, and I wasn't inclined to waste time with it. Besides that, my mind had been set against legalized marijuana for a long time, and I was convinced it had no medical value and most of the people who clamored for its legalization just wanted to get high without fear of reprisal.

Alabama is the buckle of the Bible Belt. Even before the 2010 Republican sweep, medical marijuana legislation couldn't get traction in the Democratic-controlled Alabama Legislature. It had taken the craft beer industry years to gain a foothold and pass a modest bill, and beer doesn't have a social stigma like marijuana. It didn't seem possible that the Alabama Legislature would pass a medical marijuana bill in the next decade, much less in the next session with elections looming.

Medical marijuana bills had been introduced in the Alabama House but went nowhere. The previous year, Representative Patricia Todd had introduced three medical marijuana bills, earning her the Shroud Award, an honor of dubious distinction given on the final day of the regular session each year to the sponsor of the deadest House bill of the year. I don't believe a medical marijuana bill had ever gotten a full committee vote in the House or had even been introduced in the Senate.

But if a real person cared enough about it to send an email at 1:49 a.m., the least I could do is read it and try to respond. So, completely unaware of the impact it would have on me, I continued to read.

From: sgibbs58
To: mikeball
Sent: 10/13/2013 1:49 AM
Subject: Health Issues
Representative Ball,

I am asking for your support for Alabama Medical Marijuana. First, let me state that I do not smoke pot nor does anyone in my family. We are Christians and don't even drink.

My concern is for my 14-month-old granddaughter who is an epileptic. There have been many studies to show that MMJ helps seizures tremendously. The type of marijuana we need has little to no THC so there is not much 'get high' properties to it at all. We need the other part of the plant called CBD.

Right now our baby is just 'getting by' but there has been a lot of research where the CBD oil is legal and it has helped so many patients. 20 states now have legal medical marijuana but after having my family live here for generations we just hate to move and try to start over in another state.

There are many people in Alabama with Epileptic children and most like me would go to the ends of the earth to stop the seizures so their lives can be normal. In our case our granddaughter was born with a gene deletion that has never been recorded in history so that does not give our doctor much to go on in respect to what we can expect in the future. We give her the best of care and opted for a neurologist at Le Bonheur Hospital in Memphis since he has such a great reputation with neurology and epilepsy. She has no other health problems and is smart as a whip but some days she may have up to 100 seizures.

Please consider what I am asking and just imagine if this were your child or grandchild. Low to no THC marijuana has got to be so much better than the Valium she has to take now to stop her convulsions. Please help us if you can!!!

For more info----http://en.wikipedia.org/wiki/Cannabidiol
Thank you,
Sherry Gibbs aka. Meemaw
Madison, Alabama

Also, this is who we are fighting for :) She didn't get to enjoy her first

Baby Charlotte Dalton photo was attached to the email.

birthday because she was asleep from Valium (This was the only birthday photo we were able to make)

I responded with the following email to put her off, and let her down easy:

-----Original Message-----
From: Mike Ball
To: sgibbs58
Sent: 10/14/13 11:57 AM
Subject: Re: Health Issues
Thanks for the email. I wish we could get a bill that would allow legitimate medical uses for marijuana or at least its derivatives. I would support a bill if it had the proper controls, but unfortunately the bills I've seen in Alabama were so broad, they would legalize marijuana for recreational use by making enforcement impossible. I'm not familiar with CBD, but it might be easier to legalize CBD oil with a prescription. I'll see if I can get some research done on this.
Mike

It was readily apparent that this was not a ruse from some pothead wanting to get high. It was a humble plea from a loving grandmother, desperate to find relief for her granddaughter. However, I was convinced marijuana had no medicinal value, and since CBD oil was derived from marijuana, it must be a modern-day version of snake oil. I searched Wikipedia and read a little about cannabidiol, but the article stated that available research neither proved nor disproved its medicinal value.

Knowing of my position on marijuana legalization, my legislative assistant Clif Richard was surprised when I asked him to see if he could find out anything about using CBD oil for medical purposes. Clif is also an ordained minister dedicated to ministering to the needy, mostly in the Montgomery area, and is not someone who takes substance abuse lightly. I had confidence that he would be diligent in finding any potential for abuse. When something seems too good to be true, it usually is, and I expected Clif to help me get off the hook with Mrs. Gibbs. To my surprise, what he found out only enticed me to nibble at it more.

National interest in the use of CBD oil to control seizures began a few months earlier when Dr. Sanjay Gupta, a neurosurgeon and the CNN chief medical correspondent made a drastic reversal of his long-held position on medical marijuana. His documentary, *Weed*, and his writings such as "Why I Changed My Mind on Weed" were compelling. The story of Charlotte Figi, a child suffering from a form of epilepsy known as Dravet Syndrome was a living testimony to the potential therapeutic value of CBD oil.

During the days that followed, I couldn't get the picture of little Charlotte Dalton out of my mind. She seemed to bear a strong resemblance to another little girl whose memory had been asleep in my mind for many years.

Lois was the youngest child of a large family that lived up the road from me when I was growing up. She was about three years old and was the center of attention, especially to her older brother who was about my age. He was a big easygoing and good-natured fella with a humble, kind spirit who doted on his little sister.

I was eighteen years old when I drove past their house and saw him running toward the road with his baby sister in his arms. When I stopped my car, I heard him wail, "Oh Lord, I've shot my baby sister; oh Lord, forgive me."

While I rushed them to the nearest hospital, my friend sat in the back seat holding his baby sister, saying how much he loved her and desperately wailing for the Lord to help her. When I glanced back at them in the back seat, the gaping wound in her chest made it clear that the situation was hopeless. He didn't know the shotgun was loaded until it went off. It was a tragic, horrendous accident.

Our desperate prayers while I drove them to the hospital and continuing while we waited outside the emergency room seemed useless. Lois was dead. Nothing could help that. Scrubbing Lois's blood from the crevices in the back seat of my car later that day, my mind grappled with the question that has challenged my faith many times since: Why would a powerful, omnipotent God, the very essence of love and compassion, allow such a thing to happen?

The same question was on my mind while I gazed at the face of the innocent baby in the photo that awakened unresolved sorrows that had been accumulating within me for many, many years. While I grappled with the issue during the weeks that followed, my nights were filled with desperate prayer, peaceful contemplation of scripture, and very strange dreams, all of which worked in tandem to arouse my faith and force open my mind. The world is full of suffering, and there is little we can do about most of it—but sometimes we are put a position where we can. When that happens, there is a moral obligation to do so. For those who are followers of Christ, that obligation includes self-sacrifice.

It eventually became apparent that I would be unable to avoid introducing legislation to decriminalize CBD oil for medical purposes. One person who helped me arrive at that conclusion was Dustin Chandler, whose daughter Carly had suffered from seizures since she was eight weeks old. In 2012, she was diagnosed with the same rare, incurable affliction as Charlotte Figi, who had captured the attention of Dr. Sanjay Gupta earlier that year.

When I reached out to Dustin, we hit it off immediately. He was a police officer with the Pelham Police Department and had been no marijuana advocate, either. After working through his initial shock of Carly's diagnosis, Dustin began desperately exploring options and discovered CBD. He had already done a lot of legwork, laying the foundation for grassroots support for Carly's Law that would be necessary for such a politically absurd thing in Alabama to have a glimmer of hope for success. Dustin was a highly motivated, independent thinker with enough self-discipline to listen and follow instructions. He was a perfect partner for this undertaking.

One of the first things I asked of Dustin was to visit Dr. Joe Godfrey, executive director of the Alabama Citizens Action Program (ALCAP). AL-CAP is a social conservative Christian lobbying group and could swing some Republican votes in the legislature. Dustin didn't know about my ulterior motive in sending him to see Dr. Godfrey. Without divine intervention, I was certain that our effort would fail. So, like Gideon in the Bible, I threw down the fleece.

I knew Dr. Godfrey would be predisposed against Carly's Law since he and ALCAP consistently opposed any legislation that might loosen restrictions on marijuana, alcohol, or any other substance with potential for abuse. As a social conservative lobbyist, he could be relied upon to oppose almost any law that decriminalized any form of cannabis for any reason. I prayed to the Lord that I would take Dr. Godfrey's support as a sign to introduce Carly's Law. The next day Dustin was excited when he called to tell me that Dr. Godfrey said we needed to do it.

I was still uncertain. Since Gideon threw down the fleece a second time, I sent Dustin to see Representative Allen Farley, a fellow House member who I expected to be one of the least likely members to support a bill to decriminalize any form of cannabis. Farley is a retired senior law enforcement officer and minister whose faith and moral philosophy were near to those of Dr. Godfrey. Once again Dustin reported a positive response.

I was getting close to going all in for Carly's Law, but political pragmatism and spiritual weakness made me throw down the fleece a third time. I sent Dustin to talk to Speaker of the House Mike Hubbard. Without the support of the Speaker, Carly's Law had no chance and, in the unlikely event it had his full support, it only had a slim chance.

With the 2014 elections looming, Speaker Hubbard was under a great deal of pressure facing stiff political opposition from the odd coalition aligned against him and his allies. I was concerned that Carly's Law would be a political risk that he would not be willing to take in the face of a propaganda machine geared up to challenge his supermajority, with the aid of information leaking to it from the special grand jury investigation in Lee County.

However, when Dustin made his presentation to Speaker Hubbard, I was surprised by his support even more than Dr. Godfrey's or Representative Farley's. Speaker Hubbard told Dustin that it needed to be done and said, "I'm a father and any father who loves his children would have to do this." The support of the Speaker of the House greatly improved our chances for success.

With a contentious election season looming, and being one of Speaker Hubbard's allies, I expected that sponsoring Carly's Law would surely cause me to draw a primary opponent and might even get me defeated. However, I was convinced that the Lord's hand was on it; my political career was not a major factor in my decision. If my career in politics was about to end, Carly's Law would be a good hill for it to die on.

Before I was drawn to Carly's Law, Representative Patricia Todd was planning another run at the 2014 Shroud Award by introducing it in the upcoming session. When I called her to share my desire to sponsor the bill, there was a stunned silence over the phone before my left-wing Democratic friend delightfully agreed that I should carry the bill. A medical marijuana bill sponsored by a conservative, Republican committee chairman who is also a retired state trooper is much different than one sponsored by a left-wing Democrat, even if it's the same bill.

Even so, the public announcement of my intention to introduce Carly's Law was initially met with lots of skepticism, some derision, and almost no expectation of success. By the time I introduced it on January 14, 2014, my concern for the families it would help was crowding out my interest in the upcoming election cycle, the investigation of Speaker Hubbard, the state budgets, and the myriad of other bills.

I was surprised when Senator Paul Sanford eagerly volunteered to be the Senate sponsor for what looked like a political kamikaze mission for an Alabama Republican, but he obviously knew what he was getting into. He has stated since he left office that Carly's Law was the most satisfying achievement of his legislative career.

The House version of Carly's Law was initially assigned to the Judiciary

Committee, chaired by Representative Paul DeMarco of Birmingham. I fully expected a fair hearing when he learned how CBD was different from recreational marijuana and met some of the people who would benefit from its decriminalization. As originally introduced, Carly's Law was innocuous and minimal. It would provide an affirmative defense to the charge of possession of marijuana for those who possessed cannabis oil with very low levels of THC, the constituent of marijuana with psychoactive properties, while under a doctor's care for seizures.

I recognized the added difficulty of passing a controversial bill during an election year, but a strong show of public support and good polling numbers should help calm the nerves of politicians shaky about the stigma associated with marijuana. I didn't want anyone to be politically damaged for supporting Carly's Law, including Paul DeMarco, who was the front runner for an open seat in the U.S. Congress.

To my surprise, I had no opponent when primary qualification ended. But that wasn't the case for Speaker Hubbard and many of our allies who were about to face a fierce onslaught. The families supporting Carly's Law were masterful in their grassroots efforts to communicate their message to the public as the legislative session began to progress.

By early March, the political repercussions I had previously expected dissipated. At my request, Carly's Law was included in caucus polling conducted during the session. It indicated huge support for Carly's Law—over 80 percent of Republican Primary voters. Our strategy to educate the minds and win the hearts of the public first should have made it easy for the politicians to follow. I had underestimated the moral discernment of the public at large. But the stigma attached to marijuana was ingrained deeper within some of my colleagues than I thought. One of these was Paul DeMarco.

Judiciary Chairman DeMarco not only refused to put Carly's Law on the agenda, but he also refused to even discuss the bill with either Dustin or me. Voter reaction to DeMarco's obstinance toward Carly's Law was one of the key factors that drove him from being the overwhelming front-runner in his congressional race to getting trounced by Gary Palmer, 64 percent to 36 percent.

As we approached the midway point of the session, it was apparent that DeMarco wasn't the only one determined to run out the clock and kill Carly's Law. There were indications that Speaker Hubbard's concern over the relentless propaganda war overrode the compassion he had initially shown for the innocent victims of horrible seizures. However, I kept poking at it until he revealed how far he had come from his initial favorable response to Carly's Law.

Members of the House Republican caucus were being briefed by a consultant about polling results of various issues but failed to mention the overwhelming support for Carly's Law. When the floor was open for questions, I immediately raised my hand, but Speaker Hubbard would barely look in my direction. I kept my hand up until he was forced to call on me. I asked about polling related to Carly's Law.

The consultant asked, "What's Carly's Law?"

Speaker Hubbard angrily responded, "Pot!"

He had decided that Carly's Law was not going to pass and hadn't bothered to tell me. The betrayal felt like a knife in my chest as I realized loyalty was a one-way street. Grief overwhelmed me as I rushed out of the room.

But I wasn't the only one who had been betrayed. Families of suffering children who would benefit had made countless trips to Montgomery for nothing. A rare opportunity to ease unnecessary suffering would be lost because those with the power to help didn't have the empathy to help. Families would continue to be forced to decide between breaking the law and facing possible arrest, moving out to another state, or helplessly watching their loved ones suffer.

The caucus meeting adjourned minutes later and several caucus members consoled me as I sat in a nearby stairwell and mourned before going back to my office and continuing to wallow in remorse and ask forgiveness for failing to do what I believed to be my primary purpose for being in the legislature. If I can't pass a bill that eases helpless suffering and doesn't even cost anything, what's the point of me even being here? I was trying to give up when there was a knock on my office door and Mac McCutcheon walked in.

Mac is a special friend. Like me, he's a retired criminal investigator and is a former hostage negotiator. But what really makes our friendship special is that the faith we share seems to be almost always in sync, like hearing the same radio station in our minds. I was Mac's mentor when he was first elected in 2006, but in just a few years he rose past me in the pecking order. In late 2012, he was appointed as chairman of the Rules Committee, a position second in power only to the Speaker.

Mac McCutcheon's soothing manner offset Speaker Hubbard's more intense personality. Mac understood Carly's Law and recognized the need for it. We are close friends and we had discussed it extensively. His district adjoined mine, and the grandmother who sent me the email was his constituent. In late January, near the beginning of the legislative session, he underwent an emergency quadruple heart bypass and had missed most of the session. He had only recently returned to service when he entered my office and saw me wallowing in defeat.

He unexpectedly bristled at me and declared, "You can't give up. We've got to get this done. The Lord called you and He hasn't given up on this." I knew Mac was supportive of Carly's Law, but I didn't expect him to be so adamant about getting it done. Mac helped me realize that I was not alone and the same Spirit that moved me would keep moving among us until it got done what it wanted done. I wasn't sure how, but whatever it was trying to do would get done. I went home and spent the weekend preparing myself to fight it out until the end.

The following Tuesday, Speaker Hubbard texted me while I was driving to Montgomery that he wanted to talk to me in his office. I was fully prepared for a confrontation but, when I entered his office, I was surprised to find he had a complete change of heart over the weekend and he humbly apologized. He proposed budgeting a million dollars to the University of Alabama at Birmingham Neurology Department to conduct a cannabis research project that could provide an avenue for those suffering from seizures to obtain the oil. He seemed genuinely excited about the project and was fully committed to do all he could to get it done.

We decided to move Paul Sanford's Senate bill, substituting the decriminalization bill with the newly written research bill that was more palatable to some of my skittish colleagues. On the evening on March 11, 2014, a remarkable thing happened in Montgomery. Worshipful tears flowed freely while Carly's Law was presented on the floor of the Alabama Senate. The senators were in one accord as the roll was called and each one present voted "Aye."

After passing the Senate, the rewritten Carly's Law was fast-tracked through the Technology and Research Committee, and it unanimously passed the House during the wee hours of a stormy night. Governor Bentley signed it a few days later, and it was done.

The research that resulted from Carly's Law would play an integral role in further efforts to overcome the stigma placed on the cannabis plant by over seventy years of government propaganda. The propaganda campaign has successfully prevented cannabis from being used by a huge throng of suffering humans in the manner for which it was created while utterly failing to prevent its widespread abuse.

The permanent classification of cannabis as a Schedule I narcotic appears to be more the culmination of a propaganda campaign that began in the early 1930s than medical science. The first commissioner of the Federal Bureau of Narcotics, Harry Anslinger, led the charge to stigmatize cannabis when he discovered marijuana could be the perfect nemesis to replace alcohol with the repeal of national prohibition. While alcohol was widely used across many racial and socioeconomic strata, cannabis was believed to be mostly used by Latinos, blacks, and jazz musicians.

The effort to stigmatize cannabis paid off for Anslinger when Congress passed the Marijuana Tax Act of 1937. Although the bill was initially opposed by the American Medical Association, the relentless racially tinged propaganda campaign led by Anslinger was largely unchallenged at a time when Jim Crow ruled the day, as indicated by remarks such as "Reefer makes darkies think they're as good as white men."

His propaganda campaign was heavily promoted by the yellow journalists of the day as they sopped up his unsubstantiated and unchallenged hyperbole, such as his congressional testimony:

> . . . the deadly, dreadful poison that racks and tears not only the body, but the very heart and soul of every human being who once becomes a slave to it in any of its cruel and devastating forms. . . .Marihuana is a short cut to the insane asylum. Smoke marihuana cigarettes for a month and what was

once your brain will be nothing but a storehouse of horrid specters. Hashish makes a murderer who kills for the love of killing out of the mildest mannered man who ever laughed at the idea that any habit could ever get him.

Anslinger's comments are particularly ironic in that in his later years he was hospitalized for a mental breakdown characterized by intense paranoia and became addicted to morphine that he was prescribed for heart angina.

By 1970, when Congress was developing the Controlled Substances Act, there was some question about how to classify cannabis. In response to a congressional request, Assistant Secretary of Health Dr. Roger Egeberg recommended that it be temporarily placed on Schedule I until the National Commission on Marijuana and Drug Abuse could complete its comprehensive study. President Nixon commissioned the study to gather evidence to justify permanently classifying marijuana as Schedule I and allow law enforcement to go after his political enemies, particularly the anti-war left and blacks. In the 1971 White House tapes he said, "I want a goddamn strong statement on marijuana. Can I get that out of this sonofabitching, uh, domestic council? . . .I mean one on marijuana that just tears the ass out of them."

Nixon thought he stacked the deck sufficiently when he appointed former Pennsylvania governor Thomas Shaffer, also a former tough-on-crime prosecutor and anti-drug warrior, to head the commission along with several others just as predisposed against marijuana. But the commission looked past the stigma and the political ramifications and the following year issued its report "Marijuana: A Signal of Misunderstanding." Nixon was infuriated and took the opposite approach to the one recommended by the very commission he appointed. The president instead chose to continue Anslinger's tradition and declared war on marijuana, leading to it being permanently classified a Schedule I narcotic where it remains to this day.

Carly's Law was about much more than a plant. For those who could see, it was a public demonstration of the spiritual power of the Unseen Hand that guides us to resist fear and deception with truth and love.

CHAPTER 15

Prosecutor, Persecutor, or Propagandist?

While I was engaged with Carly's Law, the political posturing and machinations surrounding the special grand jury in Lee County didn't matter much to me. I was aware that Representative Ed Henry had been subpoenaed to testify, presumably about the leak he had reported to the Attorney General's Office. It was no secret that many of Speaker Hubbard's friends and political associates were being intimidated and grilled before the grand jury, but that could mean the investigation was just aggressive and not necessarily tainted by politics.

However, when Representative Barry Moore was arrested in late April 2014, evidence of collusion between the prosecution team and the political coalition aligned against us during the primary began to emerge and the political taint on the prosecutors running the Lee County grand jury investigation became impossible for me to deny.

Although Barry Moore had no Democratic opponent in the November election, he was going to have to face his primary opponent again, only this time in a courtroom on trumped-up perjury charges. The upcoming trial added to the fodder that fed the propaganda machine throughout the summer and into the fall of 2014.

Barry Moore's perjury trial was scheduled to begin in Lee County on October 27 and continue through most of the week leading up to the general election. As the trial date drew closer, rumors began to swirl of Speaker Hubbard's imminent arrest. But such a politically toxic arrest within a couple weeks of an election was unthinkable to me, even without considering the prejudicial effect of such a high-profile arrest on the jury pool in the Barry Moore perjury trial.

Nonetheless, on Monday, October 20th, two weeks before the general election and the week before the Lee County trial of Barry Moore, Speaker Hubbard was arrested on twenty-three felony counts. The timing of the arrest was the final straw that convinced me someone in the prosecution was collaborating with our political adversaries. It looked to be a shameless manipulation of two of the foundations of our system of governance by the people: the ballot box and the jury box. Baron Coleman, John Rice, or AEA's Dr. Henry Mabry couldn't have timed the arrest better if they had been leading the Hubbard investigation themselves.

I didn't have an opponent in the November 4th general election, but my political allies and friends in the Tennessee Valley region did, including Representative Dan Williams, Representative Jim Patterson, Representative Lynn Greer, Representative Ken Johnson, Representative Terri Collins, Will Ainsworth, and Philip Pettus. So, when WVNN radio talk show host Dale Jackson invited me to come on his show the morning after Speaker Hubbard's arrest, I readily accepted, hoping to counter the propaganda being heaped upon my friends who had nothing to do with the crimes for which Speaker Hubbard would be ultimately convicted.

WVNN Newstalk Radio has been a major political force in the Tennessee Valley since the early 1990s with the rise in popularity of Rush Limbaugh. Sean Hannity spent several years at WVNN before moving on to national prominence. Dale Jackson had a large following of listeners across the Tennessee Valley and was also simulcast in the Birmingham market. I had been a regular guest on Dale Jackson's talk radio show for nearly ten years.

Dale invited me to come on the show to tap into my investigative experience to help the public understand more about the investigative process and provide additional context to the circumstances leading up to the previous day's arrest of Speaker Hubbard. I'd hoped that by explaining the investigative and judicial process, listeners might be less likely to allow the ill-timed arrest of Hubbard to unfairly prejudice them at the ballot box against my friends and political allies. I was fully engaged in a political activity known as "damage control."

I avoided speculating about any of the allegations against Speaker

Hubbard's guilt or innocence during the interview but opted instead to explain the investigative and prosecutorial process. I encouraged listeners not to decide guilt or innocence based on an indictment alone, emphasizing that information was limited and that we wouldn't know the facts until the case went to trial.

I was by no means an apologist for Speaker Hubbard, pointing out that he'd brought much of this on himself. Speaker Hubbard had wandered too close to the edges of the Ethics Law and had made himself an easy target for his political adversaries. Nobody has ever fallen from the middle of a roof—they fall from the edge. Ethics laws are the same way.

Near the end of the interview, Dale questioned whether Attorney General Luther Strange initiated the Hubbard investigation to take out a potential 2018 gubernatorial rival. I responded that the attorney general's motives seemed to be legitimate but added that I was absolutely convinced that a connection existed between Speaker Hubbard's political adversaries and the prosecution.

After the interview ended, I was invited to attend a press conference in Auburn that afternoon. Auburn was over two hundred miles away, in Lee County where the trial of Barry Moore was to begin the following week. I agreed to attend without hesitation. Had the prosecution waited until after the general election and the Barry Moore trial, the press conference would have been unnecessary and I would not have participated.

About two dozen legislators were among those who gathered for the press conference wearing "I like Mike" stickers. The mood was somber as several speakers reminded the public that an arrest was not a conviction but merely a step in a judicial process. The press conference took a turn in a direction I had not anticipated when some of the speakers accused Attorney General Strange of manipulating the investigation for political purposes.

The criticism seemed unfair and without merit. I considered the attorney general a friend and was unaware of any evidence of impropriety by him at the time. Strange had nothing to do with the timing of the arrest or anything else in the case to my knowledge. I believed the decision to recuse himself from the Hubbard case and to appoint an independent counsel to investigate was a sound one, and I had seen no evidence that Luther Strange had anything to do with the leaks and the political collusion from within the investigation.

I was despondent during the three-hour trek home from Auburn, equally dismayed by the political entanglements of the prosecution and what I believed to be reckless accusations at the press conference.

The following morning, I called the attorney general to express my regret for the unfortunate remarks made at the campaign press conference. During the lengthy phone call, I tried to be encouraging, and I expressed my confidence in him and told him that I planned to distance myself from the unfair remarks made about him at the press conference.

Although Alabama is a bright red state, Baron Coleman's former law partner Joe Hubbard was the Democratic nominee for attorney general, and he seemed to be making some headway in the final weeks of the campaign. I didn't want Luther to get unfair fallout from the horrible timing of Speaker Hubbard's arrest. I joined several other legislators who attended the press conference in Auburn in endorsing Luther Strange in his re-election.

On Friday, October 24th, I received the following email from our legislative delegation office:

"Mike: Mr. Matt Hart called and would like for you to give him a call. I asked if there was something I could reference to you, and he said he would rather tell you."

I called the number and left a message. At 1:39 p.m., Matt Hart called me back and introduced himself as the lead prosecutor of the Mike Hubbard case. He said that one of his subordinates, Mike Duffy, told him about my interview on the Dale Jackson Show the day after Mike Hubbard's arrest. He sounded agitated and offended when he accused me of impugning the integrity of him, the entire prosecution team, and the Lee County grand jury.

He didn't seem interested in my explanation that I was expressing my opinion on a radio talk show and hadn't intended to impugn anyone, although I wasn't exactly sure what the word "impugn" meant. The dictionary defines it as "dispute the truth, validity, or honesty of (a statement or motive); call into question." By that definition, his integrity had been impugned, although I didn't know he was the culprit collaborating with political operatives. I spoke the truth and it impugned him.

While he scolded me for "impugning" his integrity, he accused me of saying that I knew "for a fact" of a connection between the prosecution and the political operatives aligned to bring down Speaker Hubbard, insisting that it was impossible for me to know for a fact. At first, he barely let me get a word in as I denied saying that I knew it "for a fact" and that I was only expressing my honest opinion on a political talk show.

I tried to be nonconfrontational at first, but he continued to escalate, and I did, too. After exchanging heated words, we settled into a more civil, albeit adversarial tone for a little while. He explained that his purpose in calling me was that my law enforcement background gave me credibility with the public and people respected my opinion. Hart mentioned that he had met me once when I was an agent with the Alabama Bureau of Investigation, but I didn't recall meeting him. He tried to discredit my law enforcement and investigative experience by pointing out that I had only risen to the rank of corporal during my career while he bloviated about his specialized training in public corruption and his long career of high-profile arrests of public officials.

As he shared some his exploits it became obvious that his view of criminal investigative methodology and mine were sharply divergent. He spoke about arresting people like collecting trophies. I view an arrest as a necessary duty that arises as the result of an investigation. It was apparent that Hart was impressed with himself and tried hard to get me to feel the same. I was not impressed.

While he bragged about himself, he explained how special investigations involving politicians were different from other cases and required a unique set of skills and techniques, making sure to point out that a little ABI agent like me walking around with a notepad asking questions could not possibly understand what he did. He was wrong. The more he talked, the more I understood.

In my investigative experience covering many types of cases, all had a common framework. Due process is due process, regardless of who or what is being investigated. Good investigators purposefully and methodically allow evidence to lead them to the truth without regard for their personal bias. They do not isolate targets by alienating them from their political allies and friends, collaborating with their adversaries, and leaking damaging information to the media. If those were the special skills and techniques Hart was bragging about, they are way outside the realm of a professional law enforcement officer—they are signs of a propagandist at work.

He explained that the questionable timing of Speaker Hubbard's arrest was because the statute of limitations was about to expire on some of the counts.

"Do you know what a statute of limitations is?" he asked in a condescending tone.

"I do, but you should have known the statute of limitations when you started the case two years ago. That date didn't change and neither did election day," I responded.

Hart countered that the investigation was slowed down because he was forced to stop and investigate all the allegations of leaks and side issues, an odd excuse considering that many of the leaks and side issues seemed to be the result of his own unprofessional behavior.

He expressed dismay that my fellow representatives who were law enforcement officers and I attended the press conference in Auburn in support of Speaker Hubbard's campaign wearing "I like Mike" stickers. I was taken aback when he accused me of being thoughtless about the effect of my actions on the potential jurors in Barry Moore's perjury trial the following Monday. He seemed unaware that our actions were a natural response to his decision to roll out the Mike Hubbard indictments so close to the trial and the election.

Did he think my comments on a talk radio show outside the Lee County listening area would be more prejudicial to a Lee County jury than the Mike Hubbard arrest? Since I wasn't very well known in Auburn, I don't think my attendance at the campaign event had much effect on the jury. But it sure seemed to bother Hart, which led me to believe that influencing the jury pool in the imminent perjury trial was probably a major factor in the timing of the Mike Hubbard arrest. The hypocrisy reminded me of

Eric and Lyle Menendez's attorney arguing that they should be excused for killing their parents because they were orphans.

Hart also scolded me for comments that I had made about wanting to form a public study commission when the Hubbard case is over to find ways to improve the process surrounding ethics investigations and the use of the grand jury for political investigations. The Alabama judicial system usually doesn't use grand juries the same way they are used in the federal system. If we plan to continue doing it that way, we need to examine the process and institute some sort of judicial oversight. I explained that we needed to have the attorney general, the district attorneys, the Press Association, legislators, and other stakeholders openly participate in the process when the Hubbard case was over.

Hart showed little regard for the legislative branch of government or my effort to perform the duties of my office. He seemed convinced that, by questioning his methods, I wanted to gut the Ethics Law. He must have recognized that my effort would limit his ability to use his power as a propaganda tool and a bully's bludgeon when he told me that I would have to deal with him if I tried to reform the system. It struck me as a clear but open-ended threat. Matt Hart was not a low-level state employee or an angry constituent expressing an opinion. He headed the Attorney General's Special Prosecutions Unit that had just arrested the Speaker of the House and was about to try my colleague Barry Moore on a trumped-up perjury charge, and he was telling me that I would have to deal with him if I tried to do my job.

When the call ended, I was shaken, intimidated, disgusted, and insulted all at once. I had never seen any of the many district attorneys or other prosecutors I've known approach the sort of behavior Hart exhibited during that forty-four-minute phone call, but I was not unfamiliar with it. I have faced many narcissistic bullies in my life—just not one in such a powerful position.

The phone call from Hart was enough to convince me that he was probably the source from the Hubbard investigation to the political operatives, but that didn't prove that he intentionally collaborated with political operatives. I was convinced he genuinely believed that my remarks about a connection between anti-Hubbard political operatives and the prosecution were unfair. Unaware of the men's relationship, I believed Hart was probably just an unprofessional, pompous blowhard who recklessly spouted off information that Coleman somehow picked up.

The following Sunday, October 26, 2014, Hart telephoned Dale Jackson, who recorded the nearly hour-long conversation in which Hart did most of the talking. The conversation was consistent with the one that I had with Hart two days earlier, although his tone with Dale was less confrontational. Similarities include Hart's adamant denial of political connections, his belief that he was persecuted for fighting corruption, his disdain for prosecutors that worked traditional crimes, bluster about his previous cases, and his concern about the jury pool in the Moore case.

It was odd that he was spending time talking to a radio commentator in the Tennessee Valley the night before he was going to start the Moore trial in Auburn over two hundred miles away. Hart seemed much more concerned about my comments on Dale's show than he should have been, expressing to Dale his disdain for my commentary while attempting to minimize my law enforcement career and credibility. Hart's calls to Dale and to me were more consistent with the behavior of a propagandizing politician than a professional prosecutor.

The criminal trial of Barry Moore began the next day and lasted through most of the week. Despite the prejudicial timing of Mike Hubbard's arrest, the jury freed Moore from the trap that had been laid for him by his former Republican primary opponent and sprung on him by Matt Hart. The charges had been used as a propaganda bludgeon against Speaker Hubbard and his allies throughout the 2014 election cycle, but the acquittal of Moore a few days before the November 4th general election turned it around.

When the general election returns came in, it was evident that the Republican tsunami that swept into Alabama in 2010 had not subsided in 2014. Although Attorney General Luther Strange rode the Republican wave to another term, his Democratic opponent and Coleman's former law partner, Joe Hubbard, decisively outperformed all other Democrats on the ballot statewide. It was apparent that the timing of both the arrest of

Speaker Hubbard and the acquittal of Moore were key factors that led to Luther Strange underperforming at the ballot box.

The politically ambitious attorney general was widely believed to be already looking toward a gubernatorial run in 2018 as a steppingstone to his ultimate prize, a seat in the U.S. Senate. He didn't need a political consultant to tell him that Matt Hart's performance as "corruption fighter" would have a major impact upon whether his ambition would be realized.

CHAPTER 16

The Bamboozled Boss

Even after Barry Moore was acquitted and the election was over, Matt Hart's calls to Dale Jackson and me in response to my interview at WVNN continued to bother me while I strived to grasp their proper context. I sought help from trusted friends with prosecutorial, legal, and investigative expertise, but none could identify a legitimate reason for the calls. The interview on WVNN was constitutionally protected free speech, unlike the intimidating and manipulative phone calls to Dale Jackson and me. A public official using his position to suppress public criticism is not a form of speech protected by the First Amendment. That is something entirely different. I am not a psychologist, but I have had some experience with pathological bullies. The First Amendment was adopted to protect citizens from those bullies who are also public officials.

I believed that it was my duty to report Hart's intimidating and manipulative behavior to the attorney general, Luther Strange. Although Luther had recused himself and appointed retired District Attorney Van Davis to oversee the investigation in Lee County, the attorney general is responsible for the professional conduct of the employees of the office. I naively believed if Luther knew what Hart was doing, he would put a stop to it. There were other prosecutors in the Attorney General's Office who were quite capable of successfully prosecuting the Mike Hubbard case. However, replacing Hart was not politically expedient for the attorney general.

Despite that, I believed Luther was an honest man with the fortitude to put duty above political expedience. After the election, I sent a text message to the attorney general stating that I needed to talk to him about something bothering me. A few days later, he called me.

We had a cordial chat and I told him that I was aware of his recusal from the case in Lee County and didn't want to interfere, but he needed to be aware of Hart's troubling behavior that I'd witnessed. Luther responded that he didn't want to hear about it since he had recused. I tried to explain to him that he needed to be made aware of his employee's problematic behavior, but he wasn't interested in hearing what I had to say. The conversation ended with the attorney general telling me, "Y'all are big boys. You'll just have to work it out."

I was stunned that he refused to even listen. His sense of duty should have dictated that he would at least listen enough to determine the merit of a report of employee misconduct, especially from a loyal friend who happened to be a state representative with extensive law enforcement experience. The attorney general either lacked the fortitude to place duty above political expedience or he had been utterly bamboozled by Matt Hart. Or both.

His refusal to hear my complaint is even more shocking since it wasn't the first time someone had tried to report Matt Hart's recurrent bullying to his befuddled boss. There were others, but none more noteworthy than Sonny Reagan, a seasoned prosecutor in the Attorney General's Office and a man of deep faith with a reliable moral compass and a strong sense of duty. Reagan served in the U.S. Army as a Chinook helicopter pilot. Upon graduation from law school, he was hired by then Attorney General Bill Pryor and served with distinction as an assistant attorney general in the violent crime division until shortly after September 11, 2001, when he deployed to Afghanistan. He served nearly two years on deployment with the National Guard, earning the Bronze Star and an Air Medal. Upon completion, he returned to the Attorney General's Office. Bill Pryor had been appointed to be a Federal Judge in the 11th U.S. Circuit Court of Appeals and Governor Bob Riley appointed Troy King as attorney general.

Gambling is always a hot-button issue in Alabama politics, and soon after King assumed the office, he began an extensive evaluation of gambling in Alabama. In December 2004, Attorney General King issued a controversial finding that declared electronic bingo permissible under Alabama law governing charity bingo in certain counties. The findings resulted in the proliferation of the electronic bingo machines (or slot machines, depending upon which side of the argument you take) across Alabama. Some district attorneys did not agree with King's finding and took legal action to shut them down.

In December 2006, the Alabama Supreme Court issued a unanimous ruling that contradicted King's findings, providing the spark that ignited the electronic bingo wars in Alabama. Governor Riley believed King to be wrong and was committed to enforcing the law as he believed it to be. In 2007, his disagreement with Troy King over the gambling issue led to Sonny Reagan leaving the Attorney General's Office to serve as a legal advisor for Governor Riley. After two years of inaction by Attorney General King, a constitutional conflict erupted when Governor Riley issued Executive Order 44 in December 2009, creating the Governor's Task Force on Illegal Gambling "for the purpose of promoting and supporting uniform statewide enforcement of Alabama's anti-gambling laws."

The constitutional conflict between Governor Riley and General King was settled on May 21, 2010, when the Alabama Supreme Court unanimously ruled that the governor is the supreme executive power of the state of Alabama with the duty to ensure its laws are faithfully executed. Eleven days later, King was resoundingly defeated in his re-election bid by Luther Strange while Robert Bentley emerged as the last man standing in the rough-and-tumble gubernatorial primary to succeed the term-limited Bob Riley. The controversy was a major factor in making public corruption and gambling one of the significant factors that led to the seismic shift in favor of Alabama Republicans in 2010.

A month before the 2010 general election, eleven people, including four state senators, were indicted in federal court for charges associated with gambling legislation. Although all were eventually acquitted, the political damage was done, and the indictments fit snugly with the Republican message that provided the foundation for the historical election sweep. As I discussed in Chapter 12, ethics reform was a major element of our "Handshake with Alabama."

On Governor Bentley's first full day in office, he signed an executive order that rescinded Governor Riley's executive order creating the illegal gambling task force. The order stated, "the new attorney general, Luther Strange, has stated that he intends to enforce the laws of the State of Alabama with respect to anti-gambling, lottery schemes, and illegal gambling." With the Governor's Task Force on Illegal Gambling eliminated, Sonny Reagan returned to the Attorney General's Office.

Before being elected attorney general, Luther Strange had been an oil company lobbyist since the 1980s. When I met him during his unsuccessful run for lieutenant governor in 2006, he impressed me as someone who seemed to have a sincere desire for public service. Although Luther's law enforcement experience was limited when he was elected attorney general in 2010, a solid team of professionals surrounding him could compensate. That seemed to be exactly what he was trying to do when he hired people like Sonny Reagan with his expertise on illegal gaming issues and Matt Hart with his experience on public corruption cases.

In early 2014, Reagan reported to Chief Deputy Attorney General Kevin Turner that Hart created a hostile work environment by causing a climate of fear with his behavior that included taunting other employees and bragging about how he could send a "message" to the whole office by having employees critical of him demoted and transferred in retaliation. Reagan also reported that Hart had bragged about bringing down the entire "Riley machine" and working in concert with the press to further his cases and ruin his adversaries, including certain public officials.

Reagan reported that Hart wanted Reagan's office space and began manipulating his way to get it. After Reagan reported Hart's unruly behavior to the attorney general and his Chief Deputy Kevin Turner, Reagan was instructed in February 2014 to avoid contact with Hart and report any additional complaints to Charla Doucet, the chief of the Attorney General's Administrative Division.

As instructed, on July 22, 2014, Reagan filed a complaint with Charla Doucet, and an investigation was subsequently initiated. A few weeks later, Hart was in full damage-control mode as evidenced by the publication of a post in the *Alabama Political Reporter* on August 18 by his friend Bill Britt, who served as Hart's mouthpiece, with the headline "Sources Link AG's Chief Deputy to Plot to Remove Hart from Hubbard Investigation." The article accused Chief Deputy Attorney General Turner of attempting to derail the Hubbard investigation by orchestrating a plot to remove Hart from the case.

The article also attempted to discredit not only Turner but also Attorney General Luther Strange by speculating that Turner, who had been his driver and body man during the 2010 election in which he defeated Troy King, was holding some dirty secret over Strange. Britt reported that he'd seen Turner's recent personal cell phone records indicating calls to Speaker Hubbard and Representative Barry Moore in the previous months. Since a subpoena is required to obtain personal cell phone records, it was likely that Britt's source was Hart or someone close to him with subpoena power.

Britt cited "sources within the AG's office" reporting that Hart was notified in a letter from Turner that Hart was reassigned to an office in Birmingham and would no longer have an office in Montgomery. According to the article, the letter prompted a heated exchange between Hart and Attorney General Strange in the presence of the Special Prosecutor Van Davis, which resulted in Strange reversing Turner's orders that reassigned Hart to Birmingham. According to the source leaking to Britt from within the Attorney General's Office, Hart was temporarily relieved of his responsibility as the head of the white-collar crime unit but remained in charge of the Hubbard case in Lee County and another unrelated case in Montgomery revolving around Alabama State University. Britt ended his piece by calling upon Governor Robert Bentley and Chief Justice Roy Moore to protect Hart and demand that Strange remove Kevin Turner from his position.

Before Doucet's investigation of Reagan's complaint could be completed and Hart could be interviewed, the investigative files relative to the complaint were subpoenaed to the Grand Jury in Lee County and the internal investigation of Hart's conduct discontinued. Reagan received a subpoena and was grilled for over an hour in front of the grand jury in Lee County before he asserted his rights under the Fifth Amendment due to its accusatory nature. Like Representative Ed Henry's complaint and the ambush of Barry Moore months before, the Lee County grand jury was evidently once again weaponized by Hart to promote a personal agenda and to silence or discredit his accusers.

On September 19, 2014, acting Attorney General Special Prosecutor W. Van Davis announced the investigation had determined that Reagan "had undisclosed communications with individuals affiliated with people indicted or under investigation by the Lee County special grand jury" and that he had "taken other action to impede or obstruct the investigation." Davis added that he'd given the information to Attorney General Strange, who immediately placed Reagan on administrative leave.

Although Davis was ostensibly in charge of the Lee County special grand jury, there was little doubt in the minds of many, including mine, that Matt Hart was calling the shots and was behind the statement. I don't mean to belittle or disparage Van Davis. He was a good man who served with distinction as the St. Clair County district attorney for many years before his retirement, but his prior experience and good intentions did not prepare him for Matt Hart and his "special skills."

In 2019 Van Davis lost a long battle with cancer that lasted nearly a decade. An excerpt from a news report of his death contains a quote from him and reinforces my thoughts about him:

> Before his death, Davis described himself as a country boy who was born and raised in St. Clair County. His country upbringing helped him connect with jurors in St. Clair County. "My approach has always been never to be too flashy or technical," Davis said shortly before he retired as the head law-man of St. Clair County. "You want to get your point across. I try to be as simple and straightforward as I can. I guess it's just the way I am, the way I grew up." (*St. Clair Times*, September 4, 2019)

Van Davis was the opposite of what Matt Hart purported himself to be. He had been diagnosed with prostate cancer a few years before Luther Strange recused himself from the Mike Hubbard investigation. But when the cancer worsened, it became necessary for him to undergo experimental treatment at the UAB Hospital in Birmingham while Hart ran things in Lee County. Under the circumstances, I can understand how the country lawyer was bamboozled.

After being notified that he'd been placed on administrative leave, Reagan sent Strange a letter requesting the appointment of a neutral third-party special investigator to investigate both Reagan's allegations against Hart and the allegations by Davis that Reagan interfered with in the Hubbard case.

This occurred only a few weeks before Hart had tried to bully me prior to the November 2014 general election. On December 2, 2014, Reagan resigned from his position in the Attorney General's Office soon after Luther notified him that his termination was imminent.

Gene Sisson had served as a Montgomery police officer for nearly twenty years before being hired as an investigator by Attorney General Troy King, serving as chief investigator for the final two years of King's tenure in office. When Luther Strange took office, Sisson was assigned to work with Sonny Reagan conducting investigations into illegal gambling in Alabama. As Sisson's respect for Reagan's professionalism grew, he recognized that Matt Hart had become a tremendous distraction to their gambling investigations and prosecutions.

Sisson was aware that Reagan had complained of Hart's behavior to his superiors without result during 2014 and was concerned that Hart had been and was still using his official authority to squelch the complaint against him and retaliate, an illegal activity under the Alabama Ethics Law. When Sisson discovered that Reagan and Charla Doucet's internal investigative file had been subpoenaed to the Lee County grand jury, it seemed to be a clear violation of the state Ethics Law. Sisson felt duty-bound to report it to the Ethics Commission where it would be properly investigated. It was not.

Before the executive director of the Ethics Commission, Jim Sumner, could read Sisson's submission, he received a subpoena for it and handed it over to investigators from the Attorney General's Office. Sisson brought it to the attention of federal authorities, reporting it to the Secret Service out of concern that two of Hart's investigators had recently retired from the FBI and might still have close relationships that could cause a conflict.

On April 10, 2015, Sisson was placed on mandatory leave pending an April 28 pre-dismissal hearing based on charges arising from his attempts to report and document what he believed to be Hart's illegal conduct. Sisson's employment was terminated by Attorney General Strange on May 12, 2015. Sisson and Reagan were not the only people in the Attorney General's Office with concerns about Hart's overbearing bullying behavior, nor were they the only people to experience repercussions for it, but they both stepped out far beyond the point most people would go in their resistance.

I'm unaware of any political, personal, or business relationship between Mike Hubbard and either of them. Like me, their concern wasn't the Mike Hubbard investigation—it was Matt Hart's behavior. It wasn't about protecting people from facing justice, it was about protecting the innocent people from being bullied. When Sonny Reagan and Gene Sisson stood up to Hart, Luther Strange fired them.

After my failed attempt to report the inappropriate conduct that I had witnessed to the attorney general, my next step was unclear. The attorney general was the proper authority, but like others, he seemed bamboozled by the blustering bully. The phone call to me before the election was a failed attempt to bamboozle me too, but I saw through it. When we see something and know it's there, we can't unsee it and pretend it's not. I knew that peace of mind would elude me until I had done everything in my power to prevent what I recognized as an unscrupulous prosecutor from using our judicial system as a propaganda tool or a bully's bludgeon.

CHAPTER 17

Goliath

I was not surprised when Mike Hubbard's attorney, Mark White, called me to ask about my phone call from Matt Hart. I had talked about it to anyone who was interested and some who probably weren't. I had no qualms about sharing my testimony under oath in an open hearing. My efforts to find an appropriate authority to investigate Hart's inappropriate behavior had been perplexing, and I hoped that getting it on the record before the court might bring it to the attention of someone who could help.

The legislature was in session by the time I received my subpoena to appear in Auburn at the Lee County Circuit Court on Wednesday, April 15, 2015. The subpoena gave me a peculiar sense of relief. Although I expected Hart's doting admirers in the media to attack my credibility and try to discredit my testimony as a political ploy, the subpoena represented an opportunity to unload the burden I had felt since the phone call from Hart. They could try to smear my reputation, but my sense of duty demanded that I speak out about the unethical behavior that I had witnessed. Duty only demands that we speak the truth, not that we try to force anyone to accept it. That is between them and God.

By the time I pulled into the legislative parking lot in Montgomery the day before my testimony at the prosecutorial misconduct hearing in Lee County, my relief from receiving the subpoena had given way to fear of the persecution that was sure to be flung at me for daring to question Hart's methods. Despite hundreds of biblical warnings against fear, I can say one thing good about it: Whether we are saints or sinners, prayers flow more freely when fear drives us to our knees.

As I walked from the parking lot toward the Statehouse, I passed by a legislative security officer who placed a small cross in my hand that he had made from two horseshoe nails and wire. I'd walked past him many times for many years, and he'd never done anything like that before. We had never even spoken to one another before about anything religious. He had been making the crosses and giving them to selected people whenever the urge struck him, since having a near-death experience a few years before.

We had a pleasant conversation and swapped a few cop stories. Unless he was psychic, he couldn't have known what was on my mind or that I had been praying while I walked across the parking lot; but the Spirit that moved him to give me that little cross knew. I shared my burden with him and asked him to pray for me. He said he would pray for peace in my heart.

Throughout that busy day in the legislature, whenever the fear of having my reputation tarnished for testifying about Matt Hart's bad behavior distracted me from my duty, holding the little cross in my pocket brought immediate peace of mind. I used it to ease my troubled mind like a hospital patient uses a morphine drip to ease physical pain.

I was about to leave my office at the end of the day when a lobbyist came by to discuss some legislation with me. Although my ears were listening, my mind was someplace else. Noticing my distraction, he asked, "Are you okay?" I apologized and told him that I had a lot going on. As he stood up to leave my office, he said he was going to pray for me to have peace in my heart.

It seemed an odd coincidence that the first person I encountered at the Statehouse that morning said the same thing to me as the last person I would encounter that day. I told him about the security guard that morning and took the little cross from my pocket. The lobbyist's eyes grew and he pulled an identical cross from his pocket and responded, "I didn't know you were who the guard asked me to pray for this morning when he gave me this." God winks, and faith grows.

On the morning of Wednesday, April 15, 2015, I sat on a bench in the foyer outside the courtroom clutching a little cross in my right hand while the crowd ambled in to watch the legal gladiators in suits spar in the courtroom. I spoke to Mike Hubbard and his wife Susan Hubbard as they walked by. I put my little cross in Susan's hand.

Regardless of the guilt or innocence of the accused, family members are usually forgotten victims. Their suffering is ignored while attention is on the allegation and the legal process. They are easy targets of persecution

This is what Goliath looked like to me. (Photo courtesy of Todd Van Emst/Opelika-Auburn News)

through guilt by association. Contempt for the accused should never smother compassion for the innocent. Without compassion, there is no justice.

Among the audience in the packed courtroom were Representative Barry Moore and his wife Heather. Heather Moore is a spiritual warrior, and I can't imagine anyone better positioned to empathize with Susan Hubbard than her. I sat beside Barry and Heather all morning while we listened to the lawyer's legal wrangling until the court recessed and we had lunch. My reason for being there probably had as much, if not more, to do with their ordeal than it did Mike Hubbard's. However, to the media covering the case, Barry Moore was just an asterisk.

There was some confusion about my testimony because it had nothing to do with the ethics charge against Mike Hubbard, about which I had no knowledge. It was about Matt Hart's misconduct that I had witnessed. In this hearing, Hart was on defense like he told Baron Coleman over a year ago that he would be if his relationship with the Attorney General's Office became known. Unfortunately, it would be several months before I would learn of Hart's collaboration with Coleman and the recorded conversation.

The fear that had dogged me for several days was still present while I testified under direct examination about my interview on the Dale Jackson Show that threatened to expose Hart's surreptitious relationship with the crafty political consultant and the subsequent phone call from Hart in which he tried to manipulate my opinion to keep that affiliation concealed. It was not my first time on the witness stand, so the nagging fear didn't distract me enough to hinder my testimony much. But when Mark White finished his direct examination, something happened when Matt Hart rose from his chair and walked toward me to begin cross-examination that made my fear vanish.

As Hart faced me, standing between the tables where the opposing attorneys sat, over his right shoulder, I saw Susan Hubbard sitting in the audience several feet behind him, clutching the little cross. While my burly adversary lumbered toward me sporting his big, bushy, black beard, the word "Goliath" inundated my mind. It was like something shifted my mind into a different gear that caused every trace of trepidation and doubt to dissolve as I became intensely focused and drawn toward the huge brute standing before me. The surge of confidence and energy that I felt made it difficult for me to stay seated. The filter between my brain and mouth disappeared.

He seemed on his best behavior as he attempted to cast himself in a very different light than the narcissistic bully on the phone with me a few months earlier, as depicted by my testimony. During the cross-examination, he attempted to contort the context of the phone call to make it appear that his purpose for calling me was to exercise his constitutional right as a lowly state employee to express his opinion to a legislator. However, a public official does not have a constitutional right to use their position or authority to suppress criticism. I was determined not to allow him to manipulate my testimony under cross-examination and deceive the court. If he wanted to do that, he could take the stand under oath and perjure himself.

Hart began by asking if I had ever *impugned* the integrity of another prosecutor on the radio. The dictionary defines it as "dispute the truth, validity, or honesty of (a statement or motive); call into question." It is a right, guaranteed by the First Amendment to the U.S. Constitution, for any citizen to truthfully impugn any public official who is deceptive, especially a prosecutor. I believe it is not just a right, but a moral obligation which must be met for the existence of a healthy republic. It is a fundamental element of the system of checks and balances put in place by the founders of our nation as a means of protection from unreasonable, cruel, or arbitrary abuse of power.

I knew where he was going with the question and was looking forward to answering him. There was only one other time in my law enforcement career that I publicly disputed a prosecutor, and it was because he didn't tell the truth. I was a little disappointed when attorney Mark White objected and Judge Walker sustained. If his purpose was to portray me as someone who threw around wild accusations, that line of questioning would have probably blown up in his face, even if it was irrelevant to the case at hand.

In 1998, a retiring police chief asked me to look at a partially solved murder case that had gone cold. In 1984, a jewelry dealer was killed in a shootout during a botched robbery attempt at his home. Before the jewelry dealer died, he managed to shoot one of the robbers in the back as they escaped. The wounded robber was the only one involved in the crime who was apprehended. He refused to identify his co-conspirators and was subsequently convicted and sentenced to death by the trial judge over the jury's recommendation of life without parole.

The police chief was bothered that the other assailants, including the one who fired the fatal shot, had escaped justice and wanted to make sure that no stone was unturned before he moved on. I agreed to look at it, and with the help of the local district attorney's investigator, we went through the case again and began uncovering additional evidence and new witnesses as well as the identities of the other two assailants and the driver of their getaway car.

I located the driver of the getaway car in another state and was ready to interview him. The robber who was on death row also had a change of heart and was ready to cooperate. When I met with the district attorney to update him, I was stunned to learn that he was not interested in our progress on the case and even admonished me for reopening the case. He was concerned that the arrest of the other assailants, including the trigger man, might delay the execution of the one on death row. It was appalling to me that the district attorney was more concerned about executing the robber who got shot than bringing to justice the one who did the shooting.

I didn't like it, but he was the district attorney, and if he didn't want to pursue justice for the killer, there was nothing I could do about it. He could have at least told his investigator, and I wouldn't have wasted a month working on it. I was annoyed about his attitude and his decision, but I knew my place, so I dropped it and moved on to other cases in other counties. One of the advantages of being a state agent was that there were plenty of other local officials in other counties who wouldn't jerk me around.

Four years later when the robber was about to become the first Alabama prisoner executed by lethal injection, a newspaper reporter asked that district attorney why the other assailants were never prosecuted, since Johnson was willing to testify against them. He responded that the law doesn't allow for a conviction solely on the testimony of a co-conspirator. That was true, but it was propaganda. He didn't point out that it didn't apply to this case, since there was corroborating evidence in this case and much opportunity to get more. He wanted an execution more than the shooter behind bars.

When Dale Jackson asked me about it during a WVNN radio interview shortly before the execution, I responded truthfully, and it contradicted the district attorney. I shared my information with the person in charge of capital litigation at the Attorney General's Office and Governor Siegelman's legal advisor, but they were not about to override the district attorney's decision, even if it meant forever ending any opportunity to bring the other perpetrators to justice. When Anthony Keith Johnson was executed on December 12, 2002, any hope for bringing the others to justice died with him. The killer was seventy-eight when he died of natural causes in 2014 at a nursing home where I made monthly visits with my bluegrass band.

Throughout the cross-examination, Hart tried to substitute his testimony for mine by making his statement and adding, "isn't that true?" or "do you remember me saying?" It seemed a cowardly way of manipulating the system to give his testimony without being placed under oath and subjecting himself to cross-examination and the risk of perjury. Since it would be nearly a year before I'd discover how far he would go to hide his misconduct, I just viewed him as an obnoxious, overgrown bully attempting to pull off a ruse and hide his bad behavior.

Courtroom testimony is not usually very entertaining, but laughter erupted several times in the courtroom during our confrontation. When Hart asked how I could tell over the phone that he was angry, there were scattered snickers in the courtroom when I raised my voice and demonstrated as I said, "Listen to my voice now. Do I sound angry?"

Because Hart's questions were so easy to anticipate, and I was eager to respond, my answers came out before he was finished asking the question, prompting him to say, "I am not going to talk over you. I am going to try not to talk over you. Let me ask my question."

"Good," I responded. "That would be different from our phone call."

I wasn't trying to be funny, but laughter once again erupted in the courtroom at another point when I observed, "You were quite full of yourself," while recounting how Hart bragged about his previous cases and his expertise in ferreting out public corruption. He had also expressed a low regard for my investigative experience, referring to me as "a little ABI corporal with my pencil and pad asking questions," unable to comprehend the complexities of his line of work. I understood why he would think that, but unfortunately for him, I understood his methods enough to recognize how far outside the bounds of ethical behavior and professionalism he had strayed.

But the loudest laughter erupted in the courtroom in response to one of Hart's attempts to downplay the confrontational nature of our phone call. Hart and I agreed that we didn't cuss at one another during the call, and then he asked me about a scripture that I had quoted to him.

"Do you remember quoting a Bible verse to me that basically said justice will be had in the end by all, something to that effect? And don't worry about it?" Hart asked.

"I don't remember a scripture that says that, but I'm very likely to have quoted a scripture. When I get cranked up, if I am in the right frame of mind, I will do that rather than cuss."

The unusual cross-examination was the only time I remember meeting Hart face to face, and it provided a record of both sides of our telephone conversation. Although it served him to inject his self-serving perspective on the record while avoiding being cross-examined under oath, Hart's questions also constituted what appeared to be several potentially damning admissions, including that his call was prompted by my radio interview that was brought to his attention by a subordinate, Mike Duffy. It was an indication that he was acting in his official capacity as the chief of the Special Prosecutions Unit of the Alabama Attorney General's Office when he made the ill-fated phone call to me, not as a mere state employee, exercising his constitutional rights as a private citizen to express his opinion to a state representative, as he had led some to believe.

I have received many such calls—this was not that. The First Amendment to the U.S. Constitution was not created to give a public official the right to subdue public criticism. Its purpose is to protect the rights of those who would publicly question those who exercise power. In this case, my appearance on the radio show and public comments about the investigation and arrest of Speaker Hubbard were protected by the First Amendment. However, the private phone call from Hart acting in his official capacity to admonish me for publicly "impugning his integrity" should not be construed as constitutionally protected free speech. It was the opposite. It was a blundering attempt to suppress my exercise of free speech.

Hart admitted why he called me instead of other legislators. He was concerned that my law enforcement experience gave my opinion and judgment credibility in the public eye. At the time, the phone call seemed like a huge overreaction to my radio comments, but until I heard his conversation with Baron Coleman, I did not know how desperate Hart was to keep his relationship and unscrupulous political activities with the crafty political consultant on the down-low, especially with Representative Barry Moore's perjury trial with Coleman's former client as the star witness about to start the following week. My analysis on the Dale Jackson Show struck Hart as way too close for comfort, and I needed to be silenced or at least discouraged from making comments that might bring attention to it.

During the cross-examination, Hart clung to his delusion that I intended to weaken the ethics laws, an accusation entirely without merit. The aggressive resistance he presented to those who have questioned his motives or the methods he employed seemed to expose something very different than a heartfelt desire for open, honest government. If open, honest government were his primary concern, he would have welcomed the concept of an open discussion to determine how we can depoliticize the process of ethics enforcement instead of vehemently opposing it. Hart seemed unable or unwilling to understand that my intention was not to weaken the ethics laws or make them difficult to enforce but to exercise my duty as a legislator in an open and cooperative manner to improve the process of enforcement and clarify the law as much as possible.

The most revealing moment to me during the cross-examination occurred when Hart questioned me about saying that I was absolutely convinced there was a political agenda influencing the prosecutorial team to make sure that Mike Hubbard would not be Speaker of the House. I looked him squarely in the eye, pointed my finger at him, and forcefully responded, "I was then. I am now." He seemed stunned, and his head jerked back as if he had been struck in the forehead with something. He froze for a few moments as he thumbed through the transcript of my radio interview and grappled to formulate his next question.

I'd seen suspects respond that way when confronted in a way that made them think that I had something on them they'd been trying to hide. We called it "mind-freeze," causing their mind to race. At the beginning of the cross-examination, Hart could have assumed that my public assertion of a connection between the Hubbard prosecutors and the anti-Hubbard political faction was based upon only the timing of the arrest. However, during the cross-examination, he should have realized that the timing of the Mike Hubbard arrest was but one of several factors contributing to my conclusion. It should have caused him to wonder how much I knew about his connection with Baron Coleman.

The week after my courtroom confrontation with Hart, the Associated Press reported that Kevin Turner had resigned as chief deputy attorney general and would be replaced by Hart's former boss and mentor Alice Martin. The replacement of Turner by Alice Martin was viewed by many Alabama political pundits as a clear signal that Luther Strange was doubling down with his support for Hart.

I stubbornly refused to believe that Luther could condone Hart's methods, steadfastly clinging to the slim chance that he had not been completely taken in by Hart's schtick. Maybe Luther brought Alice Martin on board to rein in Hart's arrogant bullying and political meddling. Maybe she would recognize Hart's improper behavior and would ensure that it would be properly investigated and proper action taken. I was overly optimistic. I didn't know Alice Martin very well. Or Luther, either.

Neither Luther nor Martin would do anything that might curtail Hart's activities because their political ambitions were linked to Hart's success at "cleaning up Montgomery." Although Luther was term limited and could not run for another term as attorney general, he was planning to run for governor in 2018, and that would clear a path for Alice Martin to run for Alabama attorney general.

They seemed to be posturing their 2018 campaigns for something along the lines of those portrayed in the Coen Brothers' 2000 film *O Brother, Where Art Thou?* that revolved around cleaning up corruption. The candidate in the movie travelled across the state vowing to sweep out corruption while a little person (note: I did not use the term "midget") would come onstage with a broom and sweep up. It was apparently the same sort of gubernatorial campaign Luther Strange envisioned in 2018 with Alice Martin as the candidate for attorney general with the broom, sweeping corruption out of Montgomery.

Concealing Hart's misconduct was important to both of their campaigns. Luther Strange and Alice Martin's political future would be ruined if Hart were exposed. I had no personal beef with either them at the time, except that they were protecting the giant that I was stalking. Secrecy was Matt Hart's armor and propaganda was his weapon. He was intimidating but not invincible, and I didn't believe he could stay hidden in his armor forever. And he couldn't have without help from the attorney general and his ambitious new chief assistant.

CHAPTER 18

Humpty Dumpty

Humpty Dumpty sat on a wall.
Humpty Dumpty had a great fall.
All the king's horses and all the king's men
Couldn't put Humpty together again.

At the beginning of 2014, Mike Hubbard was riding high, considered by many to be the most powerful elected official in Alabama. But the continual sniping by his growing number of adversaries and the leaky investigation in Lee County took its toll. Although he was powerful going into 2015, his political capital was in gradual but definite decline, while Governor Bentley's was steadily increasing. His administration seemed stable and scandal free, and the grandfatherly governor drew minimal opposition during the 2014 election cycle.

Breezing to a second four-year term by one of the largest margins in modern Alabama gubernatorial history, Governor Bentley's vanity swelled right along with his popularity, his speeches peppered with comments that the people of Alabama loved and trusted him. Like many, many others throughout history, success made him think too much of himself, and nothing topples the mighty like a swollen ego.

One of the first things I noticed about Robert Bentley in 2002 when we were elected to the legislature was a noticeable air of superiority that often seems to accompany the title "doctor." Despite having that air about him, he presented himself as somewhat bland and non-threatening in contrast to his more bold and decisive primary opponents in the 2010 gubernatorial race, Roy Moore, Bradley Byrne, and Tim James.

A large chunk of Bentley's base of support in the 2010 primary consisted of a coalition of heavy support in his hometown Tuscaloosa, independent nonpartisans weary of squabbling politicians, crossover Democrats, and the Alabama Education Association. While the other campaigns slugged it out with each other in the primary, the mild-mannered dermatologist from Tuscaloosa managed to squeak past the son of former governor Fob James into a runoff with the frontrunner, Bradley Byrne.

Byrne's rivalry with Dr. Paul Hubbert and the Alabama Education Association caused the powerful lobbyist to focus his political savvy and his resources to defeating Byrne. Although the AEA was mostly wiped out in the 2010 legislative races, the gubernatorial race was another story. Their support for Bentley was a major factor in getting him elected governor. It didn't do them much good since Governor Bentley jilted them soon after the election.

The grandfatherly doctor whose only campaign promise was not to take a salary until Alabama reached full employment was perfectly postured for his runoff with Byrne. His trustworthy and politically naïve persona made him appear to be the antithesis of a typical politician and attracted right-wing conservative voters whose support split between Tim James and Roy Moore against Byrne in the primary. Along with Bentley's support from the left leaning AEA, Democratic crossovers, and independent nonpartisan voters, the primary frontrunner Byrne was doomed. Politics does make strange bedfellows.

To put my perspective in context, I wholeheartedly supported Bradley Byrne and served as his Madison County campaign chairman, although my attention was on legislative races in 2010. Byrne won Madison County handily, but I doubt my meager effort had as much to do with it as his volunteers and staff. My point in rehashing the 2010 primary is to emphasize that Governor Bentley's humble country doctor persona worked well for him, and soon after his 2014 re-election, he seemed to embrace a persona more reminiscent of Slick Willie, the former governor of Arkansas, who exemplified the saying "Sincerity is the most important thing, and once you can fake that, you've got it made." Unfortunately for Bentley, he lacked both the personality and the political skills to pull it off.

During his State of the State Address in March 2015, he boldly proposed a $541 million tax increase after having signed a no-tax pledge and echoing it throughout his 2014 re-election campaign. He couldn't say he didn't know about the general fund budget shortfall during the campaign. He could have easily just ducked the tax issue during the campaign, but he didn't. Whenever his nominal Democratic opponent brought up raising taxes because of the ailing general fund, Governor Bentley soundly rebuffed him. The governor's tax proposal could probably be justified but not his audacious deception.

By the end of the summer of 2015, it was obvious to almost everyone but Governor Bentley and whoever was giving him advice that his popularity was spiraling downward. Apparently, the Bentley administration decided that cuts in services would create public outcry and put pressure on the legislature to pass the proposed $541 million tax increase. Steps such as closing state parks and Secretary of Law Enforcement Spencer Collier's efforts to close driver's license testing sites in rural counties with low populations seemed calculated to generate more public outcry than savings. If they were trying to create a public outcry, they succeeded—but not like they planned.

Another indication of Governor Bentley's growing ego and the departure of his old persona was the ham-handed attempts to strong-arm legislators during the 2015 legislative session by openly threatening to withhold funding for road projects and other services in their districts. Leveraging projects for votes is nothing new in the political world, but it is a subtle art. The efforts of the Bentley administration at strong-arm leveraging came across to me like Pee Wee Herman trying to be a bouncer. The surest path to failure is to try to be something you're not.

The governor's $541 million tax proposal went down in flames and the legislature adjourned sine die soon after passing an atrocious general fund budget that was promptly vetoed by the governor, as expected. It would be difficult to describe the 2015 session of the Alabama Legislature as anything other than an abject failure, and Governor Bentley's recently acquired ill-fitting machismo was a significant factor.

There was a noticeable awkwardness between Governor Bentley and his wife during the inaugural events in January 2015, but they had been together fifty years, so it wasn't thinkable to most people then that their marriage was falling apart. There had been murmurs among insiders that

Rebekah Mason, a former local television news anchor who had served as Governor Bentley's spokesperson during his first term and had recently been promoted senior policy advisor, was his paramour. It was only scuttlebutt until August 2015, when First Lady Dianne Bentley filed for divorce, ending their fifty-year marriage. The divorce transformed the absurd rumor of an affair between the grandfatherly governor and his much younger aide into a reasonable hypothesis that morphed into rampant speculation that swept across Alabama, expediting the transformation of many journalists into gossip columnists.

A few weeks after the divorce announcement, Governor Bentley called the legislature into a second special session to resolve the 2015 budget fiasco that resulted from the utter failure of his ill-conceived tax proposals during regular session. Early in the session, Governor Bentley's secretary of law enforcement, my old friend (and sometimes not) Spencer Collier came by my office in the legislature to discuss his plan to shut down some of the rural driver's license offices. The plan had drawn a considerable amount of political heat. He insisted that shutting down the offices saved money, but the nominal cost savings and the timing made it look more like part of a propaganda effort to justify a substantial tax increase.

Like almost everyone else in Alabama, I was curious about whether there was anything to the alleged affair between the governor and Rebekah. Collier was a close friend of the governor and was his cabinet member in charge of the state police, so he would probably know. I didn't want to put him on the spot, but that didn't mean that I couldn't try to glean information from him. When I looked him in the eye and commented that people were probably jumping to conclusions about Governor Bentley and Rebekah, Collier responded with his most sincere-sounding voice that he didn't believe there was anything to it, either.

I didn't expect Collier to tell me anything, but if it was true, I expected him to duck the question, look away, or raise an eyebrow. He could have easily ducked it, and I wouldn't have forced the issue, but an outright lie was completely unnecessary. He had already heard a recording and confronted the governor about the relationship over a year before. Maintaining confidentiality is one thing, but deception is something else. One would think that with over forty years of combined experience in law enforcement and politics that I'd be used to it, but it still sticks in my craw.

By the time Governor Bentley called the second special session of the legislature on September 8, 2015, no one seemed to have an appetite for going into the fiscal year beginning in October without a general fund budget. Shutting down state government operations would have more immediate impact on more Alabamians than the federal "shutdowns" that we've almost grown accustomed to. Unlike Congress, Alabama has no legal provision for continuing resolutions to keep state government operating without a budget.

When we adjourned on September 16, we'd finally passed a compromise budget with some very modest tax increases and a bare-bones general fund budget. Speaker Hubbard's arrest, the pending trial, and the politics surrounding it had been a horrendous distraction, hampering the entire process. The steady stream of media criticism had taken its toll, not only on the credibility of Speaker Hubbard, but on the entire legislature as well. The ship of state in Alabama seemed to be foundering, even more than usual.

When the second special session of 2015 ended, it was apparent that the Speaker's legal issues had understandably become paramount to his legislative duties. Despite my misgivings about Matt Hart's outrageous behavior and my misplaced confidence in our criminal justice system to bring out the whole truth, I felt the darkness hanging over our legislative process and could see its negative effect taking its toll on Speaker Hubbard.

It seemed like time for the Speaker to step back from his position for both his own good and the good of the state of Alabama. Several legislators had started publicly calling for his resignation. Although it may have been time for the Speaker to seriously consider a resignation, I believed the attempt to force him out was premature and doomed to fail. Speaker Hubbard was not someone likely to be forced into capitulation by his adversaries. He would fight to the bitter end. Even in the unlikely event it was successful, the aftermath of such a coup would have probably created lasting grudges that would have a negative impact on the legislature for years.

Forcible removal of the Speaker seemed unnecessary, considering that the impending trial would resolve much of it. After the trial, it would be much easier to clear the air and move forward. A more reasonable approach seemed to rely on legislators in leadership positions to keep the ship afloat and encourage Speaker Hubbard to distance himself from his legislative duties while the legal process played itself out, and that's what happened. Sort of.

I understood the reasoning behind the burgeoning coup and was sympathetic to many of its twenty or so participants, but their perspective was different than mine because they hadn't seen what I had seen or been where I've been, and it was apparent to me that a significant amount of political turmoil we were experiencing revolved around Hart's intimidating and manipulative behavior.

I believed the best path to relieve the tension that had fallen upon the Alabama House of Representatives was for those the Speaker trusted to explain the problem and persuade him to step down. I sensed a moral obligation to lay out the choice to him, but it was his to make, not mine. I just wanted him to pray about it, preferring to rely on divine intervention instead of political force to resolve the issue.

A few weeks later, the right moment came when Speaker Hubbard called to discuss the insurgency. I told him that he should seriously consider stepping back from his position at least until after his criminal case was adjudicated. He was stunned because he knew I was a friend. After discussing the negative effects of the investigation and the arrest on the House of Representatives, he agreed to pray about it and think it through. Since he knew that I was neither a foe nor ambitious enough to attempt a power grab, I knew he would take my recommendation seriously.

He seemed more receptive to the idea of stepping back than I'd expected. He had put forth a lot of effort to become Speaker, and the harder someone strives for something, the harder they fight to keep it. I only planted a seed, and whether that seed germinated into a sound decision was out of my hands.

During the next few days, as he mulled over my suggestion that he step back from his legislative duties, Speaker Hubbard was probably closest to voluntarily stepping down than he ever was or would ever be, but he couldn't bring himself to it. Until we went back into session in February, the decision was his and his alone and he decided to hang on. In retrospect, it might not have changed anything, but I have the nagging thought that we all would have been better off had he humbly stepped down.

Instead, we entered 2016 with Speaker Hubbard determined to hang on 'til that last dog died, although he had been gradually and quietly shifting many of his responsibilities as Speaker into the able arms of the chairman of the Rules Committee, Mac McCutcheon. An impending floor vote on whether to forcibly remove Speaker Hubbard was expected when the legislature convened on February 2. House members seemed closely divided three ways among those pushing to immediately remove the Speaker, those who wanted to wait for his case to be adjudicated, and those who were not sure what to do.

Since the 2015 special session in September, I'd been moving steadily toward removing the Speaker despite my nagging questions about the impropriety of the lead prosecutor in Hubbard's case, until Baron Coleman sent a shockwave through the state capitol. In an affidavit to the Lee County court, Coleman confirmed his political collaboration with Hart throughout the 2014 election cycle. The affidavit ensured that Hubbard would remain Speaker until his trial.

In Alabama politics at that time, Baron Coleman aiding his political nemesis Mike Hubbard was akin to Iran providing the Israelis military support. Many were puzzled about the political consultant stepping out of the shadows, but he felt cornered into it.

On Wednesday, January 13, 2016, Matt Hart appeared before the legislative contract review committee to request approval for a legal services contract with a Birmingham law firm for nearly $1 million. Coleman believed the contract was for the Hubbard case and the contract was for media and public relations work in addition to legal work. Coleman had a local talk radio show in Montgomery and wanted to talk to Hart about it.

When his phone calls were not returned, Coleman raised questions about the lucrative legal contract on his radio talk show, and he received a dose of Matt Hart intimidation. Coleman was shaken as I was by it and realized that Hart may have crossed outside the bounds of the Alabama Rules of Professional Conduct for attorneys. After consulting with legal counsel, he recognized his duty under the rules to report the conduct to the Alabama State Bar. Legal counsel also reached out on Coleman's behalf to ALEA to report Hart's dodgy political collaboration to an appropriate law enforcement authority. However, when he became suspicious that Spencer Collier was a pipeline of information to Matt Hart, Coleman got cold feet and refused to continue his cooperation. On February 2, Coleman filed an affidavit that threatened to expose what Matt Hart had managed to keep hidden for years.

Coleman affirmed that he'd engaged in political collaboration with Hart throughout the 2014 election cycle, having as many as a hundred conversations that included political strategy discussions. He'd received information from his pipeline to the Hubbard investigation with the confidence that Hart knew what was going on and was on his side. Coleman used the information extensively during the 2014 election cycle.

Coleman also confirmed that Representative Ed Henry's 2013 complaint of a grand jury leak was based on information that he'd received from Hart and passed on to Joe Hubbard, resulting in Hart threatening Coleman if their relationship were disclosed. Coleman believed the grand jury threats were made to keep the lines of communication open so that they could share information with the knowledge that Coleman would use it for political purposes but also to ensure that Coleman would be afraid to implicate Hart. Coleman said that when he was subpoenaed by Hubbard's attorneys to testify in Hart's misconduct hearing in October, Hart contacted him to help him prepare for questions he might be asked about the grand jury and information Hart had provided. Coleman further asserted that he'd been contacted by law enforcement and met with them about Hart's conduct and the circumstances surrounding the grand jury information he'd received.

Upon hearing of Coleman's affidavit, most people following the story were interested in how the affidavit would affect Speaker Hubbard's criminal case. However, I was more concerned with Matt Hart's propaganda effort and political interference that had no legitimate law enforcement purpose and how he got away with it. The affidavit was evidence from an eyewitness confirming the assertion I made on the Dale Jackson Show that a connection existed between the political operatives aligned against Speaker Hubbard and the prosecution. If Hart had been collaborating with Coleman throughout the 2014 election cycle, then his adamant denial and feigned offense during that troubling phone call were intentional deception.

Baron Coleman's affidavit was further evidence to me that Hart's extensive collaboration with the very active professional political consultant during the 2014 election cycle, the ambush of Representative Barry Moore orchestrated by Hart in conjunction with Moore's primary opponent, the butt-chewing that he gave me, and the manipulative phone calls to members of the media had no legitimate investigative purpose to further the Hubbard case. The only purpose of those actions that I could see was an attempt to change the political power structure in Montgomery—an illegitimate, illegal use of his official law enforcement position.

While the prosecution of Speaker Hubbard's case was necessary, so was a proper investigation of Hart's potential crimes. There were plenty of eyes on Hubbard's wrongdoing, but Hart's seemed to be overlooked entirely. If Hart had been using his official position to attempt to influence Coleman's political actions, he would be guilty of a felony under Alabama Law, and it needed to be properly investigated like any other case. From my old days as an agent of the Alabama Bureau of Investigation, I recalled a state statute prohibiting state employees from using their official position for political purposes. If Coleman's affidavit were true and corroborated, it appeared Hart had crossed that line several times. I was eager to read Hart's response to Coleman's affidavit.

On February 8, thirty-eight of my fellow House members, including nine Democrats, signed a letter to the U.S. Attorney General Loretta Lynch and the U.S. Attorney for the Middle District of Alabama George Beck demonstrating their concern that Hart's collaboration with Coleman could have violated federal law and requesting Hart's political activity with Coleman be thoroughly investigated. I declined to sign the letter because at the time I was focused on potential violations of state law, having been conditioned as a former ABI agent to stay in my lane and let the feds worry about federal law. Surely, they were not blind to what was going on. As a state legislator, I chose to focus on my responsibility to pursue the possible violation of state law and see if our state system of checks and balances would function properly. Besides, we hadn't seen Hart's response to Coleman's affidavit.

On February 11 the state's response to Coleman's affidavit was filed. While the response was a well-made legal argument detailing why Coleman's affidavit didn't give the judge grounds to throw out Hubbard's indictment, it confirmed Hart's illicit collaboration with the political consultant. It appeared to be an admission that Hart had shared investigative information with Coleman to influence his political actions. Hart's argument to the court that Coleman was a confidential informant was a direct contradiction to the indignant denial he had made to me of a connection with political operatives. Given the secret relationship that existed between Hart and Coleman, Hart's phone call to me could not have been an honest difference of opinion as he tried to make it appear during both the call and again when he cross-examined me in Lee County six months later. Hart called me because my comments were getting uncomfortably close to the truth about his political collaboration with Baron Coleman and he was attempting to suppress them.

Hart labeled Coleman a confidential informant as a ruse to cover his tracks. Informants' identities are kept confidential to protect them from retaliation and repercussions for their cooperation, not to protect law enforcement from repercussions associated with their misconduct. Hart should have known that law enforcement collaboration with a political campaign operative that influences election outcomes is not only inappropriate but also illegal. There are legitimate reasons for law enforcement officials to maintain confidentiality with informants, but concealing their misdeeds is not among them. I would say the same for grand jury secrecy.

Attached to the state's response were affidavits that could be placed in one of two categories: political allies of Coleman during their 2014 campaign to bring down the "Riley/Hubbard machine" and law enforcement officials from the Alabama Law Enforcement Agency presented in a context to falsely imply that they had cleared Hart of wrongdoing. The first group included Jack Campbell, a longtime Republican political consultant that had been Coleman's partner in their political consulting firm "Spot On Strategies"; John Rice, who had formed the dark money group Alabama Foundation for Limited Government and the Stop Common Core PAC as a means to secretly funnel AEA money to conservative Republican candidates, most of whom used Spot On Strategies; and finally, Speaker Hubbard's opponent in the 2014 Republican primary, Sandy Toomer.

The affidavits provided by Coleman's former political allies shared a similar theme in that they attested that Hart had not leaked confidential grand jury information to them, nor had Coleman told them that Hart was leaking grand jury information to him. Of course, anyone who has heard the recording of Matt Hart in 2013 threatening to put Baron Coleman in front of the grand jury and deny their relationship can easily understand why Coleman didn't talk to them about it. After the hiccup with Representative Ed Henry and Representative Joe Hubbard, Coleman and Hart's secret information pipeline remained a secret until Coleman went public. Coleman obviously kept the nature of his relationship with Hart from his political colleagues, and I hope that Hart kept it secret from his colleagues on the prosecution team. I shudder to think that his illicit relationship with Coleman would be condoned by other prosecutors.

The affidavit submitted by Special Agent Jack Wilson of the Alabama Law Enforcement Agency (ALEA) seemed innocuous. In it, he attests that he was directed to speak to Baron Coleman about a matter involving Matt Hart that didn't involve an allegation of criminal activity, nor did it result in a formal investigation. Coleman made no mention to Agent Wilson that he was a confidential informant. Agent Wilson reiterates in the affidavit that ALEA has no investigation underway into any matter relating to Matt Hart or the Lee County grand jury.

Agent Wilson's carefully worded affidavit declared that a formal investigation had not been initiated, but it did not eliminate the likelihood that preliminary investigative work had been done. At least, I hope it was done and documented. When I was in ABI, we called them intelligence reports, not investigations. Agent Wilson's affidavit was clearly nothing more than a formal declaration that ALEA did not have a dog in the hunt, intended to extricate the agency from involvement in the Hubbard case.

Director Collier's affidavit appeared to be almost identical to Agent Wilson's and equally innocuous; however, the circumstances surrounding it detonated a chain of events that would compel Governor Bentley to fire Collier, Collier to turn on the governor, and the governor to be impeached. Matt Hart's zeal to suppress Coleman's testimony about their illicit collaboration and remove the cloud of suspicion from himself would generate other unintended consequences that would affect Alabama politics and reverberate far beyond the Hubbard case.

CHAPTER 19

Moral Obligations

As I closely read Baron Coleman's affidavit, I thought about the statute in the Code of Alabama that states, "Any person who attempts to use his or her official authority or position for the purpose of influencing the vote or political action of any person shall be guilty, upon conviction, of a Class C felony." According to Coleman's affidavit, it seemed Matt Hart had regularly used his authority and position to influence Coleman's political actions throughout the 2014 election cycle, not to mention the ambush of Representative Barry Moore, and his propaganda efforts leading into both the primary and general elections.

Evidence clearly existed of a violation of state law, and although I was no longer a criminal investigator, my legislative duty compelled me to determine if a mechanism was in place for it to be enforced impartially by someone without an underlying conflict of interest. It's a good thing I was home alone with laryngitis when I read Hart's response because I threw a running duck fit. It explained the true purpose of his telephone call to me—it was a confession that he didn't call me to express a legitimate difference of opinion but to try to bully me into shutting up about what he knew was true.

I texted Representative Ed Henry, "I just read the prosecution's response. I'm so pissed! The whole purpose of his call to me was to dress me down for saying I was convinced that politics was influencing the investigation, which he adamantly denied. Now he files a brief saying that Coleman was a key informant in the investigation, which contradicts what he so adamantly asserted in our phone call. I am so livid at the brass of that bald-faced liar. We need to do some role reversal. I am so outraged. I want to go full on "Ed Henry," but I am afraid I would go too far. What should I do?"

Surprisingly, Ed gave me sage advice: "Be Mike Ball, not me. Mike Ball will get him but thoughtfully and precisely. But if you want to blow up, tell me when and where and I'll blow up with you."

Restraint is so far outside Ed's normal pattern of behavior that I am prone to attribute his response to divine intervention, notwithstanding the little purple devil icon at the end of his text.

A couple of hours later, I received a text from a member of Governor Bentley's staff asking me to call him about an unrelated matter. When I called him, my laryngitis didn't stop me telling him in no uncertain terms about Hart's impropriety, fully expecting the governor to be informed. My expectations of the governor were understandably low. I didn't believe Bentley had it in him to stand up to Matt Hart, but not many people do. And many who did paid a price.

Over the weekend my anger subsided, and I took Ed's advice. Instead of blowing up, I began thinking about the situation more like ABI Agent Mike Ball would have. The phone call had forced me to think of Hart like a political adversary, not a suspect who I believed may have committed a crime. I read the Code of Alabama again, 17-17-4: Any person (Matt Hart) who attempts to use his official position (he was calling me to ostensibly set the record straight as the lead prosecutor in the Hubbard case) for the purpose of influencing the political action (I was on a radio program attempting to mitigate political damage that he had caused and he was trying to stop me) of any person (me) is guilty of a Class C felony. Reading the statute that way caused me to believe that I had witnessed a felony committed by the chief of the Attorney General's Special Prosecutions Division. Not only that, but I was also a victim of the crime.

The problem was that I had no one to report it to. I tried to talk myself out of it, but I couldn't explain the facts in a way that didn't put Hart's actions within the scope of the statute. What purpose could he possibly have if not to stop me speaking out about his illicit political collaborations? Wasn't it an obvious political action to publicly share my observations to the public during the final days leading up to the election to counter the political damage he had caused to my friends who had nothing to do with the crime he was investigating? If damage control by a political candidate days before an election isn't a political action, I don't know what is.

Having obtained many arrest warrants, I believe I know probable cause when I see it, and this was way beyond probable cause—I had witnessed a felony. By itself, Hart's attempt to shut me up was at least unprofessional behavior, but this new information put the phone call in context that made me believe I had witnessed an unreported felony. Witnessing a felony carries with it a moral obligation to report it to the proper authority. The question was, who was the proper authority? The Attorney General Luther Strange had already let me know that he wasn't interested. Luther would have a political disaster on his hands if his chief of the Special Prosecutions Unit were found to have committed a felony. It was not in the attorney general's best interest to properly investigate this crime. He had a clear conflict of interest.

By Monday, I had my voice back and decided to report it to ALEA, hoping that by reporting it to them my moral obligation would be satisfied. I texted Spencer Collier that I needed to talk to him when I got to Montgomery, but he didn't respond. That very day Collier was meeting Hart about his affidavit. Collier never responded to my text, and now I'm glad he didn't. One thing for sure, Collier probably wouldn't have welcomed what I had to say. Unbeknownst to me at the time, he had his own "Hart problem."

I needed to find someone with impeccable legal credentials to help me sort through the legal and ethical morass I had wandered into. I believe Othni Lathram to be the most competent, trustworthy nonpartisan legal authority in Montgomery. Othni is the director of the Legislative Services Agency, which includes the Alabama Law Institute, the Legislative Fiscal Office, and the Legal Research Division. Legislators of every political stripe rely on Othni for his fair and balanced legal advice when drafting and seeking information regarding legislation. He has no political agenda as far as I can tell. I don't even know his political philosophy. As far as I can tell, his only agenda is to try to get it right. He not only has a staff of attorneys and personnel available to him to research these matters, but he is also widely connected with legal scholars and his counterparts in Alabama and across the country. Also, his relationship with legislators is protected by attorney-client privilege. Othni was the person that I could absolutely rely upon for wise counsel. I went to him and laid it out to him and asked, "Am I seeing what I think I am seeing?"

"Yes, you are," he replied.

"So, what do I do?," I asked.

"You have a moral obligation to report it to the proper authority," he stated.

"I know that, but who is the proper authority?" I inquired.

"I don't know," was his truthful but unhelpful response.

Othni didn't know the proper authority because Attorney General Luther Strange had a conflict of interest, his political future staked on Matt Hart cleaning up Montgomery corruption. Besides, Luther had already blown it off once when I tried to report it. If it turned out to be true now, how would that make him look? I still didn't know what to do, but my discussion with Othni was helpful because he confirmed my belief that I had witnessed a violation of the law and that my legal reasoning was sound. He used the term "prima facie," which is how lawyers describe something so obvious it stares at you in the face the first time you look at it. I would have been glad if it were not true, but the more I looked at it, the stronger it got. I have yet to find evidence to disprove it. Before I left his office, I asked Othni to research it and let me know if he found anything that might further enlighten me on it.

My moral obligation to report this crime to the appropriate authority was a heavy burden that I desperately needed to unload. But I couldn't do that until I found someone with the appropriate authority, without a conflict of interest, who would ensure its proper investigation and adjudication. I was a public official and this was public information, so I shared it with anyone who would listen. Not everyone would listen—some were afraid to hear it, and I don't blame them. Good people with legal, investigative, and prosecutorial experience listened to me as I searched for something that might refute the evidence or help me figure out what to do. I had no success.

I spoke to the executive director of the Ethics Commission, Tom Albritton. Although the crime I'd discovered was not a violation of election law and not under his purview, I respected his legal expertise and judgment and hoped Tom could help me figure out what to do. But his response was almost identical to what Othni said. I had a moral obligation to report it to the appropriate authority and he didn't know who it was. I asked him to think about it and let me know if he figured out who I should report it to.

Before I left Montgomery that week, I checked with Othni about his research surrounding the statute that I believed Hart had violated. There was very little case law surrounding it, and he could only find two instances of a prosecution under the statute. The most recent case was the former secretary of state and current chair of the Democratic Party who'd been charged under the statute for improperly soliciting employees of her office for help with her campaign. She eventually pled guilty to a related misdemeanor charge. The only case of an actual felony conviction under the statute that Othni found was that of a small-town police chief in the 1990s who used the authority of his office to compel an employee to engage in city elections. The police chief was charged and subsequently pled guilty to a felony violation of 17-17-4. It was prosecuted by a local district attorney following an investigation conducted by the Alabama Bureau of Investigation. The ABI agent who conducted the investigation was Mike Ball. Maybe that's why I remembered that obscure statute that others overlooked.

On Friday, February 19, 2016, the U.S. Attorney for the Middle District of Alabama George Beck held a press conference in response to the letter from my legislative colleagues requesting a federal investigation. Much of what he said confirmed my thinking that many of the issues cited in the letter were state issues that should be addressed according to state law. Beck suggested that the legislature exercise its constitutional power to investigate the attorney general for the impeachable offense of willful neglect of duty and incompetence. He said that he would seek additional guidance from the Justice Department regarding areas of concern that could have federal jurisdiction, such as using a grand jury to influence an election and civil rights violations relative to influencing an election. Beck added that if there was a federal investigation, it would not play out in the media. The feds have their business, and we have ours, but we sure could have used some help.

I continued to try to find the appropriate authority to report the felony that I had witnessed, when it occurred to me that the statute was tucked away in election code, and I could report it to the Alabama secretary of state. I discussed it with a friend, Brent Beal, who was an attorney on the secretary of state's legal staff. When I recounted my discovery and my struggle to find the appropriate authority to investigate it, Brent arranged a meeting in Montgomery with Secretary John Merrill and the Secretary's Chief Legal Officer Joel Laird, a retired circuit judge who had spent twenty-six years on the bench. There seemed to be no question that the complaint had merit, and they made a formal request for investigation to ALEA. My burden was finally lifted, and my conscience was clear. I innocently believed that would satisfy my moral obligation to report the crime that I had witnessed to the appropriate authority.

The moral obligation to report a crime to the proper authority is not absolute in every situation. There was already plenty of evidence available for any reasonable person to know that CBD oil was effective in helping to control seizures. I knew parents who administered this illegal substance to their children with remarkable results. The moral obligation not to report them and even to protect them was even greater than the moral obligation to report a powerful public official abusing his position to influence political action and cover it up.

Law exists to prevent needless suffering by bringing some semblance of order to our society so we can live in peace and avoid hurting one another. Law made by humans is not sacrosanct in and of itself unless it prevents needless suffering and protects the weak from being abused by the powerful. However, if a law inflicts needless suffering, it is immoral and should be changed. That's why we have the legislative branch of government.

Giving comfort to those who suffer is morally right, and a law that prevents it is immoral, at least according to the moral compass I follow. Following the moral compass my daddy gave me has caused my faith in God to steadily grow while my faith in politics and the law has diminished greatly. Anyone can do the right thing when it is also popular and legal, but when political expediency, legality, and morality collide, most people naturally choose conformity over morality. That's because there is a price to pay for choosing morality over political expediency or even legality, but a clear conscience is worth it to me.

Jesus said it would be better for those who harm the little ones if a millstone were tied around their necks and they were cast into the depths of the sea. Strong words, but I believe them. If forced to choose between the consequences of disobeying a law made by humans or wearing a millstone necklace, it's a no-brainer.

CHAPTER 20

Leni's Law

It was only a small step, but the unanimous passage of Carly's Law in 2014 by the Alabama Legislature authorized and funded medical research of cannabis. It was an important step toward removing the stigma that decades of government propaganda had wrapped around an innocent plant. It took an entire year after the Alabama Legislature passed Carly's Law before layers of federal bureaucracy were navigated and the research could finally begin. Even then, the protocols imposed on the study were extremely restrictive, limiting it to a relatively small number of participants. The heartless bureaucracy had no sense of urgency for the multitude of victims who suffered from debilitating seizures in Alabama.

People tend to see only what they look for, and they usually only look for what they want to find. Our efforts to pass Carly's Law opened some eyes, but people can be quick to revert to their preconceived notions if they don't see immediate results. By the summer of 2015 when Governor Bentley called the legislature into special session to address our failed efforts to pass a general fund budget, many eyes had shut again. The news that UAB had finally received federal approval and the study was about to get underway brought a splinter of satisfaction and gave real meaning to my legislative service when just about everything else in the legislature seemed to be coming apart.

I was savoring that bit of good news during an otherwise dreary time when Amy Young called to congratulate me that the UAB study was finally getting underway. Amy is the mother of Leni Young, who has suffered from severe chronic seizures since she was a baby. Leni's entire family have been united in giving her their full support as she has struggled her entire life just to survive. When I held her the first time and we worshipped together, her soul seemed imprisoned by the side effects of the medication that was

Leni and me in a moment of worship. (Photo courtesy of Grace Photography)

necessary to control the seizures and keep her alive. The only thing she had was love. But she had an abundant supply.

Celebration turned to sorrow when Amy told me that Leni did not qualify for the UAB study and their family would be forced to move to another state where Leni could have legal access to CBD oil. While Amy accepted it as God's will for their family to move and was upbeat and positive about it, I didn't take it so well. However, our perspectives were very different. Amy could clearly see the path where her moral obligation led. My moral obligations seemed to be leading me down a lonely path into the middle of a snake-infested jungle with no way out.

When Amy's call ended, I spoke to UAB's legislative liaison Porter

Bannister about Leni's plight, but he was unable to help. The protocols excluded Leni from obtaining cannabis through the study because of her other medication. The Young family became medical refugees from Alabama and chased their shred of hope to Oregon, while I continued to lose mine amid the darkness in Alabama. Instead of celebrating the fruits of what should have been my most significant legislative achievement, I sat in my office and mourned its failure to fulfill its purpose for the multitude of families like the Youngs who could not afford to wait for blind politicians and stubborn bureaucrats to come to their aid.

It was not my first struggle with severe chronic depression. My first episode was during the weeks following my daddy's death. Some might compare it to sadness, but this is something different. It is deeper, more intense, and seems like it will never end. It is a dark, lonely cloud that descends on the soul in its attempt to smother the hope out of its victim. Trying to survive inside the belly of a whale is the best description that I can think of.

Over fifty years have passed since I fought through my first episode with the darkness, and only by divine providence have I managed to survive many since, some of them just as severe and even more long-lasting than the first one, with almost no professional counseling or medication. I would not recommend that approach to others, it is far too dangerous. But by the time I recognized what I was fighting, I had learned through trial and error to not only escape from its clutches, but to even draw strength from each encounter.

It is the central question that surrounds the story of Job. Many people overlook the scripture indicating that the Lord did not just allow Satan to torment Job but instigated it. It seems contradictory that a benevolent God would unleash Satan to inflict pain and suffering upon those He loves. But according to the Bible, that is exactly what happened in Job's case. When Job was sufficiently humbled, he was able to recognize God's grace and that everything worth wanting was a gift received through it. By resisting bitterness and resentment while submitting to the Almighty One, Job became more complete. Everything that feels bad is not bad, and I have emerged from every struggle with the darkness better prepared for the next one.

I was still struggling with the darkness several months after the phone call from Amy when I woke during the night, unable to sleep. I opened Facebook on my iPad and saw that Amy had posted a video of Leni watching *Frozen*. It had only been a short time since the family had moved to Oregon where they could begin treating Leni with cannabis. I saw joy on Leni's face as she giggled and squealed with delight while watching the animated movie. Seeing Leni's joy chased away my despair and opened my mind. The contrast between the little girl watching the video and the near lifeless body that I held the night that Carly's Law passed the Senate reminded me of Lazarus's being raised from the dead.

While I watched Leni watching *Frozen*, my happiness was tempered with regret that we had failed to pass Carly's Law as originally introduced. Had we done so, not only would Leni's family have been able to stay in Alabama where they had lived for generations, but Leni would have been spared over a year of unnecessary suffering. I recalled many others that I knew who have also needlessly suffered during that time and tried to imagine the multitude that I didn't know.

The light of Leni's joy drove away the darkness that had been trying to consume me for weeks. While the light cleansed the darkness from my mind, the concept of Leni's Law came to me. We needed to pass something like the original version of Carly's Law that would protect as many victims of debilitating illnesses as possible from being arbitrarily prosecuted for possession of low-THC cannabis oil. I had no idea how they could legally obtain it, but if they possessed it, at least they wouldn't need to worry about defending themselves against an unjust law imposed by obtuse bureaucrats and politicians. It was the next right thing, and I had to do it to keep the darkness away.

I drafted Leni's Law and introduced it in the House soon after the legislature went into session in early February 2016. My trustworthy partner in the Senate, Paul Sanford, introduced a companion bill. The effort to pass Leni's Law was very different from Carly's Law. Our dedicated little band had strengthened both in numbers and in faith. We had learned to allow the light to guide us through the process one step at a time. A significant number of legislators recognized the power that drove our movement. I will never stop grieving for the small number who will probably never get it.

Results from the UAB research authorized by Carly's Law and many other sources provided more scientific evidence of the efficacy of cannabis than we had before. Because of mounting evidence that indicated low potential for abuse and enormous potential for palliative care, Leni's Law was broader than the original Carly's Law in that we did not limit its protection to only those suffering from seizures.

Leni's Law was fashioned to provide an affirmative defense from prosecution for possession of CBD oil containing under 3 percent THC to anyone under a doctor's care for a debilitating illness. We did not legalize it, but we were able carve out a degree of protection from prosecution in the unlikely event some overzealous police officer and a morally challenged prosecutor went after them. I did not believe most police or prosecutors would pursue a case under the circumstances outlined in Leni's Law.

District attorneys that I have encountered during my law enforcement career seemed to have a sound sense of justice and were usually reasonable when exercising prosecutorial discretion. The niche that I was trying to carve from the marijuana possession law was narrow and would have little effect on their ability to prosecute the law against people who abuse cannabis but would bring tremendous peace of mind to many sick and afflicted. Unfortunately, their continual resistance to our efforts to bring relief to suffering people, coupled with those who willfully ignored the corruption in the Attorney General's Office that I tried to bring to their attention, forced me to the realization that the esteem in which I had held prosecutors for so long was undeserved. After all, they are only humans. And politicians.

When I introduced Carly's Law in 2014, I also held Attorney General Luther Strange in high regard. Although he was not exactly supportive of our efforts, he didn't seem opposed to it, either. However, it was different with Leni's Law in 2016, and he dug in against it. I don't know if it was because of my run-in with Matt Hart, or the influence of his Chief Deputy Alice Martin who he brought in to protect Hart soon after I testified in his misconduct hearing. When I spoke to her about Leni's Law, she let me know in no uncertain terms that she did not empathize with the plight of the people who would benefit from Leni's Law. Even though it was widely believed that Martin pulled Luther's strings, I still thought highly of Luther and hoped that he would do the right thing. I believe in miracles, but I can't make one happen.

By the time that we had the public hearing in the House Judiciary Committee on Leni's Law in March, I had given up on that miracle. The attorney general dug in against us, but we didn't need his support. Plenty of legislators understood what Leni's Law was about, and we had the votes to pass it. Although the chairman of the House Judiciary Committee Representative Mike Jones was opposed, he gave his word that he would allow it to move forward and not arbitrarily kill it, which was better than what Carly's Law got from the previous House Judiciary chairman Paul DeMarco.

To his credit, Jones placed Leni's Law on the agenda for a public hearing in a timely manner. It was obvious that public sentiment was in our favor and had steadily grown over the previous couple of years. After I made brief opening remarks, Leni's dad Wayne Young made a remarkably informative and compelling presentation via a video link from Oregon. It was the first time that a live video feed had been used by the Alabama Legislature in a public hearing, and it was remarkable to hear him tell Leni's story while speaking in favor of the bill.

After Wayne finished his presentation, Luther Strange rose from his seat beside Alice Martin to speak against Leni's Law. It would be an understatement to describe him as uncomfortable. He seemed awkward and ill-prepared as he spoke. I felt sad and disappointed as I listened to his inane talking points in opposition to Leni's Law. It aggravated me to hear the career oil company lobbyist passing himself off as spokesperson for the entire law enforcement community trying to describe the difficulty Leni's law would present for a police officer during a traffic stop. His testimony struck me as asinine.

After Luther spoke against Leni's Law, it was time for members of the Judiciary Committee to ask questions, and part of me yearned to embarrass him with questions that would reveal his ignorance about police, traffic stops, and what effect Leni's Law might have on it. But my indignation melted when I looked at the families filling the committee room and remembered that Leni's Law wasn't about me showing off my experience and Luther's lack of it. The focus was on the plight of the victims of this unjust law. Anyway, the attorney general's position on the bill didn't really matter because we had already counted plenty of votes in both the House and the Senate. Besides that, he had already embarrassed himself enough with his own testimony.

Although Jones allowed Leni's Law to move out of the Judiciary Committee, he insisted on substituting for a more restrictive version that would have substantially limited legal access to the point that Leni and her family would still be unable to come home, even for a brief visit. The House unanimously passed Jones's restrictive version of Leni's Law.

On April 27, 2016, on the twenty-seventh legislative day, Senator Sanford substituted it on the Senate floor with a version that essentially restored it to its original form. The restored bill passed the Senate twenty-nine to three, with Holley, Stutts, and Williams opposed. Although a freak storm blew through Montgomery during an otherwise calm day and temporarily knocked out the power in the Statehouse while I was standing at the microphone, the House concurred ninety-five to four when the power was restored. Farley, Faulkner, Weaver, and Jones opposed.

Representative Farley's opposition to Leni's Law puzzled me. Farley was one of the early supporters of Carly's Law when it was almost identical to what was now Leni's Law. He and his wife Muriel were faithful servants for the Carly's Law families and an integral part of the spiritual movement that made it happen. If you will recall, Farley's and Dr. Joe Godfrey's support was an important factor in helping me determine whether I should commit to Carly's Law in the first place. Both firmly opposed Leni's Law, which was the same thing with a different name.

Their opposition to Leni's Law reminded me that I had used them like Gideon's fleece when I sent Carly's dad Dustin to gauge their support before I committed to pass Carly's Law. Their natural tendency was to oppose anything that had anything to do with cannabis, but something moved them to support it against their natural predisposition. But I didn't need to throw down the fleece before taking on Leni's Law, and by then, Farley and Dr. Godfrey had reverted to their initial stance against cannabis in any form. Farley's and Dr. Godfrey's support for Carly's Law and their subsequent opposition to Leni's Law only reminded me that among the greatest of God's miracles is the power to change a mind, even when it's only temporary for a specific purpose.

Leni's Law was another small but significant step toward providing protection from prosecution for Alabamians attempting to obtain relief from debilitating ailments by using a substance that has fewer adverse side effects than many commonly used over-the-counter medicines. Since the

Governor Bentley should be careful where he puts his finger.

passage of Leni's Law, there have been many who have been helped and whose lives have been saved because of it. Senator Paul Sanford has said that his work with Carly's Law and Leni's Law was the most meaningful accomplishment of his nine years as an Alabama Senator. His "damn the torpedoes" style made him the perfect Senate sponsor. I don't see how it could have happened without him.

After overwhelming passage by the legislature, all that remained for Leni's Law to become law was for Governor Bentley to sign it. Although he signed both Carly's Law and Leni's Law, Governor Bentley was never exactly eager to make CBD oil available to these families. He only signed Carly's Law after it was carved down to only the UAB study. I was concerned Governor Bentley might be reluctant to sign Leni's Law, since I had instigated his impeachment only a few weeks before its passage. Fortunately, he knew these families had captured the hearts of the public and by then he didn't have any political capital to spare.

One of the most frustrating things about politics is the dichotomy between what happened and what is reported. Despite his lack of cooperation and reluctance to help, Governor Bentley signed both Carly's Law and Leni's Law, and he received credit for something that he hindered more than helped. As a result, he had many great photo ops with the families. My personal favorite is a photo of Governor Bentley when he met Leni in 2014 soon after we passed Carly's Law. In the photo, Governor Bentley reached out his hand to Leni and she bit his finger. Maybe Leni intuitively knew something the public didn't.

CHAPTER 21

The Luv Guv

When Baron Coleman publicly exposed his illicit collaboration with Matt Hart throughout the 2014 election cycle in February 2016, it prompted several people, including some legislators, to encourage Governor Bentley to exercise his constitutional authority to appoint an independent counsel to investigate. I was not one of those people, although I had a brief conversation with a senior member of the governor's staff about the crime that I had witnessed.

I had already reported it to the secretary of state, who requested that the Alabama Law Enforcement Agency (ALEA) investigate. I also spoke with other law enforcement authorities about the situation and still had confidence that our justice system could work without attempting to persuade our indecisive governor to decisively invoke his constitutional authority. There were others in Alabama with the legal authority to investigate Hart's illicit relationships with political operatives, but my exhaustive efforts to find one that also had the moral and political courage to take action to ensure the case was properly investigated and prosecuted would be a miserable failure.

Governor Bentley was entangled in his own imbroglio and wanted no part of the one that engulfed the Hubbard case from its inception. He'd instructed members of his administration to keep their distance and was already wary, especially when he learned that Baron Coleman had gone to the ALEA ready to expose his relationship with Hart and to provide several potentially incriminating recordings of their conversations together. However, when Coleman discovered that Collier was probably sharing information with Hart, he decided against sharing further information and his recordings, fearing retaliation. Without the full cooperation of Coleman making a clear allegation of a criminal act, an investigation was not opened. Even if they had found a violation of state law, who would prosecute it?

Baron Coleman's potentially incriminating affidavit to the Lee County Circuit Court sent Hart scrambling, much like Representative Henry's original complaint had done in October 2013. In his strategy to discredit Coleman, Hart desperately wanted to obtain an affidavit from Spencer Collier, but he didn't want him to testify and be subject to cross-examination by Hubbard's attorneys. On February 8, 2016, a meeting was held with Governor Bentley and Collier in the presence of the governor's legal advisor David Byrne, ALEA executive counsel Jason Swann, and ALEA Special Agent Jack Wilson. Governor Bentley was told that Matt Hart had written an affidavit for Collier to sign, but he refused to sign it because it wasn't accurate. Hart had carefully crafted an affidavit to give the mistaken impression that Coleman's allegations had been proven by ALEA to have no merit when no investigation had even been made. The governor told Collier not to sign the document.

Governor Bentley had no objection to Collier or anyone else testifying in the Hubbard case. Bentley had cooperated with the investigation and had himself testified before the grand jury that indicted Hubbard. He would eventually testify in the trial that ultimately convicted Hubbard. However, the affidavit Hart wanted Collier to submit was unrelated to the guilt or innocence of Speaker Hubbard but was about Hart's collaboration with Baron Coleman. It was an attempt to discredit Baron Coleman and suppress his testimony about their inappropriate collaboration. Collier seemed unable to recognize that Hart was trying to use him to help suppress testimony of a witness who had come to ALEA with potentially incriminating evidence.

When Collier refused to sign the original affidavit, Hart negotiated with the governor's legal counsel David Byrne and ALEA counsel Jason Swann to produce an affidavit Collier would sign that satisfied Hart. Bentley was furious when he discovered Collier had signed the affidavit. According to Bentley's account, Collier told him that he felt threatened by Hart if he didn't give him what he needed. After speaking with Collier several times over the next few days, the governor was convinced that Hart had coerced Collier into giving an affidavit attempting to discredit Coleman's misconduct proceedings against Hart.

The appointment of a special counsel to investigate the actions of the rogue prosecutor continued to grow as an option for Bentley until February 16, when he was astonished to learn that Collier had changed his mind about being coerced by Hart to sign the affidavit. Muddled by Collier's sudden change of mind about Hart and Byrne's participation in the preparation of Collier's affidavit against his expressed wishes to remain neutral, Bentley called a meeting with Byrne, Rebekah Mason, the governor's media spokesperson Jennifer Ardis, Bentley's attorney Joe Espy, Collier, his chief of staff Hal Taylor, ALEA counsel Jason Swann, and two other people from ALEA.

Early on, Collier interrupted the meeting and wanted to speak privately with the governor and Rebekah. Collier told them that he'd spoken to Matt Hart the previous day (which explains Collier's sudden change of heart, understandable after a meeting with Hart) and that Hart had good things to say about Bentley but said there were people working for him that had committed felonies. Collier told them he believed Hart was referring to Rebekah.

Collier told the governor and Rebekah that he was afraid of Matt Hart and didn't want to testify under subpoena, further telling the governor, "You don't want to testify either." According to Bentley, Collier told him he would be doing the state a service if he got rid of Matt Hart. Collier said that Hart had questioned his chief of staff Hal Taylor until midnight the previous day and he believed Taylor might get indicted. What the squeaky-clean Hal Taylor could have possibly done to get indicted remains a mystery to me.

After the meeting, Bentley decided Collier was stressing out and needed some time off. The following morning Governor Bentley called his friend into his office and put him on medical leave for three months to have a scheduled back surgery, recuperate, and get off pain medication he'd been taking because of injuries incurred in a wreck in 2012. Collier was contrite and offered to resign, but Governor Bentley refused to accept, telling him, "No, I want you to get well and come back in three months." They had a cordial discussion about the governor's decision to appoint Stan Stabler as acting director of ALEA while Collier was out on medical leave.

Stan Stabler was a top-notch criminal investigator in the Major Crimes Unit of the Alabama Bureau of Investigation (ABI) for many years before joining the Executive Protection Unit around the time of Governor Bentley's re-election campaign. Assisting the governor's security details is among the many tasks that ABI agents are called upon to do. As a top-notch agent assigned to Mobile, Stabler was frequently called upon to assist the executive protection unit.

I'd never heard a word spoken against Stan Stabler during the twenty years that I knew him as a fellow ABI agent before 2016, but that changed when he wandered into a starring role in the governor's soap opera.

Soon after Stabler assumed the mantle of leadership at ALEA, he was besieged by career employees with reports of improper purchases of personal items, personal use of state resources, and other violations of ALEA policies and procedures by Collier and some of his subordinates. Thinking like an investigator and not a politician, acting Secretary Stabler assigned Agent April Bickhaus of the ALEA Integrity Unit to conduct an internal inquiry and determine the merit of the allegations.

Agent Bickhaus's exploratory investigation uncovered evidence that indicated Collier had committed several policy and procedure violations that would have been firing offenses had someone of lower rank committed them. Two obvious potential violations of the Alabama Ethics Law that jumped out to me were the purchase of personal clothing items that far exceeded the yearly $875 stipend provided for non-uniformed arresting officers and falsifying notarized law enforcement subsistence pay forms to reflect that he was working on days that he was purportedly at home nursing a bad back.

Purchase orders indicated Collier had exceeded the annual clothing allowance each year over a period of several years, sometimes more than doubling and tripling the amount allotted for arresting officers.

State police officers were eligible to receive a $12-per-day stipend for days they are at work for six hours or more; however, they are not eligible to claim the stipend if they are only on call and not at work. Records indicated that Collier claimed full subsistence for days that he was not at work and reimbursement for personal clothing purchases far above his legal allotment for several years running.

There were other potential violations that could also rise to the level of criminal violations under the Alabama Ethics Law, but the clothing allowance and subsistence pay fraud seemed most obvious and easy to prove when I later saw the records. During my career as a criminal investigator with the former Department of Public Safety, I'd received the annual clothing allowance and the monthly subsistence allowance. I was familiar with the associated paperwork, policy, and procedure, and the findings cited in Bikhaus's report clearly presented evidence to indicate potential violations of the Alabama Ethics Law. It would have been willful neglect of duty not to investigate.

Bickhaus's report also raised questions about Collier failing to meet the Alabama Peace Officers' Standards and Training Certification (APOSTC) as a police officer while he was director of Homeland Security and using his position questionably to appoint himself a police officer, allowing himself to receive $2,544 in subsistence pay from July 2011 through July 10, 2012, when Collier sent a letter to the state personnel department rescinding his self-appointment as a police officer. Collier did not receive subsistence pay until after the legislature passed Senate Bill 108 in March 2013, which made Collier a law enforcement officer statutorily because of his position, thus allowing him to resume his monthly subsistence payments without obtaining APOSTC certification.

As the House sponsor of SB108, I was well aware of Collier's extensive effort to get it passed, but I was unaware that Collier was ineligible for subsistence because of his failure to meet certification standards as a police officer. Had I known Collier allowed his certification to lapse and the language inserted in the bill qualified him for a benefit he was not already receiving, it would have certainly raised an eyebrow and would have needed to be addressed. Although I don't believe qualifying himself for subsistence pay was his primary motivation in passing the bill, it did seem to be a potential violation of the Alabama Ethics Law.

When I read Bickhaus's report a year later, I realized that there was a great deal that I didn't know about Spencer Collier's tenure as the leader of the Alabama Law Enforcement Agency. One of the troubling things that I learned from the report was that from the time Collier was appointed the head of ALEA, he apparently was unable to report to work most of the time, ostensibly due to the back injury he received from his traffic wreck in 2012. For several years prior to his forced leave of absence in 2016, Collier only came to work one or two days a week, yet on the subsistence claim form completed and signed each month, it indicated that Collier had worked five days a week for at least six hours a day throughout much of the time he was at home.

On March 8, Agent Bickhaus accompanied Stabler and ALEA attorney Michael Robinson to share her findings with Governor Bentley, who was Collier's supervisor and appointing authority. Until then, Bentley had no intention of firing Collier, but he couldn't ignore the information he'd been given by Agent Bickhaus. It indicated a repeated pattern of firing offenses by Collier and possible criminal violations of the Ethics Law. But it didn't matter because Collier would be protected from prosecution by the Attorney General's Office.

A week later, on March 14, Agent Bickhaus was ordered to refer the matter to the Attorney General's Office for criminal investigation and continue the administrative interrogatory. She turned the criminal investigation over to Hart's mentor and protector, Chief Deputy Attorney General Alice Martin. Later that day Agent Bickhaus was accompanied by legal counsel for ALEA and the governor's legal counsel to an unnamed agency that also referred the ethics charges to the attorney general. Agent Bickhaus had several other meetings to share information and witness contact information in cooperation with the Attorney General's Office until she was informed by an attorney general's investigator that the matter could not be further investigated without Matt Hart's authorization.

Collier and Bentley had been loyal friends since they were first elected to the legislature, but Agent Bickhaus's findings fell on the friendship like a bucket of bricks. The governor knew he had to fire Collier despite their friendship. On March 22, Governor Bentley made the following announcement:

"After placing Spencer on medical leave a few weeks ago to allow him to recover from back surgery, acting ALEA Secretary Stan Stabler identified several areas of concern in the operations, policies, and procedures at ALEA. After an internal review, the ALEA Integrity Unit found several issues, including possible misuse of state funds. I am disappointed to learn these facts, and (Tuesday) I relieved Spencer Collier of his duties as ALEA secretary."

Former friends who feel betrayed make the most bitter enemies. Spencer Collier struck quickly when he learned that an internal investigation into his use of state resources was underway at ALEA and that he'd been fired by his former friend. The next day, he pulled no punches at a press conference held at his lawyer's office. Collier believed the governor's senior policy advisor Rebekah Mason was at the core of a plot between Governor Bentley, Stan Stabler, and others to destroy him in retaliation for cooperating with Matt Hart in the Hubbard investigation. Of course, none of those people could hurt Collier because they had turned their case over to Matt Hart.

At the press conference, Collier incorrectly asserted that Special Agent Jack Wilson had completed an investigation in Baron Coleman's allegations and had cleared Matt Hart. Although great pains had been taken by Hart's admirers that now included Collier to give the impression that ALEA had cleared Hart of any wrongdoing, that was not the case. A preliminary inquiry had been made and they declined to investigate because of the lack of cooperation by the reporting witness.

The witness had refused to cooperate and turn over potentially incriminating evidence because he rightfully feared it would be given to Hart. The affidavits Hart obtained from Collier and Wilson were carefully worded to leave the court and the public with the false impression that he had been investigated and cleared by ALEA. Although it seems to have worked, it was not true, and Collier erroneously repeated that falsehood at his press conference.

Another false accusation made by Collier at his press conference was that Governor Bentley and Rebekah Mason conspired to terminate four ALEA employees merely because they were loyal to Collier. That was not true. Acting Secretary Stabler had dismissed three, not four, employees, two of which were state retirees working part-time for Collier. One of them was Collier's driver and the other was Collier's assistant who by some accounts was doing much of Collier's work while he was at home nursing his back injury.

Secretary Stabler didn't need either Collier's driver or his assistant. The other employee was a friend of Collier's with no apparent law enforcement experience that he had appointed as the assistant director of Homeland

Security with an $80,000 annual salary, against the wishes of the director of Homeland Security. By eliminating these unnecessary positions, Stan Stabler had saved his budget nearly half of what Collier's scheme to shut down driver's license offices in rural counties would have saved. Good.

But nobody remembers the false accusations Collier made at his press conference, because the accusation that was true was a doozy. As a loyal friend and employee, Collier had been obliged to protect Governor Bentley. Bentley's decision to fire Collier may have been good for the citizens of Alabama, but firing his old friend wasn't good for him. When he fired Collier, Bentley removed Collier's biggest reason for keeping quiet about the governor's intimate relationship with his senior policy advisor. Collier was not obliged to keep it secret anymore.

Collier probably felt relieved to release what he had kept hidden since at least early August 2014, when he first heard the recording of Governor Bentley engaging in sexually intimate banter with his senior policy advisor, who many believed controlled the governor's office. Collier's press conference was a precursor to the imminent release of a recorded conversation that unleashed a media frenzy and undermined what little credibility the governor had not already squandered.

Collier's opening salvo was a huge success. The press would give the governor and his paramour their undivided attention and shift the spotlight from Collier or Hart to whether Governor Bentley and Rebekah Mason were lovers. Its blistering heat melted the hapless governor's ability to govern.

Spencer Collier's press conference was masterfully done. Governor Bentley's ongoing relationship with Rebecca Mason was the perfect vehicle to shift the clouds of suspicion to Governor Bentley and present Collier as a hero for blowing the whistle, despite poor leadership at ALEA, evidence of potential ethics violations, and the inept handling of Baron Coleman's failed attempt to report Hart's illicit political meddling.

Public interest limits the number of scandals that it can process or villains it can focus its ire upon at a time. Pulling the curtains back on Bentley's romantic relationship with his senior policy advisor sucked up what little media oxygen was left from the ethics charges against Speaker Hubbard.

Spencer Collier's press conference drove nails in the coffin that buried

Bentley's reputation and political career, but most of the nails would be driven by Bentley himself. To say he was politically inept would be an understatement, but that had been a large part of his appeal to Alabama voters. People seemed to appreciate that he was not one of those slick politicians, like Bill Clinton. But he could have used the former president's skills.

It has been said that sincerity is the most important thing in politics and if you can fake that, the rest is easy. If you can't fake it, you'd better have it for real. Nobody could fake sincerity like President Clinton. He knew how to handle the political fallout from what his chief of staff labeled "bimbo eruptions." There are many differences between Clinton's trysts and Bentley's obsession, but the most striking difference is love. Bill Clinton was an experienced lothario who was in love with himself, but he didn't fall in love with the objects of his affection.

It seemed Governor Bentley fell in love with Rebekah to the point of obsession. The obsession was so great that it seemed to overshadow every other relationship in his life, including his family, friends, and the people of Alabama. Even if he'd have had the political skill of Bill Clinton, Bentley was so smitten that he couldn't cut her loose and escape the political morass that he was mired in. His pathetic response sunk him deeper.

Robert Bentley's best moments as governor came in the aftermath of terrible tornados that swept across Alabama in 2011. He should have learned then that you can't begin recovering from a storm until after it's passed. He must've missed that lesson, because almost immediately after Collier threw down the gauntlet, Bentley picked it up, put it on, and hit himself in the face. The embattled governor called a press conference in which he demonstrated what might be the gold standard for political ineptitude. For aspiring students in the field of political media and public relations, the video is worth watching, not only for the lessons that can be learned from it, but also for the artistic value as the embodiment of political incompetence in action.

There is a great deal of misunderstanding about the complexities surrounding the art of an apology. A sincere apology is an outward communication of repentance. It can only occur after one recognizes what they have done wrong and is willing to publicly admit it. I don't believe that a public apology is always a necessary ingredient for recovery from the effects of our wrongs, although recognizing and admitting them to ourselves and to God is always a mandatory first step. However, there are times when circumstances dictate a public apology, and when we are facing that time, it should be given only after much prayer and circumspection.

The first thing we should know about a sincere apology is that it can only be made voluntarily. If the apology is made because of coercion, it is not an apology at all—it is a surrender to adversaries. Those who demand an apology are seeking surrender, not reconciliation. It does not signal that we intend to exercise grace toward the vanquished. Those who demand an apology seldom deserve one, and those who give one because of a demand are seldom sincere.

A sincere apology is not a response to an external force but an internal one. A sincere apology is not just an expression of regret, but also a clear admission of wrongdoing. Voicing apologetic words to satisfy others or to evade the consequences of your actions is not an apology. It is attempted manipulation. At his press conference, Governor Bentley gave the most poorly executed, fake apology I have ever seen.

He opened by apologizing to his family, Rebekah Mason's family, and the people of Alabama, immediately followed by a denial of ever having a physical relationship with his senior advisor or using state resources to promote any inappropriate relations with her. When "I'm sorry" is immediately followed by denials, it is usually safe to say it is a fake apology. A sincere apology should be preceded by a clear admission of something. There might be mitigating circumstances that require some explanation to place the apology in the proper context. But it isn't an apology until you lay out what you're apologizing for.

After his alleged apology, when reporters pressed the governor to explain what he was apologizing for, he feebly seemed to suggest that it was for getting caught talking dirty to his staff member. He wasn't even sure what he'd said nor did he even know what was on the recording, but he knew it had captured him engaged in sophomoric banter while in pursuit of the object of his affection. The governor must've thought that if he didn't commit sexual intercourse, all would be well. He didn't seem to understand that he was dealing with an impending media frenzy, and emotion, not law and facts, is what matters.

His responses to questions by reporters made it apparent he was engaged in a pathetic attempt to mitigate Collier's revelation. A reporter asked if he loved Rebekah Mason, and the governor of Alabama responded that he loves all his staff and his cabinet, some more than others. I wish one of the reporters would have asked him how many of his staff he'd talked to in romantic babble. The governor appeared at the press conference to be unrepentant and smitten with Rebekah Mason. I wondered if he would be able to competently execute the duties of his office any longer.

When that press conference was finished, so was his credibility with the people of Alabama. The public persona of the honest grandfatherly doctor who cared for the people of Alabama and could be trusted to act in their best interest had been replaced by that of a lecherous old coot who couldn't be trusted to keep his hands off the employees.

I believed the bumbling attempt to deceive the public in that press conference ensured that he'd never regain the credibility necessary to govern effectively. We weren't even two years into his four-year term. It was depressing. The saddest part was that Governor Bentley and even many around him seemed to be oblivious to the magnitude of the effect of his peculiar relationship with Rebekah Mason.

All misdeeds are not equal. Some are more equal than others, as Orwell might have said. A public official being engaged in an illicit sexual liaison is certainly not acceptable behavior. But Governors Bentley's romantic obsession with Rebekah Mason seemed to be a more serious threat to the government of the state of Alabama than the former governor of South Carolina's tryst with his Argentine paramour was to his state, or even former President Clinton's indiscretions in the Oval Office were to the United States. I've seen no evidence that either Clinton or Sanford ever ceded any of their powers to the women involved or that any of the women involved wielded any political influence because of their relationship. This was different. There was ample evidence that because of Governor Bentley's infatuation, Rebekah Mason may have become the most powerful member of the executive branch of state government.

The public obsession with the salacious details of the governor's amorous relationship overshadowed more serious questions that needed to be asked. The degree to which he and his senior policy advisor might have had genital contact was not even in the vicinity of the most important question I concerned myself with as a legislator. The question that concerned me most was how much power Rebekah Mason wielded as the result of the governor's obsession.

The recording of Bentley talking to Rebekah about their fondling in the his office and his pathetic reaction made it clear to me that it was time to consider impeachment, not just because he had a tryst or an illicit affair, but because of the effect the relationship has had on his ability to competently fulfill the duties of his office.

Robert Bentley was never a great leader, but for a time he seemed adequate. His biggest political asset had been that the citizens of Alabama mostly trusted him, but he squandered most of that trust away, and it was irreversibly gone. Hubris seemed to have blinded him to the seriousness of the threat to his administration posed by the potential conflict of interest created by his personal and professional relationship with Rebekah Mason.

However, Governor Bentley was term limited and didn't have to worry about re-election, so he acted as though he could do as he pleased and no one could do anything about it. If he thought that, he was wrong because it was starting to look more and more to me as though impeachment was the best legal mechanism to get the entire sordid mess with Bentley, Mason, Collier, Hart, and others out in the open where the light of truth could shine on it.

CHAPTER 22

Spotlights

Governor Bentley's sad attempt at a public apology was not a miserable failure merely because it was a poorly executed public relations ploy. Even had it been perfectly executed by Slick Willie himself, its timing would have doomed it to failure. Within hours of the governor's public apology/denial, recordings of his mindless romantic banter with his senior policy advisor were released to the public. Listening to grandfatherly governor cooing to his paramour about kissing, fondling, putting a lock on the door, and moving the desk of his secretary so they wouldn't be disturbed created a mental image that can't be easily erased. The recording appeared to prove what Governor Bentley had denied and the additional public scorn it generated was like pumping bullets into the body of his already dying credibility.

Although Spencer Collier pointed out during his dramatic press conference that the governor could be guilty of a felony if he used campaign funds or state resources to facilitate his love affair, it would not be nearly as easy to prove as charges stemming from something such as falsifying notarized subsistence allowance claim forms or using state funds to purchase personal clothing items. Collier and whoever he was collaborating with played the propaganda game perfectly to train the media spotlight on the hapless governor and his relationship with his alleged paramour and away from Collier's potential ethics violations that had been reported by the career employees at ALEA. By blowing the whistle, Collier portrayed himself as the heroic victim of the villainous Governor Bentley.

It has been said that a good offense is the best defense, but Collier need not have worried about defending himself against ethics charges. His allies in the Attorney General's Office were playing the same game as Collier, and they would work hard to find an Ethics Law violation on Bentley while they buried potential ethics violations reported to them by ALEA that did not fit their agenda.

It is important to remember that this occurred just a few weeks after the secretary of state had requested an investigation by ALEA pursuant to the crime that I had reported, and Bentley had been separately advised to appoint an independent counsel to investigate. Bentley and ALEA had the power to undermine the self-aggrandizing agenda of Matt Hart and Alice Martin. Spencer Collier's retaliatory attack upon the credibility of the governor and the leadership at ALEA also helped insulate his protectors from scrutiny.

From the midst of the darkness that had descended over Alabama's state government, I was desperate for the light of truth to expose it all. The light of truth is a flood light that does not discriminate when it exposes corruption. Propaganda is different. It is a spotlight that selectively chooses whose corruption it exposes. By brightly shining on its selected target, it is not only useful in destroying adversaries, but it is also useful for individuals who wish to conceal their own corruption. This is what Jesus was talking about when he said, "Men seek darkness rather than light when their deeds are evil."

It appeared obvious that the spotlight held by the propaganda machine operating out of the Alabama Attorney General's Office that had destroyed Speaker Hubbard's credibility leading up to his trial was being redirected to Governor Robert Bentley. I believed that the people of Alabama desperately needed to know the whole truth, and using the legislative process as a floodlight seemed to be the best way to illuminate those dark places where corruption lurked behind the spotlight.

Astonishingly, the Alabama Legislature has neglected to give itself subpoena power, which makes most attempts at legislative oversight a sad joke. Legislators are usually good politicians but poor investigators. The legislative branch of government was designed to be the most political branch of government, but it is also supposed to be the most open branch. Since you can't have politics without propaganda, the legislative process is messy because it consists of partisan politicians pointing their spotlights at the hypocrisy of their opponents. Collectively, the spotlights in the legislature could expose the corruption that was being hidden under the shroud of secrecy within the Attorney General's Office.

Impeachment is rare in Alabama, and there wasn't much precedent to rely upon, but the Alabama Constitution gave the legislature broad authority to exercise that important check on executive power. The Constitution of Alabama, Section 179, lists the grounds for which the governor may (not shall) be removed from office by the process of impeachment. They are enumerated as "willful neglect of duty, corruption in office, incompetency, or intemperance in the use of intoxicating liquors or narcotics to such an extent, in view of the dignity of the office and the importance of its duties, as unfits the officer for the discharge of such duties, or for any offense involving moral turpitude while in office."

Since the 1901 Constitution of Alabama was adopted, articles of impeachment had only been filed once against a statewide constitutional officeholder, Secretary of State John Purifoy. In his 1914 campaign for secretary of state, Purifoy was alleged to have paid an opponent $1,000 to get out of the race. Believing Purifoy had committed an offense involving moral turpitude in connection with his office, the House Rules Committee brought the Articles of Impeachment to the House floor for a vote; however, a report submitted by a minority of the members of the Rules Committee recommended that the full House of Representatives reject the impeachment because the Constitution requires the offense to have occurred while in office. Since the alleged offense occurred prior to Purifoy's term of office that began in 1915, the House declined to impeach him.

An impeachment proceeding is quite different from a criminal proceeding. Impeachment is not intended to be a method to punish a public officeholder for an offense but a means to allow the legislature to ensure that the officers of the executive branch of government do not exceed their power or fail to fulfil the duties of their office. A criminal proceeding should never be political, but impeachment is a political mechanism that serves as a check on the power of the executive branch of government.

Even if it is never used, the power to impeach is an integral component of the internal checks and balances of a constitutional republic. It is a means of legislative oversight that is a very broad sweeping power given to the legislative branch of government. It could easily be abused, but the internal checks and balances within the legislature make it very difficult to invoke.

When I looked at Section 179 of the Alabama Constitution with a view to the situation, I considered the grounds for impeachment that might be applicable to the current governor. Since Governor Bentley was a teetotaler, the one about the intemperate use of intoxicating liquor and narcotics wasn't in play. Had he a drunken or drug-induced stupor, it would have at least given a logical explanation for some of his recent behavior. All we would have needed to do to remedy the situation would be to get him sober. But sadly, it wasn't that simple.

"Willful neglect of duty" seemed to have potential as grounds for impeachment. It would require some investigation, but if the governor had allowed his love affair with his senior policy advisor to interfere with the execution of the duties of his office to the degree that it caused him to cede to her the power of his office, a case could be made for willful neglect of duty. Allowing an intimate personal relationship with his senior policy advisor to interfere with his interaction with his staff and cabinet might also be considered as willful neglect of duty.

"Corruption in office" was another broad term that could apply to the situation as grounds for impeachment, keeping in mind that each legislator makes their own decision and must decide for themselves what they think the terms mean to them. "Corruption" is a very broad term and legislators are not bound by the definitions as applied in the criminal statutes. Impeachment is a separate body of law. Since I'm not a lawyer, I applied common sense to my application of the law and chose the dictionary definition of corruption. I could see the potential for finding grounds for impeachment using any of the four definitions of "corruption" given by Merriam-Webster:

1. dishonest or illegal behavior especially by powerful people (such as government officials or police officers)
2. inducement to wrong by improper or unlawful means (such as bribery)
3. departure from the original or from what is pure or correct
4. decay; decomposition

"Incompetence" as defined by Meriam-Webster also had great potential. The first definition didn't seem applicable since Governor Bentley was legally qualified, but convincing arguments could be made for incompetence as grounds for impeachment by applying the other two definitions to the recent situation surrounding the governor:

1. one who is not legally qualified
2. inadequate to or unsuitable for a particular purpose
3. a: lacking the qualities needed for effective action; b: unable to function properly

The final ground for impeachment listed in Section 179 of the Alabama Constitution was any offense involving moral turpitude while in office committed under the color of the office. Since it used the word "offenses," I took it to mean a violation of criminal law, which would require a criminal investigation by a law enforcement agency and maybe more of a criminal-style prosecution. I expected the Attorney General's Office to thoroughly investigate Bentley for any criminal offenses that he might have committed; however, the removal of a sitting governor from office is a designated power of the legislative branch, not the executive.

The governor's peculiar behavior since his re-election and the odd circumstances surrounding the firing of Spencer Collier cried out for an independent legislative investigation. Since I was unaware of a legitimate investigative body within the legislative branch of Alabama state government, an impeachment resolution seemed to be the only way to get there. The whole truth had to be brought to light and thrown out in the open before the burgeoning drama with its hidden duplicity could come to a successful conclusion, including the duplicity within the bowels of the Attorney General's Office.

After a few days contemplating our options, I spoke to Representative Ed Henry about impeachment as a means of getting the whole truth out in the open. When I said that one of us needed to introduce an impeachment resolution, Ed was ready to jump in with both feet. It seemed logical, because he was more suited than me to be the ringmaster of the media circus that had come to town. I'd been continuing to grow weary of political drama for a couple of years, but my protégé was more than ready to lead the circus into town. Besides, Leni's Law was my priority during the 2016 regular session.

On Tuesday, April 5, Ed introduced a resolution, co-sponsored by nine other legislators and me. That day I made the following comment at the press conference:

"Well, this is a sad day that we have to initiate this process, and it is a process. This begins a lot of discussion about how this unfortunate set of circumstances has affected us all. It's certainly not a glad time for anybody, and as this process goes forward, we will carefully weigh out the issues. This is really about the checks and balances of government that the founding fathers have put in place. The legislative branch of government doesn't operate exactly like the judicial branch or the executive branch. The impeachment process—it is fortunate that it hasn't been used very often. We do have term limits in Alabama, and we don't have recall. This is a process where, when circumstances rise to a certain level, that it can hold a constitutional officer accountable. As this goes forward, I think it's very important that we look at this as objectively as possible and consider the ramifications of what has happened and also how this will affect the people of Alabama going forward. There is a crisis of confidence and this needs to be resolved. Thank you very much."

As a standing committee chairman and one of those considered to be close to the leadership, many were surprised to see that I was on the podium, since Speaker Hubbard and some members of the inner circle of leadership were not pleased with the impeachment resolution adding more turmoil in an already boiling pot. But I had to be there since I'd instigated it. The lengthy investigation of Speaker Hubbard and the impending trial made many legislators scandal weary and eager to get it all over with. I was, too. That's why I wanted everything out in the open as soon as possible. I believed impeachment was our only hope to do it.

The impeachment resolution was referred to the House Judiciary Committee, chaired by Representative Mike Jones of Andalusia. The Committee was given the responsibility to investigate the facts and provide an accurate report to the legislature. Each member needed a sound, factual basis derived from an independent investigation with which to base their decision on whether to impeach the governor.

The impeachment process would not move quickly because there was a consensus among the members of the Judiciary Committee that getting it right was more important that doing it quick. When the House adjourned the week after the impeachment resolution was introduced, the Committee prepared to work through the summer. That was fine with me, because my goal was to get the whole truth out in the open more than to remove the governor from office.

I was glad to see the last day of the 2016 session finally arrive. The drama surrounding Bentley's tête-à-tête with his senior policy advisor, Spencer Collier's affidavit, Speaker Hubbard's impending trial, and Matt Hart's attempts to keep Baron Coleman under wraps were all distractions that exacerbated the leadership failure and prevented finding meaningful solutions to the significant problems of state government, such as over-crowded prisons, exploding Medicaid costs, deteriorating infrastructure, and a myriad of other issues.

Although we managed to do a few good things during the regular session, including Leni's Law, a significant part of the session had been taken up with filibustering, led by Democrats in the sharply divided Jefferson County delegation over some highly contentious local issue. By the last day of the session tensions were high, and we were grating on one another's nerves.

Filibustering is a procedural ploy that involves talking to burn up time and slow down or stop the legislative process. It is a tactic that allows a minority to block legislation they don't have the votes to stop. A filibuster is forceable resistance to the will of the majority. It is often thinly disguised as debate and can be irritating to the majority.

A filibuster makes the legislative process difficult and can even bring it to a complete halt. The antidote to the filibuster is cloture. Cloture is the procedural method employed by the legislative majority to shut off debate and force a vote. It is a forceful response to forceful resistance. An excessive number of filibusters and clotures is a good sign that the legislative process is probably not working very well.

Although we easily had the votes to cloture, Speaker Hubbard usually restrained from invoking cloture, but many majority caucus members were fed up with the filibusters. At the final caucus meeting of the session (which I incidentally missed), the Republican supermajority decided they'd had enough and resolved to pass partisan senate bills that had been blocked by filibustering Democrats for several days by cloturing them as many times as necessary.

Tension built throughout the long day as the cloture petitions came one after another. The political resistance of a rebellious minority was being put down by the political force of the ruling supermajority. A couple of hours before midnight, the clerk called a politically charged bill creating a monument commission designed to protect Confederate monuments from local governments. Several Black Democrats went ballistic and legislative train jumped the track.

I didn't have the stomach anymore for partisan squabbles and political gamesmanship. Throughout most of that contentious final day, I preoccupied myself with other things, like email, surfing the internet, sneaking off to my office, wandering around the Statehouse visiting with folks, or sneaking off to play my guitar. Music is cathartic for me and gives me respite from the spiritually draining political squabbling.

After a long day of political tension with the insurgent minority being procedurally stifled by repeated cloture petitions, some of the Black Democrats exploded when the bill designed to protect Confederate monuments was called. I was sitting on my back-row seat beside Representative Phil Williams from Huntsville who detested political drama as much as me. An angry legislator at the microphone raged at the Republican majority and accused them of being oppressors for their repeated cloture motions. The monument bill was the final straw. After several minutes of haranguing, the legislator began to sing, and others joined in:

> We shall overcome, we shall overcome,
> We shall overcome someday.
> Oh, deep in my heart, I do believe,
> We shall overcome someday.
> The Lord will see us through, The Lord will see us through,
> The Lord will see us through someday.
> Oh, deep in my heart, I do believe,
> We shall overcome someday.
> We're on to victory, We're on to victory,

We're on to victory someday.
Oh, deep in my heart, I do believe,
We're on to victory someday.
We'll walk hand in hand, we'll walk hand in hand,
We'll walk hand in hand someday.
Oh, deep in my heart, I do believe,
We'll walk hand in hand someday.
We are not afraid, we are not afraid,
We are not afraid today.
Oh, deep in my heart, I do believe,
We are not afraid today.
The truth shall make us free; the truth shall make us free,
The truth shall make us free someday.
Oh, deep in my heart, I do believe,
The truth shall make us free someday.
We shall live in peace, we shall live in peace,
We shall live in peace someday.
Oh, deep in my heart, I do believe,
We shall live in peace someday.

Other minority members joined in the protest song associated with the civil rights movement. As fellow musicians, Phil and I savored the beautiful harmonious voices that filled the meeting room of the Alabama Legislature. As we listened to the song, I listened to my friends on the other side of the political coin and how much I'd appreciated their friendship over the years. As I listened to the singing, I prayed that the contentious spirit would leave, and I was about to get a bird's eye view of that prayer being answered.

As the song neared its end, Phil and I talked about Representative A. J. McCampbell's majestic baritone voice underlying the harmonies. When the song ended, I walked from my seat on the back row into the well where my colleagues had been singing to compliment A. J. for his singing. When I told Representative McCampbell that I enjoyed his singing, some of the other minority members heard something I neither said nor meant.

I was utterly baffled when my colleagues began to rage at me and falsely accused me of being racist and making fun of them. Nothing could have been further from the truth, but it didn't seem to matter while the vicious and hurtful verbal assault continued. I stood there in the spotlight utterly bewildered, innocently trying to understand what I'd done wrong to provoke their wrath. I know my own heart, and there was nothing ugly in it, only hurt. It was only a couple of the minority members that put me in their spotlight, but it was painful to see some who I consider friends stand idle and silent while I helplessly incurred the wrath inflicted by false accusations.

Proclaiming my innocence from within the miasma of collective rage only caused the rage directed at me to swell. My very presence was offensive to those who were consumed by their anger toward their oppressors who had voted cloture on them all day, and I was guilty of that, but that was legislative politics. The wild accusations of racism were utterly false. Their anger blinded them.

The Alabama House of Representatives was silent, except for me asking, "What'd I do? What'd I do?" while two House of Representatives security officers escorted me off the floor and into the lobby outside. I am not resentful about what happened, and I am only bringing it up because there is a great deal to be learned from that episode. Being wrongfully persecuted, falsely accused, and ignominiously led from the chamber was the worst moment of my twenty years of legislative service, but the experience gave me a personal perspective of the magnitude of what happened to Jesus on a much greater scale.

Something else good also came out of it.

Seeing me being escorted from the spotlight in the chamber while being innocent of any ill will or malice seemed to bring my colleagues to the realization that it had gotten out of hand. When I reentered the chamber a few minutes later, the spiritual atmosphere on the House floor was entirely different. Belligerence and resistance had yielded to cooperation and fellowship. The onerous highly politicized monument bill had been carried over, and the minority had stopped filibustering.

There was agreement that it was in everyone's best interest to cooperate with one another and pass as many non-controversial bills as possible before time ran out. We passed all the noncontroversial senate bills on the calendar before adjourning session sine die. For what it's worth, Representative Phil Williams and I were the only two Republicans in the legislature opposed to that overreaching, politically motivated monument bill that excessively expanded the power of state government over local governing bodies.

Hurtful as it was, my experience that evening helped me better understand why the ultimate scapegoat, Jesus, was put through something much worse to appease an angry mob.

When I went to the well to pay a compliment for the beautiful singing, those who looked at me through a prism of racial animosity saw a white devil; those who looked at me through the prism of political rivalry saw a member of the oppressive majority that had run over them all day; but those whose view passes through the prism of grace could see me for who I am: a friend. Incidentally, I believe those who persecuted me that day know that now.

The most humiliating part of the whole ordeal was after I returned to the House floor while things were calm and running smoothly. Representative Ed Henry couldn't resist needling me about creating a disturbance and getting escorted out of the House Chamber. "Wow," he crowed, "I've never been so bad that I've been escorted from the chamber."

My friend Ed loved spotlights, whether he was pointing one or standing in it. We all carry around our spotlights that we shine on the sins of others, while hoping to hide our own. But the Light of Truth is a flood light, and it illuminates all darkness. Eventually.

CHAPTER 23

See Proverbs 24

On March 29, 2016, Circuit Judge Jacob Walker III entered a carefully worded order that denied motions filed by the Hubbard defense to dismiss the indictment against him based on Matt Hart's misconduct, clearing the way for Speaker Hubbard's trial to begin. Contrary to what Hart and his apologists would have us believe, the ruling did not clear Hart of prosecutorial misconduct. The ruling simply stated that he found nothing that provided legal justification to dismiss the indictment against Hubbard. Judge Walker's order cautiously tiptoed around Hart's political machinations and the legal landmines they created to move Hubbard's case to trial. Judge Walker also denied the motion filed by Hart claiming that Baron Coleman was a confidential informant and their communications privileged.

On Monday, May 16, jury selection began, and over the next dozen days, the prosecution called witness after witness. There seemed little dispute over the facts of the case, much of which was already known before the trial. However, by the time the trial reached its conclusion, the circumstances surrounding the Speaker's downfall were much clearer.

Before he become Speaker of the House in 2011, Mike Hubbard's business career was already more successful than his political career. As founder and CEO of a multimedia company, much of his initial success revolved around his acquisition of the multimedia rights that he had acquired for Auburn University Athletics. In 2003, Hubbard sold the rights to International Sports Properties, agreed to work for the company, and received a generous salary until his election as Speaker of the Alabama House of Representatives.

Soon after International Sports Properties merged with two other companies to form IMG College, a major multimedia sports marketing firm, Mike Hubbard was elected Speaker of the Alabama House of Representatives and was informed that his political career took too much time from his job and that he was going to have to choose between the two. His $60,000 annual salary as Speaker of the House was a pittance compared to his previous income, and he began seeking ways to make it up.

By engaging in new business dealings with principals and lobbyists, Hubbard tried to tap dance along the boundaries of the very ethics law that he had worked to tighten up in 2010. He frequently sought guidance from Jim Sumner, the director of the Ethics Commission, about his business dealings, which should have served as a clue that he was near the edge of an ethical precipice. A few years later Mr. Sumner's opinion would change after the was "enlightened" by Matt Hart.

The line between legal and illegal according to the Alabama Ethics Law is fraught with gray, murky areas where no one knows for sure where the line is. When Hubbard wandered into that swamp, it was almost inevitable that he would eventually wind up on the wrong side of the line, where Matt Hart was waiting to bag himself a big trophy.

The gist of the Alabama Ethics Law is to prohibit public officials from using the powers of their office for personal or private use. Witness after witness testified to circumstances that indicated Speaker Hubbard used the influence and the power associated with his public position to help generate personal income. The jury heard the evidence and after deliberation, found Speaker Hubbard to be guilty of twelve of the twenty-three charges for which he was charged.

After the verdict, Matt Hart made the following statement to WSFA-TV in Montgomery:

"I feel like the whole team from the attorney's general special prosecution division has been working for Mr. Davis is vindicated by this and our methods we were accused but at every step of the way the court never found any basic of those things this kind of prosecution when you are investigating and prosecution people of the highest levels of power government you are going to get that sort of tactic that is what it shows was a tactic" [sic, from WSFA website].

Hart's statement to WSFA was muddled and confusing, but if it was an attempt to say that Hubbard's guilt proved his innocence, it was wrong. The jury found Mike Hubbard guilty of the crimes for which he was charged, but Hart's case had not even been investigated by a proper authority, much less adjudicated. Whether Mike Hubbard was guilty or not of the crimes for which he was charged is irrelevant to the crime that I had witnessed. Although it was disappointing that nothing about Matt Hart's illicit collaboration with Baron Coleman was mentioned during Hubbard's trial, I understood why.

Mike Hubbard's and Matt Hart's offenses were separate and should have been investigated and prosecuted separately. The judicial system clearly provided a mechanism for Hubbard's offenses to be thoroughly investigated and prosecuted, even though he appeared to be the most politically powerful person in the entire state of Alabama. But the lack of action surrounding Matt Hart's offenses indicated to me that a serious flaw existed in our system that could be exploited by someone skilled in the art of propaganda who possesses a certain type of ego. The flaw cannot be fixed until it has been exposed, but the secrecy that is built into our judicial system to protect its credibility can also undermine its integrity.

The purpose of the Ethics Law is to prevent public officials and employees from exercising the power and authority over others outside the scope of the duties of their public position. It is unethical to wield it to fulfil any personal agenda, regardless of whether it is for monetary gain, sexual gratification, to satisfy personal grudges, or to gain unfair political advantage. There is no legitimate investigative purpose that justifies the protracted collaboration between Hart and Coleman throughout the 2014 election cycle that outweighs the damage done to our electoral system by providing propaganda fodder attempting to tilt the scales in favor of Coleman's clients.

During the year or so after we hastily reformed the Ethics Law in 2010, confusion began to emerge about some of its aspects, and as chairman of the House Ethics and Campaign Finance Committee it was my responsibility to consider ways to make the law more effective, clear, and consistently enforced.

I wanted to publicly bring together various stakeholders and legislators to have an open dialogue so we could update the law with more humility and less hubris than the newly elected Republican majority had in 2010. But once the investigation of Speaker Hubbard began, I recognized it would need to wait until the investigation was complete. Besides, I expected to learn a lot from observing the process. I was certainly right about that.

When the trial of Speaker Hubbard finally ended in the summer of 2016, I believed the appropriate time had arrived to begin the re-examination of our Ethics Law. Of course, by then the deficiencies, inconsistencies, and inefficiencies of its enforcement mechanism had become woefully obvious to me.

On August 15, 2016, Governor Bentley called the legislature into special session to consider a lottery or other legislation that might provide funding for still-ailing general fund. True to form, the governor had no legislation drafted, nor did he have an inkling what the legislature wanted to do. With a pending impeachment resolution against him and a recently empaneled attorney general's special grand jury probing his relationship with his senior policy advisor, I was not the only legislator who believed our besieged governor may have called the legislature into special session to consider the politically popular lottery, divert the spotlight away from his drama, and regain some of his squandered political capital.

If that was the intended purpose, the poorly planned special session was a miserable failure. It only seemed to further spotlight his inability to lead the state and further called his competence into question. However, the special session was our first opportunity after the conviction of Mike Hubbard to finally pass a resolution establishing the study commission could help improve our Ethics Law and the enforcement process.

Senator Arthur Orr, a friend who I had worked with on issues regarding ethics and transparency since his election in 2006, drafted a resolution that would create a study commission composed of legislators, the attorney general, a district attorney representing the DA's Association, a circuit judge representing the Judges Association, a representative of the Alabama Press Association, the governor's legal counsel, the executive director of the Ethics Commission, a representative of the County Commission's Association, a representative of the League of Municipalities, a representative of the Council of Association Executives, an attorney appointed by the Alabama Law Institute, and an attorney appointed by the Bar Association. There was a great deal of support from not just legislators, but also members of the broad range of organizations that would participate in the proposed study commission. But Attorney General Luther Strange was adamantly opposed to it.

Senator Orr, our new Speaker of the House Mac McCutcheon, House Judiciary Chairman Mike Jones, and several other legislative leaders pleaded with the attorney general for his cooperation, but he dug in against it. Riding high from the recent conviction of Speaker Hubbard, the attorney general was convinced that Alice Martin and Matt Hart should craft their own "strong" ethics package. He was willing to meet lobbyists and stakeholders privately, but the attorney general wanted his handlers to have full control of drafting the legislation. I wanted changes to the law to be addressed publicly by the legislative branch, but the attorney general was determined to do it privately. He seemed to have forgotten that the Constitution designated lawmaking to be the duty of the legislative branch, and the Attorney General's Office was part of the executive branch.

It was widely believed the term-limited Attorney General Luther Strange was posturing to use ethics and corruption as the centerpiece of his 2018 gubernatorial race in tandem with his Deputy Chief Alice Martin's campaign to replace him as attorney general. They were privately working on an ethics law that would enhance their power to prosecute and persecute other public officials. The bill was expected to be introduced during the 2017 regular session.

The legislative leaders pleaded with Luther Strange for weeks to participate in the study committee, at times thinking Luther might relent and participate, but Alice Martin and Matt Hart were dug in against it. It didn't even matter if Luther chaired the study commission, they wouldn't budge. The last thing Matt Hart wanted was an open dialogue about his methodology of enforcement. Without the approval of the attorney general, the legislative leadership had little appetite to go out on a limb and proceed with the study commission on the heels of the Hubbard conviction.

As time began to run out of the session and negotiations stalled, I decided to try to force the discussion about the study commission out of the shadows of the dark corridors of political power. If Luther was going to oppose it, he should do it in the open and state his reasons. I called a press conference for Friday, September 1.

Before the press conference began, I texted a scripture to the attorney general: "Here's a bible passage I'd like to share with you . . . A froward man soweth strife: and a whisperer separateth chief friends. Proverbs 16:28 KJV"

I began the press conference by announcing that the three ethics bills in my committee would not be rushed through during a special session, and I intended to handle ethics bills carefully, deliberately, and openly. Then I announced my plan to introduce the ethics study commission resolution as a move toward adopting comprehensive reforms. When a reporter asked about my run-in with the Attorney General's Office, I tried to be non-adversarial and expressed regret for having been dragged into the mess. The study committee was an attempt to move forward.

I hoped that the scripture and the message that I conveyed at the press conference would convince the attorney general that I was neither protecting Mike Hubbard nor engaging in political gamesmanship. I would have preferred a private meeting with Luther, but he wouldn't talk to me. Public or private I wanted a response of some sort. I got both.

The day after the press conference, Luther Strange issued the following public statement:

"I am strongly opposed to Representative Mike Ball's idea of a commission to review Alabama's Ethics Law. The whole point of such a commission would be to undermine the law. Alabamians want our ethics laws enforced, not gutted."

Although I believe someone else probably wrote those words, the malicious, false allegation that I was trying to gut the Ethics Law stung, especially coming from someone that until then I had naively thought of as a friend. Soon after Luther publicly opposed the ethics study commission, accompanied by the false accusation of malicious intent, he decided to respond to the text message that I'd sent him before the press conference:

"See Proverbs 24:25."

Luther had thrown down the gauntlet. The scripture read: "But it will go well with those who convict the guilty and rich blessing will come on them." He had not stopped gloating over Speaker Hubbard's conviction. He must not have read verse 17.

The Bible is all good, all the time; unfortunately, humans are not. It is like a mountain where great nuggets of truth are mined by diligent miners equipped with a tender heart and an open mind through a process of prayerful study and humble contemplation. Unfortunately, when pride, malice, bitterness, envy, and a myriad of other diluting agents are present during the mining process the treasure can be rendered worthless. By distorting the truth and twisting the context to suit our own ends, we are imitating the original propagandist who tempted Jesus in the wilderness.

During the days that followed, I carefully contemplated Proverbs 24 and noticed that verse 25 began with the word "But," which indicated that it was connected to the previous verse. Together the verses read, "Whoever says to the guilty, 'You are innocent,' will be cursed by peoples and denounced by nations. But it will go well with those to who convict the guilty, and rich blessing will come upon them." Reading verse 25 by itself conveyed to me the attorney general had rejected my notion that Matt Hart was a froward man who stirred up strife and was also a whisperer who had come between our friendship.

The scripture was Luther's way of declaring Hart innocent of any wrongdoing while praising him for convicting Hubbard. I am not a lawyer, so probably shouldn't quibble over words, but Hart did not convict the former Speaker of anything—the question of Hubbard's guilt was settled by the jury that convicted him. For the record, I've never proclaimed Mike Hubbard's innocence. Throughout the investigation and the trial my position has always been that it was a question for the jury to decide, not me.

I had no evidence that the question of Matt Hart's guilt of the offense I had witnessed had been properly investigated by an appropriate authority. As far as I could tell, nobody wanted to even look at the case, because there was no one to prosecute it. The local district attorneys were powerless because if a grand jury returned an indictment, the attorney general could take over their case and make it go away.

I began to consider that reporting the offense to the secretary of state had not satisfied my moral obligation to report it to the proper authority. The proper authority was the attorney general and I had not reported it to him. I had tried to report the misconduct in November 2014, but Luther Strange refused to even listen to my complaint. But I had uncovered additional evidence that indicated the misconduct I'd witnessed was a crime, and it had still not been reported to the proper authority: Luther Strange. I decided that's what I would do when the session ended.

The following Tuesday, September 6, as the special session waned, I introduced Senator Orr's resolution authorizing the ethics study commission. As expected, the resolution went nowhere. There was little appetite to stand up to the attorney general, who was secretly working on legislation with Matt Hart and Alice Martin that would expand their power even more.

After discussing the situation with several experienced legal authorities, I was confident that when I reported the crime that I'd witnessed directly to the attorney general, the ramifications to his political career would create and obvious conflict of interest. He would have no ethical alternative other than to recuse himself and appoint an independent counsel to investigate the case, like he was purported to have done with the Mike Hubbard case.

The day after the special session ended, I sent the Luther the following text message:

"I only want to tell the truth that I see. No one that has looked at this has told me that it is not true. I want to tell it to you. I believe you are a good man trying to do the right thing. Mike Hubbard and Matt Hart have deceived and hurt many innocent people. I believe Matt Hart has committed a crime that you don't know about. I only want the truth to come out. This shouldn't be so complicated. I don't want to hurt you, but this will hurt you sooner or later. I only want to know if I am wrong. I am glad the truth has come out about Mike Hubbard. He brought all of this on himself." "Please listen to me."

A couple of hours later Luther texted me back, "That's a serious accusation. I'm interested in the truth and the actual evidence. I'm out of town. Would you be willing to meet confidentially with Alice Martin and an investigator tomorrow in North Alabama?"

"Yes, can I have someone with me? This is serious to me. I want this handled appropriately," I asked.

"Of course. Please bring anyone you'd like," he replied.

"Thank you. I want to clear the air," I said.

I wanted Speaker McCutcheon with me, but he was out of state officiating a wedding. I should have known I'd have to do this alone. The next day, September 9, 2016, I met Alice Martin and an investigator from the Attorney General's Office at the Madison County Legislative Office in Huntsville.

Alice Martin's conflict of interest was even more blatant than the one Luther Strange had. If Matt Hart were proven to be guilty of the crime that I was reporting, her political career would be ruined. She was plotting a 2018 run for attorney general because the eyes of term-limited Luther Strange were set on the governor's office. Alice's electoral career would be doomed if the man who directed her North Alabama Corruption Task Force during her tenure as the U.S. attorney for the Northern District of Alabama and now the chief of the Special Prosecutions Division of the Alabama Attorney General's Office were found to be guilty of political corruption. Despite that, I innocently hoped the facts and circumstances I presented to her would force her to recognize the need for a special counsel to perform a fair and impartial investigation without a conflict of interest.

I spent a couple of hours outlining the facts that supported my belief that Hart had used his position to illegally attempt to influence my political activity, specifically his attempt to suppress my efforts to mitigate the political damage that he had caused while I exercised my constitutional rights on the Dale Jackson Show. I told her about Hart's phone call, the Barry Moore case, and how I originally just thought that it was only bad behavior, but when Baron Coleman came out in the public and Hart admitted their collaboration, I realized the true purpose of Hart's call: to keep me from talking publicly about a possible political connection that might expose his collaboration with Baron Coleman.

The nature of her questions made it clear to me that she was not interested in finding out if my allegation was true. She asked limiting questions like "Exactly what is the crime that you think he committed and what specific act did he do?" I tried to explain it to her, but she didn't seem receptive to what I was saying. It shouldn't have been a surprise since Luther brought her on board as his chief deputy the week after I testified in Lee County.

She asked me if I felt like I was a victim. I replied that I was technically a victim according to the law, but I couldn't allow myself to feel like a victim until I could be assured that someone was properly investigating my case. Alice Martin was no novice when it came to making a complaint against Matt Hart go away. She was polite and professional as she held her poker face, giving little emotional reaction until near the end of the interview when I responded to her follow-up questions. The follow-up questions indicated to me which areas of my complaint might be problematic for them.

I saw her eyes tear up when I responded to her questions about my call to Luther right after the election, consulting with Othni, the director of the Ethics Commission, and finally reporting it to the secretary of state, who requested an investigation by ALEA. As we amicably parted, I thanked her for coming and taking the time to listen. I told her the burden was off my shoulders and was now on theirs. My eyes were teary when I asked her to tell Luther that I missed our friendship and looked forward to the day that we could reconnect.

I had presented the attorney general with a clear choice between ethics or politics. He could do his duty and ensure that this crime would be properly investigated by special independent counsel, or he could try to cover it up for the sake of political expediency. A week later, I received a letter dated September 16, indicating that political expediency won the day, and my complaint was summarily dismissed. On the following page is the confusing letter where the attorney general arbitrarily proclaimed Matt Hart's innocence without a fair, unbiased investigation.

The legal rationale in the letter was muddled, but its purpose was clear. It was a thinly veiled attempt to make my complaint go away without proper investigation by an authority without a conflict of interest. It was a poorly written, confusing misinterpretation of the law, with a few cherry-picked facts thrown in that overlooked the crime that I'd reported.

It was patently absurd to assert that Matt Hart was legally exercising his First Amendment rights as a private citizen when he indignantly chewed me out for noting what turned out to be evidence of his illicit activity with a political consultant. I was on the radio exercising my First Amendment rights when he attempted to prevent me from questioning his motives and exposing his relationship with Baron Coleman. A public official trying to

STATE OF ALABAMA
OFFICE OF THE ATTORNEY GENERAL

LUTHER STRANGE
ATTORNEY GENERAL

501 WASHINGTON AVENUE
P.O. BOX 300152
MONTGOMERY, AL 36130-0152
(334) 242-7300
WWW.AGO.ALABAMA.GOV

September 16, 2016

Via Email & First Class Mail
Rep. Mike Ball
Alabama House of Representatives, District 10
105 Canterbury Circle
Madison, Alabama 35758

Re: Complaint

Dear Rep. Ball:

We have completed a review of your complaint that Alabama Code §17-17-4 may have been violated by an employee of this Office. The purpose of §17-17-4 [previously codified as §17-1-7(b)] is to prevent tacit political pressure where an official could *use* their position, through the use of reward or threats of reprisal, for political actions taken by persons over whom they have some authority related to elections. Title 17 relates to *election* offenses. See State v. Worley, 102 So. 3d 435 (Ala. Crim. App. 2011), AG Opinion 2007-075 to the Honorable Bob Riley, and AG Opinion 96-00242 to the Honorable Fob James.

Based on a review of your talk show interview and your testimony before Judge Walker about the contents of the telephone call which followed that interview, no violation of this statute occurred. The only 'threat,' that a legislator would "have to deal with me" if attempts were made to weaken state ethics law or the use of grand juries for investigation, is not criminal conduct. It is nothing more than what any state employee or citizen can lawfully do – and what is done every day in the state house – engage in protected First Amendment speech to educate and influence legislative action.

Accordingly, no further action will be taken and this matter is closed.

Sincerely yours,

Luther Strange

LS:klg

This is the Strange response to my criminal complaint despite the Attorney General's apparent conflict of interest. The letter appeared to be clear evidence of an impeachable offense: Willful Neglect of Duty.

suppress criticism is not protected by the First Amendment. The purpose of the First Amendment is to protect those who do what I was doing on the radio from those who do what Matt Hart was doing.

The letter made it evident to me that Luther Strange willfully neglected to perform his duty as attorney general and appoint an independent authority to properly investigate the crime I'd reported. It looked like a pathetic attempt to cover up a politically embarrassing crime. Thanks to Governor Bentley, I'd become very familiar with Section 179 of the Alabama Constitution, which governs impeachment. The letter looked like clear evidence of willful neglect of duty—grounds for impeachment.

I wasn't sure what to do until the legislature returned to regular session in February 2017 and an impeachment resolution could be filed against the Attorney General Luther Strange. The case for the impeachment of the attorney general seemed clearer to me than the one pending on Governor Bentley. Since Speaker Hubbard's conviction, most of the spotlights were trained on the wounded governor, and nobody seemed interested in shining light on the ambitious power grab and cover-up emanating from the Attorney General's Office.

But I had a letter from the attorney general proclaiming Matt Hart's innocence of something that I had witnessed, and Proverbs 24:24 gave me reason to believe that would change:

"Whoever says to the guilty, 'You are innocent,' will be cursed by peoples and denounced by nations."

CHAPTER 24

Mexican Standoff

Although the language in the September 16, 2016, letter from the attorney general was confusing, its message was clear. Luther Strange had no intention of fulfilling his duty to enforce the law of the state of Alabama impartially and would not hold Matt Hart to the same standard of legal scrutiny that they had held upon others, including Mike Hubbard. Although willful neglect of duty is an impeachable offense, Alabama law also provides another constitutional remedy when an attorney general shirks his duty.

The governor is designated by the Alabama Constitution as the chief magistrate of the state and is authorized to override an attorney general's refusal to enforce the law. Under normal circumstances, my next course of action would have been to simply go to the governor. But a constitutional crisis is never a normal circumstance, and this one was exceptionally peculiar. Governor Bentley was under an impeachment investigation that I'd helped initiate and was also under a grand jury investigation headed by the perpetrator of the crime that I had reported. Besides that, I believed the governor had neither the moral clarity nor the backbone to fulfill his duty by appointing an independent counsel to impartially execute the law in this case.

I planned to pursue an impeachment resolution against the attorney general, but the regular session of the legislature would not begin until early February. Meanwhile, I hoped to share my discovery with others who might be interested in knowing what had happened. It was disappointing that most people didn't care to hear what I had to say for several reasons.

One was that the presidential campaign between Donald Trump and Hillary Clinton was in full swing, and the air was filled with allegations of impropriety by competing political operatives. Another reason was that Governor Bentley's scandal had heated up with the attorney general's special grand jury led by Matt Hart, the House Judiciary Committee impeachment investigation, an Ethics Commission investigation, and the media bearing down on the beleaguered governor. Coming on the heels of a couple years of the Hubbard case, many were growing weary of political scandals, and people might have mistakenly thought I had a political agenda.

After the resolution authorizing the ethics study commission failed in the special session, the attorney general and his cronies were privately working on a comprehensive, tough ethics law that would tip the balance of power even more heavily in their direction. They were expected to introduce their bill in the next session to begin in February 2017 and use it as a launching pad for the 2018 gubernatorial and attorney general's race.

However, they may not have thought it all through. They may not have realized their bill would come to the Ethics and Campaign Finance Committee that I chaired. I was eager to get their bill in my committee and put it on the committee agenda as quickly as possible so I could invite Luther Strange to appear before the committee to answer questions about ethics investigations. I was especially looking forward to hearing him publicly explain his letter and why he should not be impeached.

The noted philosopher Iron Mike Tyson once said, "Everybody has a plan until they get punched in the mouth." A strange press release from the attorney general, dated October 20, 2016, found on the following page, was a punch in the mouth that forced me to rethink my plan to wait until February to do something in response to the attorney general's letter to me.

To the unsuspecting public, this statement exonerated Spencer Collier of any wrongdoing, but given what I knew, it was very different. I'd seen more than enough evidence to recognize it as a big "thank you" to Spencer Collier for cooperating with Matt Hart as he struggled to keep his relationship with Baron Coleman secret. Although it was better worded, the press release reminded me of the September 16 letter that I had received from the attorney general.

The attorney general had every right to decline prosecution if the case had been assigned to someone without a conflict of interest, but it seemed evident to me that Collier was being protected as a reward for his collaboration with Matt Hart. When I reported Hart's crime to Alice Martin the

NEWS RELEASE

Luther Strange
Alabama Attorney General

FOR IMMEDIATE RELEASE
October 20, 2016

For More Information, contact:
Mike Lewis   (334) 353-2199
Joy Patterson (334) 242-7491
Page 1 of 1

STATEMENT OF ATTORNEY GENERAL LUTHER STRANGE
REGARDING FORMER ALEA SECRETARY SPENCER COLLIER

(MONTGOMERY) –*This statement is being issued because substantial information related to the Attorney General's investigation has been put in the public domain.*

On February 17, Governor Robert Bentley placed then-ALEA Secretary Spencer Collier on sick leave for allegedly disobeying his instructions regarding Collier's interaction with State prosecutors.[1] Shortly after the Governor's action, ALEA initiated a broad internal inquiry into Collier's conduct as ALEA Secretary.

On March 22, Governor Bentley fired Collier, stating publicly that he relied on the ALEA inquiry in doing so.[2] Governor Bentley and ALEA issued public statements that the results of the ALEA investigation indicated possible "misuse of state funds" and were being referred to the Office of Attorney General Luther Strange.[3] That day, the Office of the Attorney General received the complaint and other information from ALEA.

To determine the facts with certainty, the Special Prosecutions Division of the Attorney General's Office conducted a complete investigation of the ALEA allegations against Collier. For efficiency, and to ensure public confidence in the investigation, all of the information from ALEA was presented to the Montgomery County Special Grand Jury. Numerous witnesses, including senior ALEA leadership, were called to testify before the Special Grand Jury.

The investigation conducted by Attorney General Strange before the Special Grand Jury was a criminal investigative proceeding. In the course of the investigation, no witness provided credible evidence of criminal "misuse of state funds." No witness provided credible evidence of any other criminal violation on the part of former Secretary Collier. Finally, no witness established a credible basis for the initiation of a criminal inquiry in the first place.

After receiving all of the information provided by ALEA to the Attorney General, and after receiving substantial additional evidence, the Montgomery County Special Grand Jury declined to act on the allegations against former Secretary Collier. For these reasons, the investigation of former Secretary Collier is now closed.

---

[1]   http://www.al.com/news/index.ssf/2016/02/states_top_cop_placed_on_leave.html
[2]   http://governor.alabama.gov/newsroom/2016/03/governor-bentley-announces-termination-spencer-collier-alabama-law-enforcement-
[3]   http://www.montgomeryadvertiser.com/story/news/politics/southunionstreet/2016/03/22/alea-review-finds-possible-misuse-state-funds/82122208/

I was flummoxed by this press release issued by the Attorney General exonerating Spencer Collier while excoriating the Alabama Law Enforcement Agency for requesting an investigation. It reinforced my opinion that political ambition within the Attorney General's office had overridden their moral obligation to objectively investigate corruption wherever it could be found and ultimately prompted me to make a formal request to Governor Bentley to appoint a special counsel to investigate what I believed to be corruption within the Attorney General's Office.

previous month, I told her that I had previously reported it to ALEA. She couldn't know for certain how much ALEA had documented.

A press release exonerating someone while a grand jury is in session is very unusual in Alabama. I tried to think of a legitimate reason for it but kept coming back to the cover up and the letter that Luther had sent to me. I had seen receipts at ALEA that directly contradicted what the press release said. It looked like the Attorney General's Office was bolstering Collier as part of an effort to discredit Governor Bentley and ALEA.

In 2010, Justice Glenn Murdock wrote a unanimous Alabama Supreme Court ruling in a case that arose from the "Electronic Bingo War" between then Governor Bob Riley and then Attorney General Troy King. At issue was whether the governor of Alabama had the authority to appoint persons to engage in law enforcement activities that included the prosecution of the law without the approval of the attorney general or the local district attorney and whether the attorney general had the right to assume control from the governor of such activities and litigation.

The following excerpt illustrates the court's rationale in ruling that the governor held "supreme executive power" that included a duty to ensure the laws of the state were properly executed and that the attorney general of Alabama did not have the authority to assume control over the governor's law enforcement activities:

> Article V of the Alabama Constitution of 1901 creates and defines the "executive department" of government. Section 112 of that article provides: "The executive department shall consist of a governor, lieutenant governor, attorney-general, state auditor, secretary of state, state treasurer, superintendent of education, commissioner of agriculture and industries, and a sheriff for each county." The very next provision of that article states as follows: "The supreme executive power of this state shall be vested in a chief magistrate, who shall be styled 'The Governor of the State of Alabama.'" Ala. Const.1901, § 113 (emphasis added). Section 120 of that article then provides that "[t]he governor shall take care that the laws be faithfully executed." Ala. Const.1901, § 120 (emphasis added). As hereinafter discussed, these express constitutional provisions, all of which are of course unique to the office of governor, plainly

vest the governor with an authority to act on behalf of the State and to ensure "that the laws [are] faithfully executed" that is "supreme" to the "duties" given the other executive branch officials created by the same constitution. See generally Black's Law Dictionary 970 (8th ed.2004) (defining a "magistrate" as "[t]he highest-ranking official in a government, such as the king in a monarchy, the president in a republic, or the governor in a state.-Also termed chief magistrate; first magistrate"). See also Opinion of the Justices No. 179, 275 Ala. 547, 549, 156 So.2d 639, 641 (1963): "The laws of the state contemplate domestic peace. To breach that peace is to breach the law, and execution of the laws demands that peace be preserved. The governor is charged with the duty of taking care that the laws be executed and, as a necessary consequence, of taking care that the peace be preserved."

The ruling clearly pointed out another constitutional mechanism within the law in addition to impeachment by the legislature to ensure the attorney general faithfully executed the powers of his office. There were several reasons I didn't immediately go to Governor Bentley upon receiving the garbled letter that clearly indicated the attorney general had failed to faithfully execute the responsibility of his office due to a clear conflict of interest. One reason was he'd already declined to appoint an independent counsel in early spring when several others had urged him to do so.

If the governor had the courage to do it, he would have and should have done it then. Instead, he tried to duck it, resulting in the affidavit fiasco, which led to the firing of Collier, the release of the recordings, and an impeachment resolution against him. I believed the failure to appoint an independent counsel then was also part of the potential grounds for impeachment. Had he done his duty, Governor Bentley might have survived his term and Collier might have stuck with him and kept his job. It would have taken courage, which is not exactly an attribute for which Governor Bentley was known.

Another reason that I didn't immediately go to Bentley after receiving the letter from the attorney general was that as a member of the impeachment committee, I was forbidden by the rules from talking to the governor about any material fact related to the impeachment. What I needed to report was certainly related to his impeachment. Then there's that little thing of being one of the main instigators of the governor's impeachment made it unlikely that the governor would be receptive to my request. Finally, the Attorney General's Office had convened a special grand jury spearheaded by Matt Hart to investigate the governor, the subject of the matter that I believed the governor should appoint a special counsel to investigate.

I decided that going public would be a best recourse. On Monday, October 24, during my regular gig on Dale Jackson's radio show, I made a public accusation, calling Hart by name and accusing the attorney general of covering up a crime in his letter to me. Talk radio was my media outlet of choice because I wanted an easily accessible public record of my words, unfiltered by a newspaper or television reporter. After putting it out on the public airwaves, I waited for a response.

The next day I talked to a member of Governor Bentley's staff who asked me if I needed the governor to do anything. I requested the governor appoint an independent counsel to investigate the offense that the attorney general had covered up. A little while later, the staffer called back and asked if I would put the request in writing. A few minutes later, I sent a written request to Governor Bentley, which is shown on the following page.

During this time, I received a friendly but odd phone call from my fellow former Alabama state trooper Spencer Collier encouraging me to speak to the chairman of the Impeachment Committee Mike Jones about getting rid of the special counsel, Jack Sharman. Collier insisted that the special counsel was a waste of taxpayers' money and that Sharman and his team did not have the expertise to properly investigate the governor. He said the Bentley investigation was a law enforcement matter and should be left to the attorney general and the special grand jury.

Although Collier was a former legislator, he didn't seem to grasp that impeachment was a legislative responsibility, entirely separate from the criminal investigation. The impeachment investigation would delve into matters that may be impeachable offenses but not criminal offenses, such as willful neglect of duty or incompetence. Collier was insistent that the impeachment investigation be stopped.

Since Collier was eager for justice to rain down on Governor Bentley, it

ALABAMA
HOUSE OF REPRESENTATIVES
11 S. UNION STREET, MONTGOMERY ALABAMA 36130

REP. MIKE BALL
DISTRICT 10
105 CANTERBURY CIRCLE
MADISON, ALABAMA 35758

HOME: 256-772-8730
CELL: 256-565-6225
EMAIL: mikeball@knology.net

October 25, 2016

The Honorable Robert Bentley
Governor of the State of Alabama
State Capitol
600 Dexter Avenue
Montgomery, AL 36130

Governor Bentley:

I have reason to believe that in the 2014 election cycle, Matt Hart, violated Alabama code §17-17-4 by using his position to influence political activities. I reported the matter to the Alabama Attorney General on September 9, 2016 and a proper investigation into this matter was declined.

As such, I herein request that you appoint a special prosecutor to fully investigate this matter.

Respectfully,

Mike Ball

I had hoped this letter would finally result in a proper investigation of the apparent political corruption within the higher echelons of the Attorney General's Office.

239

was puzzling that he wanted the impeachment stopped until he expressed his displeasure that the lawyers questioning him had asked about his conversations with Matt Hart. He said that he refused to discuss sensitive law enforcement information with them and was offended that the attorneys had asked to see text messages between him and Hart. He said that he refused. Collier strongly urged me to do whatever I could to stop the entire impeachment investigation, but he only succeeded in making me more firmly convinced that the impeachment committee special counsel was doing what he was supposed to and needed to continue his work.

Collier did most of the talking during the entirely nonconfrontational conversation and I neither disputed nor agreed with his comments, staying noncommittal as I told him that I planned to take a hands-off approach and let the special counsel finish his work. I didn't believe that fiscal responsibility was the primary motive of Collier's call. It seemed more to me that there was something between him and Hart that he wanted to keep hidden and the impeachment process threatened to expose it.

After submitting the letter to Governor Bentley requesting an investigation, he wanted a meeting. The rules adopted by the impeachment committee forbade committee members from speaking to Bentley or his staff about material fact relative to the impeachment, but pursuing this seemed more important than serving on the impeachment committee, so I agreed to talk to the governor.

On November 1, I had a meeting at ALEA with the director Stan Stabler before walking over to Governor Bentley's office. As I entered the receiving area of the governor's office, I was slightly embarrassed to hear applause when I walked past a small gaggle of staffers. It was no secret why I was there.

The governor and I had a long discussion and I went over my run-in with Hart and the events leading up to my discovery that probable cause existed for me to believe that the chief of the Attorney General's Special Prosecutions Unit had committed a felony. We discussed the governor's constitutional duty to ensure that this crime would be properly investigated by a proper authority that had no conflict of interest in the matter. We discussed the letter that Luther Strange sent me that seemed to constitute evidence of an impeachable offense.

The governor and I agreed that he not only had the authority to appoint an independent counsel, but he also had the duty to do it. He said that he intended to appoint one and we discussed the qualities of a potential independent counsel. We needed someone beyond reproach, and since such a creature did not exist in the political world, it would likely need to be someone who no longer had a political agenda. Maybe a retired judge. When I left his office, Governor Bentley seemed determined to do his duty and appoint an independent counsel who would finally get to the bottom of this mess and get it resolved once and for all.

When I left the governor's office, I felt relieved of that pesky moral obligation to report this crime to the proper authority . . . again. However, I was uncertain that he would follow through since our governor was not known for being resolute. At that point the Attorney General's Office had been bearing down on investigating Governor Bentley. It was no secret that I had requested the governor appoint an independent counsel to ensure Hart's illicit collaboration with Baron Coleman would be properly investigated and adjudicated, and he was the only person with constitutional authority to do so.

If the governor did his duty and appointed an independent counsel, we would have had the counsel investigating Matt Hart's relationship with Baron Coleman and the subsequent cover-up, the legislative impeachment committee investigating Governor Bentley, and the attorney general's special grand jury looking for whatever Matt Hart and Alice Martin wanted them to. It looked like we were on the verge of mutually assured destruction between the governor and the attorney general, the Alabama version of a Mexican standoff. If the governor appointed the counsel, a political apocalypse would commence in Alabama.

In addition, the pesky impeachment threatened to blow everything out in the open.

The same day I was meeting with the governor, November 1, the chairman of the House Impeachment Committee, Representative Mike Jones, was meeting with Attorney General Strange, Alice Martin, and Matt Hart to inform them that the impeachment investigation would proceed full-bore with the expectation that it would be completed by the end of the year. It

STATE OF ALABAMA
OFFICE OF THE ATTORNEY GENERAL

LUTHER STRANGE
ATTORNEY GENERAL

501 WASHINGTON AVENUE
P.O. BOX 300152
MONTGOMERY, AL 36130-0152
(334) 242-7300
WWW.AGO.ALABAMA.GOV

November 3, 2016

Rep. Mike Jones, Jr.
District 92
Alabama State House
11 South Union, Suite 419
Montgomery, AL 36130-2950

Dear Representative Jones:

In your letter of June 7, 2016, you informed me that the work of the House Judiciary Committee and the investigative work of my office might intersect with certain issues and witnesses. I appreciate your willingness to efficiently and effectively communicate with my office.

At this time, I believe it would be prudent and beneficial to delay the work of the House Judiciary Committee. I respectfully request that the Committee cease active interviews and investigation until I am able to report to you that the necessary related work of my office has been completed. My staff will continue to coordinate with the Special Counsel for the Committee, Jack Sharman, as necessary and appropriate.

Thank you for your time and consideration.

Sincerely,

Luther Strange

Luther Strange

LS/MMH/sp

Yet another strange letter from the Attorney General, this one to the House Judiciary Chairman halting the governor's impeachment investigation. The timing of this letter, only days after my request to Governor Bentley to appoint an independent counsel seems to indicate the desire of the Attorney General and his inner circle to control the narrative to suit their personal political ambitions and egos.

was the last thing they needed. The impeachment investigation would likely reveal what they were trying to hide and I'd been trying to get exposed. They asked Representative Jones to stop the impeachment investigation because it would interfere with their "related work." Jones subsequently received letter from the attorney general halting the impeachment process.

Halting the impeachment investigation relieved pressure on the Attorney General's Office as much as the governor. They recognized the danger a public airing of their dirty laundry by the special counsel hired by the House Judiciary Committee posed, but they were also in a position of mutually assured destruction with one another.

I was given assurances that the appointment of an independent counsel would come on the heels of the general election. It would have been the shot that would end the Mexican standoff. I also expected Hillary Clinton would cruise to victory in the 2016 general election. I was 0-for-2. The unexpected upset of Hillary Clinton by Donald Trump ultimately ended the Alabama governor's resolve to appoint an independent counsel.

When I had talked to the governor on November 1, he was in a corner with few options. He was ready to do the right thing but for the wrong reason: self-preservation, not duty. He and others in his administration could feel heat from the Attorney General's Office breathing down his neck. They were deeply concerned that indictments might fall on them from the special grand jury any day.

Until I sent the letter requesting the investigation of Hart and the cover-up that gave him political cover and leverage, Governor Bentley was their helpless prey. Although the governor sincerely believed he had committed no crime, he was fearful of the trophy hunters in the Attorney General's Office prosecuting him criminally for an inadvertent misstep.

With the balance of power shifting toward the governor, the attorney general began turning the heat off with the watchful guidance of Alice Martin and Matt Hart, cooling down the governor's motivation to appoint an independent counsel. With the impeachment investigation stopped, the Alabama governor and attorney general spent the days leading up to the November 8 general election in a stalemate.

After the Trump victory it was expected that Senator Jeff Sessions would accept a cabinet appointment in the new administration, creating an opportunity for Governor Bentley to appoint a U.S. Senator. The power to appoint a U.S. Senator gave Bentley even more leverage against the attorney general than I had given with my request for investigation. The governor now had a carrot to go with his stick.

For years, Luther Strange had dreamed of becoming a U.S. Senator, but the path leading to it from the Attorney General's Office was fraught with ethical landmines. If Governor Bentley appointed someone other than him, Luther would be forced to run against an incumbent, a steep hill to climb that would be made steeper with the political bombs waiting to explode, such as the impeachment resolution that I was anticipating.

On November 18, President-elect Trump announced the nomination of Senator Jeff Sessions for U.S. attorney general. A few days later Luther Strange told *The Weekly Standard* that he would run for the seat and would not seek an appointment from Governor Bentley; although, he would accept an appointment, if selected.

Since shortly after October 25, when my formal request for investigation was made, I had remained in touch with Spencer Collier's replacement at ALEA Stan Stabler and members of the governor's staff. I had received assurance that the governor intended to ensure that a proper investigation was made pursuant to my request.

But that changed November 30 when a dumbfounded friend told me that Governor Bentley changed his mind about appointing an independent counsel. He said the governor said he knew the Hart case merited a proper investigation, and he had found a different way to get it done and end the conflict with the Attorney General's Office.

Luther Strange would gratefully accept an appointment to U.S. Senate, creating a vacancy for the governor to appoint an attorney general who could address my request without a conflict of interest that would prevent him from properly addressing my request for investigation. The die was already cast, but Bentley had to make it look good by pretending to seriously consider other candidates for the coveted Senate seat.

Governor Bentley did not believe that he had committed a crime. He was not worried about a fair, impartial investigation, but he recognized the danger posed to him and his administration by trophy-seekers in the Attorney General's Office.

In December, Governor Bentley interviewed at least seventeen potential candidates for the appointment, only one of which had a real chance—but he made it look good. I don't see how interviewing for an appointment is not asking for a job. Luther Strange would later deny asking for the appointment, with good reason. There is an inherent conflict of interest attached to soliciting an appointment from someone being investigated by his office.

It wasn't the attorney general's first time to put political expediency ahead of ethics, and I had a letter to prove it. It was astonishing to hear that Governor Bentley was even considering appointing someone who he knew had willfully failed to execute the duty of his office by collaborating with his subordinates to discredit ALEA and bury evidence of criminal acts for the sake of political expediency.

On Wednesday, February 8, 2017, Representative Ed Henry was also astonished by Governor Bentley during a meeting in the governor's office speaking on behalf of one of the finalists for the Senate seat, Representative Connie Rowe. Ed was unaware that it was already a done deal when he told Bentley that Luther Strange was corrupt. The governor replied that he knew Luther was corrupt but that he had to get him out of Montgomery so he could appoint an attorney general who could straighten out the mess.

Ed Henry was visibly upset when he returned to the Statehouse and summoned me to his office. Several other legislators including Representative Rowe were already in his office when he told me about his meeting with the governor. My longtime friend begged me to speak to Governor Bentley and talk some sense into him, unaware of what I'd been doing since we adjourned for the special session in early September. Ed had wandered into a political rabbit hole where talking sense is a waste of time.

The next day, February 9, 2017, in an affront to the office of both the governor and the attorney general of the state of Alabama, Governor Bentley ended the Mexican standoff by appointing Attorney General Luther Strange to the United States Senate. In a joint press conference with Bentley the same day, the freshly appointed U.S. senator made the mind-boggling statement,

"We have never said in our office that we are investigating the governor. I think it's actually unfair to him and unfair to the process."

If the Attorney General's Office was not investigating Governor Bentley, why did he authorize the special grand jury in July 2016 and request that the legislature suspend their impeachment investigation because it might interfere with "other related work"? It was obvious to the public that the appointment of Attorney General Luther Strange to the U.S. Senate smelled rotten, but the source of the stench was hidden—until now.

CHAPTER 25

A Bully by Any Name Smells the Same

I admire the little boy in the "The Emperor's New Clothes." Following the conventional wisdom of your respective tribe is much less trouble than honestly speaking the truth. Truth leads to conflict with those who manipulate it to gratify their own purposes. The world of politics is filled with these propagandists battling one another. Without humility, pride transforms even the most genuine, forthright truth seeker into one of them. The price for choosing truth when it conflicts with established power, cultural traditions, or public opinion is persecution and rejection. Look at Jesus.

If someone in authority would have objectively looked at the evidence and answered my questions about the misconduct that I had witnessed, my mind would've been set at ease and I could have let it go. But of the many who had the time or inclination to listen, the only indication I received from anyone with legal authority or expertise that my allegation against Hart had no merit was the loopy letter from Attorney General Strange, likely prompted by his ambitious Chief Deputy Alice Martin, that should have led to his impeachment but instead sent him to the U.S. Senate. It would have been a relief to me if their response could have shown me where I was wrong, but all it revealed was their determination to cover up the ethical lapses in the Attorney General's Office.

I showed the letter to an alleged journalist from a major statewide news outlet that even agreed with their assertion that Hart's call to me was merely a citizen exercising his First Amendment rights. I had made several attempts to share my perspective with him after he bashed me in an editorial the year before without bothering to get the whole story. It was my mistake to treat an opinion writer like a reporter. I was under the impression that telling him the truth would matter, but his opinion was steadfast. Trying to change a made-up mind, other than your own, is a waste of time, regardless of the evidence. The writer's contempt for Matt Hart's prey made him an unwitting victim of propaganda promoting the pernicious prosecutor's predatory proclivities.

We humans are naturally inclined to follow our herd, and we doggedly resist evidence that contradicts the conventional thinking of whatever flock we identify with. The sincerity and intensity of our beliefs or the number of people who share them doesn't add one iota of truth to them. Good investigators know that the truth is the truth, whether the person speaking it is good or bad. More than a few times, I've found that some of the best witnesses are what many might consider to be the worst people. Sometimes the opposite is true. True words are sometimes spoken through false teeth. It all depends on getting the context right, and that requires us to exercise the dying art of thinking.

After his bizarre decision to appoint Luther Strange to the U.S. Senate, my expectations were understandably low when Governor Bentley began vetting attorney general candidates. Since his re-election in 2014, Bentley's decision-making process seemed to have no logical paradigm. He interviewed several candidates for the job, including Matt Hart's protector, Alice Martin, who eagerly solicited the governor for the job, although he wasn't about to appoint Matt Hart's chief protector as Alabama attorney general, especially if one considers that he was one of the main reasons that Bentley had created the vacancy in the first place. I was pleasantly surprised when the hapless governor made what seemed to be a good choice in Steve Marshall, who'd served sixteen years as the district attorney in Marshall County.

I'd known Steve Marshall during my career as an ABI agent and only knew good things about him. He'd been appointed by Democratic Governor Don Siegelman and ran unopposed twice as a Democrat before switching parties in 2011. Like most district attorneys I've known, Marshall didn't seem to be a highly partisan politician, and considered politics a chore that must be attended to allow him to promote justice by applying the law as fairly and impartially as he could. It was a pleasant surprise—the last thing I had expected was for Governor Bentley to do something that made sense.

My hopes that the new attorney general would untangle the mess in his office rose precipitously when Marshall replaced the politically ambitious Chief Deputy Attorney General Alice Martin with Clay Crenshaw, a thirty-year career employee in the Attorney General's Office and a consummate professional with no apparent hint of political aspiration. In a roundabout way, it looked like Governor Bentley's cockamamie scheme to clean up the mess in Montgomery by sending Luther Strange to Washington might be fruitful.

I hoped that politics would not corrupt the new Attorney General Marshall, and he would apply the same ethical standards within his office that he did to everyone else, which would have meant Matt Hart's days were numbered. Because he had been appointed by Governor Bentley, Marshall recused himself from the investigation of the governor and appointed retired Montgomery County District Attorney Ellen Brooks to take charge of the special grand jury that U.S. Senator Strange didn't say was investigating Governor Bentley. I was hopeful Brooks would get to the bottom of the entire mess and let the chips fall where they may. With Luther Strange and Alice Martin out of the picture, the impeachment committee resumed its investigative work in preparation for public hearings.

On April 5, the Ethics Commission issued a finding of probable cause that Governor Bentley had committed a felony violation of the Ethics Law and three felony violations of the Fair Campaign Practices Act. Two days later, on Friday, April 7, Governor Bentley held a press conference and announcing he had no intention of resigning. A few hours later, the impeachment committee special counsel Jack Sharman released his initial report to the committee that was devastating to the governor's defense.

The governor's counsel attempted several legal delays which were unanimously rebuffed by the Alabama Supreme Court. When I noticed that Justice Murdock recused, I figured that it could have been because I'd spoken to him for guidance while I was struggling to figure out what to do during the ordeal. Justice Murdock had written the opinion that affirmed the governor's duty to enforce the law in the event the attorney general failed to do so, and he was someone that I'd known and trusted for many years. Much of what had happened seemed so surreal to me that I didn't completely trust my own judgment. I knew this was over my head and I wanted to make sure that I perceived it properly and was doing the right thing. Justice Murdock was one of many credible people from whom I sought counsel throughout this ordeal (Proverbs 20:18).

After Sharman's report was released and the Alabama Supreme Court gave the Judiciary Committee the green light, the governor saw the writing on the wall, and negotiations for a plea bargain on the charges referred by the Ethics Commission began moving toward a resignation ahead of his now inevitable impeachment.

The following Monday, April 10, 2017, the Chairman Jones opened the impeachment proceeding by announcing the recusal I'd made months earlier after my discussions with the governor and other members of his staff in violation of committee rules. The committee later recessed amid reports that Governor Bentley was expected to enter a plea with Supernumerary District Attorney Ellen Brooks in the Montgomery Circuit Court. About an hour after the committee recessed, Bentley pled guilty to two misdemeanor charges and shortly thereafter resigned from office.

The resignation of Governor Robert Bentley meant the end of the special counsel's investigation and the end of the opportunity for the impeachment process to bring the entire story out in the open. Had the impeachment continued, I expected the full circumstances surrounding the firing of Spencer Collier which revolved around Matt Hart to come out in the open.

My confidence in the entire process continued to be shaken when the television news coverage of Governor Bentley's resignation showed Matt Hart working alongside the retired District Attorney Ellen Brooks right in the thick of things. With the governor's resignation, the impeachment investigation was over and another opportunity to put the whole story out in the open was gone.

Lieutenant Governor Kay Ivey assumed the mantle of the governor's office with a long resume of public service and a steady hand to steer the foundering ship of state. However, the stench of Bentley's appointment of Luther Strange to the U.S. Senate still reeked in the nostrils of the people of Alabama. Governor Bentley had made the interim U.S. Senate appointment under a law that required a special election to be held "forthwith."

Governor Bentley interpreted "forthwith" to mean the 2018 election cycle, over a year away. Had he appointed anyone but Luther Strange, there probably wouldn't have been much of a clamor for a special election. But the public hated the smell of the appointment of Luther, even if they were in the dark about the specifics of it.

In one of her first measures to clear the air, Governor Ivey called a special election for the interim U.S. Senate seat held by Luther Strange, setting the primary for August 15. The Alabama Republican Party had a deep bench of highly qualified candidates who wanted to run, but the incumbent Luther Strange was the darling of the Washington insider crowd, having had a long career as a Washington lobbyist before being elected attorney general. Ignoring the dubious circumstances surrounding the appointment a few months earlier, the Republican Senatorial caucus cleared the field for Luther, discouraging credible primary opponents by drying up their funding sources and threatening to blackball consulting firms that worked against Luther.

Congressman Mo Brooks and former Chief Justice Roy Moore, two confrontational Alabama politicians, notorious for sticking a thumb in the eye of the political establishment, were among the top Republican contenders willing to take on the Washington powerbrokers and undo Bentley's blunder. Roy Moore remained the front runner throughout the initial primary because of his solid base of largely rural, evangelical, right-wing voters.

Although Judge Moore had a solid voter base, his controversial, confrontational nature had a negative effect on many voters, making it difficult for him to expand his base. Having been removed from his office as chief justice of the Alabama Supreme Court twice for defying the federal courts wasn't exactly a plus for him, either. But in a low-turnout Republican special primary with a large number of candidates, his loyal base could be relied upon to carry him into a runoff.

I spoke out about the circumstances surrounding Luther's Senate appointment, but it was too complex and bizarre for people to grasp. I blew my whistle as hard as I could, but it must have been a silent dog whistle and all the watchdogs must have been sleeping, because none of them barked. My warnings were probably written off as wild smears by a pissant politician, just a little static lost in the blaring political smears flooding Alabama during the election cycle.

At one point, it seemed that Luther might finish third, but a Trump endorsement coupled with a multimillion-dollar campaign targeted toward knocking Mo Brooks out of the runoff put Luther into a very clear second-place position and into a September 25 runoff with Roy Moore. The political geniuses in Washington must not have realized how much Luther Strange had been tainted by the circumstances surrounding his appointment. He was probably the only Republican contender the controversial Roy Moore could have defeated in a runoff.

I've never been a huge fan of Roy Moore, primarily because he usually came across as overly smitten with himself as the final arbiter of God's word. Self-righteous, defiant, in-your-face religiosity has never squared with my personal experience with Christianity. But the taint of Luther's appointment overshadowed all Judge Moore's weaknesses. Even the unabashed support of President Donald Trump himself could not mask the smell.

The Alabama Democrats nominated former U.S. Attorney Doug Jones, who would have taken full advantage Luther's ethical lapses with plenty of help from the local and national media. I would have probably been treated like Benedict Arnold by many of my Republican friends for telling the truth. I was spared that when Roy Moore handily defeated Luther Strange despite being outspent ten to one by the tainted Washington insider.

Despite Republican Roy Moore being a weak general election candidate and Doug Jones being as strong a candidate as the Democrats could have found, Moore looked destined to win, until a story broke in *The Washington Post* in early November that unleashed a flood of sexual allegations dating back forty years. Regardless of the veracity of the allegations, the timing of the story reeked of a well-orchestrated media ambush perfectly timed for maximum political effect.

Soon after the story broke, the Roy Moore campaign began to founder while the Doug Jones campaign clicked on all cylinders. In a special election where turnout is paramount, Democrats were energized and Republicans were demoralized. On December 12, 2017, the Democratic nominee Doug Jones eked out a stunning upset over the Republican Roy Moore in bright-red Alabama. Ironically, the Democrats probably did us a favor considering the havoc the Roy Moore media circus would have wreaked on Republicans across the nation during the following years.

The following Saturday, I almost skipped the Republican Men's Club meeting in Huntsville. It is the largest, longest running monthly Republican meeting in Alabama and is obligatory for serious local and statewide Republican candidates for office to make an appearance at this meeting. That morning, I was in no mood for politics. It was my daddy's birthday and I planned to visit his grave later that day.

My partisan zeal had been already waning for several years, and it was a discouraging time to be an Alabama Republican. We'd even managed to bungle our way into losing a U.S. Senate seat to a Democrat in a deep-red state. Unlike most people, it didn't look like an upset to me—more like the natural consequence of a toxic blend of systemic internal power struggles, moral and ethical failures, arrogance, incompetence, and leadership lapses that snowballed its way to culminate in Republicans blindly squandering away a United States Senate seat.

The success of Alabama Republicans at the polls over the previous decade made us overconfident and oblivious to our vulnerability, but that morning the atmosphere at the Republican Men's Club was gloomy, as if we were in a stunned stupor, only partially awakened from a bad dream. But the biggest reason I was in no mood to go to the meeting was that one of the scheduled keynote speakers was none other than Alice Martin, who had announced her 2018 campaign for attorney general.

For years, she had been posturing to run for attorney general as a corruption fighter cleaning up Montgomery, evocative of the gubernatorial campaign in the Coen Brothers' 2000 film *O Brother, Where Art Thou?* I envisioned Alice Martin on the campaign trail holding a broom and bragging about how she would sweep corruption out of Montgomery, while sweeping Matt Hart's iniquities under the rug for the sake of political expediency.

Although I had no desire to hear Martin bloviate, a sense of obligation to my political allies and friends who were still licking their wounds from the stinging loss of a U.S. Senate seat drove me to halfheartedly attend the meeting. When I arrived, an officer asked me to sit at the head table and innocently seated me next to my least favorite person at the meeting, Alice

Martin.

It's been said that coincidences are how God winks at us. I believe it is true. After several minutes of self-aggrandizing spiel about her corruption-fighting prowess and moral superiority from the podium, I couldn't resist an overpowering urge to remind her that I hadn't forgotten what she had covered up and it wasn't going away. When she returned to her seat beside me, I smiled and leaned toward her and said, "I'm really looking forward to 2018, so we can tell the rest of the story."

Since we were sitting at the head table in front of several hundred people, we both tried to appear cordial as we carried on our snarky exchange.

"You've been walking around with a smirk on your face, like you think I've done something wrong," she responded in a soft voice accompanied by a smirk of her own that strongly suggested feigned innocence.

"That's because I know you've done something wrong," I replied with another smirk disguised as a smile for the benefit of the onlookers.

"And what is that?" she asked in an overexaggerated, poorly faked inquisitive tone.

"You should know, you're the corruption fighter," I answered.

"You're an asshole" she observed.

"You have a way of bringing that out and you're the expert," I opined.

"Just shut up," she shot back.

"You should know by now, that's not going to happen," I reminded her.

I used to be a state trooper, so it wasn't the first time I'd been called an asshole. But it was first time I'd been called one by someone of such high status and it was the first time I enjoyed it.

Calling me "asshole" was an expression of her disdain that someone of my low station would be uppity toward her. It inspired me to contemplate the word and its connotations. I discovered an interesting book on the subject by an alleged moral philosopher (whatever that is, I guess it's good work if you can get it) Aaron James. In 2012 he wrote *Assholes: A Theory*, which provides an excellent definition of the pejorative that helped me further understand Alice Martin's special message to me.

Aaron James defines an asshole as follows:

"A person who considers himself of much greater moral or social importance than everyone else; who allows himself to enjoy special advantages and does so systematically; who does this out of an entrenched sense of entitlement; and who is immunized by his sense of entitlement against the complaints of other people. He feels he is not to be questioned, and he is the one who is chiefly wronged."

Ms. Martin recognized I'd been acting like one but was probably too self-absorbed to recognize that it was only a temporary state for me. I was talking down at her from a higher moral high ground, intentionally trying to make her uncomfortable, as I had with criminal suspects many times before. Unaccustomed to interacting with someone who usurped her usual position of moral superiority, she became irritated and called me an ugly name.

Being one and acting like one are two different things. Dr. James's definition does not describe my usual state. For me, it is just a mode of behavior that can be useful in certain situations with certain people. It feels good to give those people their comeuppance with their own medicine. The sense of satisfaction feels so good that it brings an inherent danger of addiction. If we become addicted, we cross a line from acting like one to being one. When we take ourselves so seriously that we do it indiscriminately with everyone who disagrees with us we are over the line. It should be used like medicine. Keep it to a minimum and reserve its use for special people on special occasions.

Just because everyone acts like one occasionally doesn't mean they are one. It's often just a temporary condition we fall into based on circumstances; a temporary lapse of self-control that can arise from a situation that causes us to allow our feelings to control our behavior with little or no regard for its effect on others. Most people can eventually recognize when their own bad behavior has been hurtful and feel regret. If you are one of those, I have good news. You are not an asshole, at least not yet. Everybody acts like one, sometimes. However, if you never feel regret for hurting someone and you believe that regret is for chumps, you are an incurable asshole, although you will never admit it. Because you're an asshole.

I recognize the name Alice Martin called me is offensive; but instead of offending me, it caused me to think. I am not trying to offend but to provoke thought. That was what Jesus did when he reserved his harshest admonitions for those who fit perfectly within Aaron James's definition. Jesus used other terms such as hypocrites, blind guides, wolves in sheep's clothing, and whitewashed tombs that are beautiful on the outside but on the inside are full of dirty dead wicked bones. Outraged at how those people abused their power and authority by standing between the sick and needy and their only hope, Jesus flipped over their tables and gave them a whipping as he chased them away. But the stubborn assholes came back, and they had him crucified. They always come back. But so does Jesus.

When our paths cross with a narcissist bully, we have three choices: avoid, join, or resist. Avoidance is the most sensible thing to do most of the time, but sometimes that is just not possible. Joining them is usually less desirable because stress created by their perpetual power struggles is spiritually draining. However, sometimes it is necessary to join one to resist another one, which is the purpose of partisan politics. But there is another way to resist them, and that way is Jesus's way. The way of truth and grace is not for the timid.

A great deal of law enforcement training is geared toward the use of physical force, but I have learned to recognize many other types including emotional, spiritual, and political force. All of them have similar dynamics. We should be naturally reluctant to use them because it is painful to those on the receiving end and it can create all sorts of unintended consequences. There are some people who derive pleasure by forcefully imposing themselves on others and derive satisfaction from making others cower. Empathy and remorse are alien to them. Those people should never be trusted with power over other people, but their ambition often makes them most successful in attaining it.

As aggravating as they are, these difficult people have contributed greatly to my spiritual growth throughout my life. They have been used like the needle in the hand of the Lord to stitch me into who I am. They have had an uncanny knack for showing up at the most inopportune times to aggravate, irritate, persecute, and torment. However, by making me feel helpless and vulnerable, they drive me to my knees and into the waiting arms of the Shephard who comforts, protects, and strengthens me, while preparing me for the next encounter.

Though they do great harm to many victims, bullies are themselves victims of a spiritual disease. Pride destroys the soul like cancer ravages the body. Pride has many variations, just like cancer. Regardless of how it is packaged, pride transforms human souls into something they were never intended to be. We have many different names we hang around the necks of those we judge to be afflicted, like bully, jerk, narcissist, psychopath, chiseler, crook, braggart, shark, brute, prick, gangster, ogre, and blowhard. Afflicted females have been referred to as shrew, nag, witch, battle-ax, temptress, fishwife, seductress, and bitch. Our evolving society seems to be phasing out female descriptors and using the male terms in a more gender-neutral manner. Regardless, they are all assholes, and a bully by any name smells the same.

CHAPTER 26

Experts

In the 2018 general election, the Alabama Democrats put forth some decent candidates, emboldened by the Doug Jones victory over Roy Moore in the 2017 special election for U.S. Senate. The effort to mobilize their base had some of the organization and energy leftover from their stunning upset victory the previous December. But without a strong foil like Roy Moore, they could not rekindle a political fire with enough intensity to overcome their lack of a coherent political philosophy that might appeal to most Alabamians.

Governor Kay Ivey won a decisive victory in the June 5 primary without a runoff over several reasonably strong and credible candidates. The idea of a steady hand to right the ship of state after all the political drama we'd been through during the previous years was appealing to most Alabamians. Ivey was a solid veteran of Alabama politics and appealed to voters as a pillar of stability.

The hottest political race in Alabama in the 2018 election cycle was the Republican primary race for attorney general. As expected, Alice Martin ran as the great corruption fighter who would sweep Alabama clean. Despite the public being uninformed of her involvement in the chicanery that emanated from the Attorney General's office during her tenure, she fell short of making the primary runoff, finishing with 23 percent behind Governor Bentley's appointee Steve Marshall (28.3 percent) and former Attorney General Troy King (27.8 percent). The race appeared close until the sudden tragic death of Marshall's wife on June 24. In the July 17 runoff, the incumbent prevailed by a huge margin.

To my bewilderment, Matt Hart was still the chief of the Special Prosecutions Division in the Attorney General's Office a year after Marshall's appointment to the vacancy created by Governor Bentley after my request for investigation. I believed Attorney General Marshall and his Deputy Clay Crenshaw would have taken appropriate steps to ensure my complaint was addressed and Hart would be held accountable, like anyone else. I was wrong, and it became abundantly clear who was being held accountable a couple of weeks before 2018 candidate qualifying ended on February 9 when, along with other legislators, I received a grand jury subpoena from the Special Prosecutions Unit demanding my previous four years campaign finance records.

Sharks are attracted to blood in the water. I had not had an opponent since 2006, but in 2018 they came from every direction. The subpoena was another cut added to the editorializing about me that began soon after I testified on April 15, 2015, in open court about Matt Hart's misconduct. Despite my severely waning political zeal, I managed to defeat my "tea party" challenger in the June 5 Republican primary by the largest margin of any local or statewide Republican in Madison County. The November general election was a bit closer, thanks to a Libertarian who managed to siphon some votes that probably helped the Democratic nominee in a swing district.

To my surprise and to their credit, none of my 2018 opponents mentioned the subpoena or took cheap shots based on the criticism I'd received from the alleged journalists who'd been enamored by Matt Hart. Despite spending the entire campaign season with little enthusiasm for not getting to fight the battle I wanted and was prepared for, I managed to get re-elected to a fifth and final four-year term, 54 percent to 41 percent to 5 percent.

Although I was already sick of politics, I made no bones throughout 2018 that corruption and cannabis were the two main reasons I was running for re-election. I received a great deal of encouragement throughout my district and began my final term determined to do everything in my power to complete my work, so that when 2022 came around, I could walk away with a clear conscience.

After the 2018 election was over, the discrete letter I received from the attorney general's corruption experts informing me they'd found no evidence of impropriety with my campaign finances did not make up for suspicious timing of the subpoena, nor did it pay my attorney fees. Speaking of suspicious timing, two weeks after the general election, Matt Hart abruptly resigned from the Attorney General's Office. According to his doting admirers in the media, who likely heard it from Hart himself, Attorney General Marshall made him an offer he couldn't refuse.

My biggest question was what took so long, and I didn't like the obvious answer. Steve Marshall was acting like every bit as much of a politician as his predecessor, Luther Strange. His actions indicated to me that political expediency was at or near the top of his ethical decision making, in some ways even worse than the former oil company lobbyist, Luther Strange. Marshall had been a district attorney for sixteen years and should have known going in at least as much as I did about Matt Hart. He may have taken steps to contain the brutish bully in charge of his public corruption unit, but leaving him there for an entire year before sending him on his way with a polite thank you soon after the 2018 election cycle reeked of someone more concerned with appearance than justice.

A few months after leaving the Attorney General's Office, Hart was hired by the same law firm where he steered a legal services contract worth nearly $1 million that had begun the chain of events ultimately leading the political consultant and Montgomery radio host Baron Coleman in January 2016 to publicly reveal their furtive collaboration—which ultimately gave me probable cause to believe Hart had committed a felony. I have yet to receive an indication that any sort of investigation has been made nor a satisfactory explanation why he was not held accountable for his conduct as he seemed to pride himself in holding others.

My top priority going into the 2019 regular session of the legislature was to update Carly's Law and Leni's Law. The ongoing research at the University of Alabama at Birmingham authorized by Carly's Law in 2014 had been productive in identifying the medicinal value of cannabis, but the five-year authorization was about to expire. Dr. Jerzy Szaflarski led the research that had produced convincing evidence of the efficacy of cannabis for medical use. One study published in the journal *Epilepsy & Behavior* in 2018 based on the UAB research revealed a two-thirds overall reduction in seizures.

In addition to reauthorizing Carly's Law, some last-minute language discretely slipped into Leni's Law in 2016 created some confusion regarding the amount of THC permitted and the legislative intent. My top priority for the 2019 regular session was to reauthorize the UAB research and clear up the ambiguities slipped into Leni's Law. Leni's mom Amy Young, Carly's dad Dustin Chandler, and I decided to get the old band back together to get it done. Speaker McCutcheon's policy director and general counsel Andrew Wescott was tasked with getting a bill drafted.

As we began working on the bill, our like-minded little band grew with the shared mission to allow access to cannabis to as many suffering people who could be helped by its proper use, without expanding its abuse as a recreational drug. In December 2018, the U.S. Congress passed a bill that completely legalized low-THC cannabis for any purpose. In one swoop, the CBD oil was available to anybody, anywhere, for any purpose, just a couple of years after Leni's Law had generated substantial opposition to being made available to people with debilitating illnesses under a doctor's care. I didn't hear a whimper from the religious right, from where most of the opposition came.

I knew we needed to do something in the 2019 session, but we couldn't do anything until we received the blessed assurance that had led us since 2014. January 2019 came and went with no bill while our little band continued to search for our next step. On February 13, Dustin set up a brainstorming meeting in Birmingham. Joining us were recently retired Alabama Court of Civil Appeals Judge Terri Willingham Thomas, women's midwife activist Jennifer Crook, Speaker McCutcheon's legal counsel Andrew Wescott, and the person who probably knew more than anyone else in Alabama about the medical efficacy of cannabis, Dr. Jerzy Szaflarski.

When Jerzy (Dr. Szaflarski is exceptionally unpretentious, preferring that we call him by his first name) first began studying cannabis after the passage of Carly's Law, he was skeptical about the efficacy of cannabis for treating seizures. However, his continuing research produced evidence that convinced him not only of its value in the treatment of seizures but also of other ailments related to the neurological system.

At that meeting I expressed my preference for simple legislation narrowly crafted for a specific purpose. I tried to limit our conversation to extending the authorization for UAB to continue cannabis research, clarifying the murky language in Leni's Law that had been mysteriously substituted, and expanding the use of CBD oil with a higher THC content than allowed under the Farm Bill for those under a doctor's care for a debilitating illness.

But Jerzy and the others were insistent that simple protection from criminal prosecution wasn't enough. There was an untold multitude of people who evidence had indicated could benefit from treatment with cannabis in therapeutic dosages under the supervision of a licensed physician. Such treatment would require a regulatory mechanism that would provide for the legal growth, processing, and sale of cannabis in a manner that could assure the medication distributed to the patient was of the appropriate quality and consistently labeled in a manner conducive to the practice of medicine.

It didn't take me long to figure out Jerzy was the reliable expert I had been seeking since beginning my journey with cannabis in 2014, one who really knows what he knows and is honest enough to admit what he doesn't know. He projected a wonderful mix of humility, confidence, and reason that assured me he could be counted as a source for accurate, unvarnished truth about anything within his realm of expertise. I recognized him as an unadulterated scientific thinker, like many of my constituents scattered throughout my legislative district surrounding the Redstone Arsenal—especially my next-door neighbor of seventeen years who had passed away in May 2015 at eighty-two.

Dr. Richard Fork was a visionary laser scientist at the University of Alabama in Huntsville. He held several patents, including one for a space-based laser system for powering spacecraft that's probably the first commercial endeavor to provide energy generated in space and delivered in space. He was fascinated with lasers as a source of energy and was engaged in developing technology that would use powerful laser pulses to bust up asteroids endangering Earth.

Dr. Fork received his doctorate in physics from Massachusetts Institute of Technology in 1962 and was co-author of the original paper on the demonstration of a mode-locked laser that has helped form the basis of work resulting in five Nobel Prizes for advancements in various aspects of mode-locked laser technology. He authored numerous publications on lasers including "Deflecting Asteroids with Femtosecond Optical Pulses," "An Advanced Optical System for Laser Ablation Propulsion in Space," and

"Mode-locked Lasers Applied to Deflecting a Near Earth Object on Collision Course with Earth." I haven't gotten around to reading any of those page turners, but you get the idea. He was brilliant. But to me, he was just my sweet, elderly neighbor who occasionally needed a helping hand.

Once, he called me because he'd locked his keys in his car, so I grabbed my "slim-jim" and a coat hanger and opened the door in a couple of minutes. Dr. Fork was awestruck, as though he had witnessed a magic trick. He was full of questions about opening car doors and how I happened to develop my dubious talent.

Like most things, I'd learned it out of necessity. I've absentmindedly locked in my own car keys many times. As a state trooper, I came across people who had locked the keys in their cars. I even inadvertently locked my keys in my patrol car on a traffic stop with the blue lights flashing on the side of the road. Thankfully a friendly motorist stopped and happened to have a coat hanger.

I usually mowed Dr. Fork's yard when I mowed mine. Since he was trying to save the planet from destruction, the least I could do was cut his grass. Besides, pushing the mower is a great stress reliever. When he tried to pay me, I wouldn't accept the money. But he insisted, so I suggested he could give me a six-pack of craft beer. It turned into a mission for him to find the perfect beer to suit my palate. Each week he brought me another six-pack with an explanation of its composition and the brewing process and quizzed me about the previous week's selection. I felt like being in the middle of high-level research; but no matter, the beer was good. Who else had a premier scientist carefully researching and selecting their beer just for them?

Another time, some huge limbs fell in his yard, and I offered to cut them up and haul them off. He gratefully accepted and wanted to help me. Since it was his yard, it was an offer I couldn't refuse. Dr. Fork was getting up in years and was not accustomed to heavy manual labor. I kept a close eye on him while he loaded limbs and I cut them up. When my utility trailer was loaded, he was eager to go to the landfill with me because he had never been.

Being a former roofer, a trip to the dump is routine. But it was a high adventure to Dr. Fork, and that made it special for me. We shared childhood stories and I enjoyed hearing about his life from running a paper route as a young boy in Michigan to the present. We had a delightful day.

He reminded me of my six-year-old granddaughter Clarke the way he bombarded me with one question after another about the landfill and the various equipment associated with it. The questions posed by the great physicist were a little more complex than my granddaughter's, but their attitude was identical. His childlike wonder and awe were keys to his academic brilliance. He was honest and humble enough to realize how much he didn't know. What he knew didn't make him smart—it was recognizing what he didn't know. Ignorance can't be cured until we acknowledge it. Dr. Fork's genius was the result of a humble spirit, honest heart, and open mind working in unison.

One day, I was in my recliner trying to stave off an impending bout of depression after being at odds with some alleged experts and high-ranking public officials and had just finished reading a blistering editorial taking cheap shots at me. I was feeling dejected, wallowing in a deep funk that can linger for days when my doorbell rang. It was Dr. Fork with a bottle of wine.

Dr. Fork handed me the bottle while telling me that he'd seen me on the evening news and was fascinated at how I kept up with legislative issues and was willing to take on any issue. It gave him a peculiar urge to let me know he appreciated me being his state representative. He went on to say how much he treasured our friendship. Compliments continued to gush from the lips of the renowned physicist until it began to feel awkward. It was entirely out of character for the usually mild-mannered and reserved professor. I tried to graciously accept the wine and cut off the conversation or at least change the subject. Frankly, struggling with the blues makes a person want to be alone, and I was eager to get back to my wallowing, but he wouldn't shut up.

He said he'd watched me trying to always do the right thing and help my neighbors and that I was the best neighbor he'd ever had. It was totally out of character for my usually reserved and reticent elderly neighbor. He got so worked up that he started poking his right finger into my left shoulder proclaiming, "You're a genius, you're a genius, you. . .are. . .a. . .f—king genius."

We looked at each other, both of us stunned that he'd lost his self-control and gotten so carried away that he used used the F-word. Cuss words don't usually shock me. I was a street kid, a Marine sergeant, and a career police officer. I'm no stranger to cussing, but it was startling to see my humble neighbor so assertive and uninhibited. Seeing my surprise, he paused for a moment and continued poking his finger into my shoulder and changing his rant to "You are a FRIGGING genius, a FRIGGING genius," before abruptly turning around and going home.

I went back into the house and had a good laugh at the absurdity of it all. One of the top physicists in the country had just gone ballistic trying to convince me that I was a genius. I couldn't help thinking that he must not be as smart as everyone thinks. But the episode turned out to be more than just a good laugh, and it snapped me out of the funk I was in.

It serves as a reminder that genuine experts don't stubbornly bend facts to match their own conclusions, like lawyers or politicians. They are more like investigators whose minds keep turning with new evidence, like a cement mixer. Their search for truth never stops because they are aware of how much they don't know. Every day, they learn something new that forces them to rethink what they have learned before. Each bit of new information their minds process into their previous conclusions brings their opinion a little closer to the absolute truth that only God possesses.

Pride creates counterfeit experts, some of whom are so good at pretending, they even fool themselves. Their egotism invariably tricks them into confusing their biased conclusions based on their limited knowledge with undistorted truth. When their conclusions harden like concrete in their minds and become stigmas, they cannot be changed. They can only be broken by the powerful force of truth and grace. Unfortunately, pride causes many to live and die in ignorance, thinking they know things they don't and deceiving others in addition to themselves along the way.

There are some clear symptoms displayed by pretenders that can expose them to us. They include constant fault-finding, a harsh tone, superficiality, defensiveness, religious presumption, craving for attention, and lack of concern for others. Since Jonathan Edwards's essay "Undetected Spiritual Pride, One Cause of Failure in Times of Great Revival" brought these symptoms to my attention a few years ago, I began noticing hypocrites and frauds everywhere I looked, especially in the mirror. The mirror doesn't lie when we are standing naked in front of it.

Since then, I can't help but remember Dr. Fork's tirade on my front porch and feel his finger poking my chest whenever I smell an air of superiority wafting from someone peering down at me. His words are like a spritz of air freshener as I hear him in my mind saying, "You. . .are. . .a. . .frigging. . .genius." It always evens things up.

Dr. Fork knew lasers, and Jerzy was the expert that convinced me of the necessity of making cannabis available in a form that would be beneficial for patients when used in collaboration with a physician. His expertise as a scientist and medical researcher clearly pointed him in the right direction, but his ignorance of Alabama politics and the legislative process cloaked the mountains looming and the many pitfalls that would need to be navigated before we could get where we needed to be. But I'd been in the legislature a long time and had developed some expertise that Jerzy lacked, and our little band had been around the horn a time or two.

With the 2019 session looming in only a couple of weeks, none of us knew of any state with legislation that could provide the regulatory structure that we envisioned for Alabama. Our vision was to find a way to allow access to cannabis for the multitude of ailing, afflicted people who could be helped without encouraging its expansion for recreational use. The next day Leni's mom Amy discovered a bill that had been filed only the previous week by a stalwart conservative in the Tennessee General Assembly, Senator Janice Bowling. Bowling's SB486 appeared to be just what Dr. Szaflarski had prescribed for Alabama. The following Monday, I made the two-hour drive to Nashville in search of Senator Bowling and more information about our bill and the experts who had helped her draft it.

CHAPTER 27

Marijuana Mike

I liked Tennessee State Senator Janice Bowling from the first time we met. For those who are not well acquainted with the legislative process, things move very fast during session, and it's important to be able to size up folks quickly. Coming from two different legislatures probably made it easy for us because we didn't have a lot of other issues to distract us and we could focus on our common cause. I wanted to know as much about her SB486 as quickly as I could, especially its inspiration and development.

It seemed that I had struck the mother lode. Her vision for the regulation and use of cannabis for medical purposes was identical to mine, and she had already put in the work to develop legislation to accomplish it at the state level.

Bowling, a native of Selma, Alabama, taught special education soon after graduating from Auburn University. When her husband was stationed at Arnold Air Force Base, their family moved to nearby Tullahoma, Tennessee. She served as alderman in Tullahoma for sixteen years before she was elected senator in the Tennessee Assembly in 2012.

It is safe to say that Senator Bowling's politics line up better with the modern right-wing populist movement led by Donald Trump than mine, which tended to be more in line with the Reagan-Bush conservatives who once dominated Republican politics. Unfortunately, both factions tend to stigmatize marijuana users, and Bowling was just as unlikely a candidate as I had been to sponsor to cannabis legislation. But there is something more powerful than politics that compels certain people to turn against the grain, and we had a common experience with it.

Representative Jeremy Faison is another state legislator who had experienced it. In 2018, it gave him the gall to ask the ultraconservative Bowling to support medical cannabis legislation. Bowling was taken aback that Faison would dare ask her to consider supporting legislation authorizing the use of cannabis for medicinal purposes, given that she was already absorbed with trying to ease the widespread opioid epidemic.

After Bowling thoroughly excoriated the lowly representative, he responded simply to her, "I know you research your issues before you vote. . .just read the research. That is all I ask!" When Bowling got off her high horse and started investigating, the evidence led her to the shocking revelation that, had the cannabis plant been properly researched, regulated, and utilized for medical purposes instead of abused, stigmatized, and outlawed, the opioid epidemic might have never happened!

Bowling spent an entire year developing a bill that would provide the state-level regulatory structure for growing, processing, and distributing cannabis for medical use, without opening the door for widespread distribution for other purposes. She elicited help from former Washington State Representative Glenn Anderson, with twelve years' service, and former Colorado State Representative Dan Pabon, an attorney with eight years' service. Both were living in Tennessee and had extensive experience developing legislation for regulating cannabis for medical purposes.

On February 6, 2019, Bowling introduced SB486. It was assigned to the Senate Judiciary Committee, where it was summarily executed on March 17. However, the previous years' work of Senator Bowling and her collaborators was not in vain. Our little band of collaborators in Alabama had discovered SB486 the week after it was introduced in the Tennessee Assembly.

On March 20, three days after SB486 was killed in the Tennessee Assembly, it was resurrected in the Alabama Legislature as HB243, where it was sent to languish in the Health Committee of House of Representatives. It would have been destined to die had it not been for language extending the Carly's Law study in the bill that had almost universal support.

The Health Committee Chair Representative April Weaver was a career professional nurse, whose politics, training, and experience led her to be a protector of the status quo and a staunch opponent of cannabis at the state level for medical purposes. She represented Shelby County, which was a hotbed of opposition to medical cannabis. She politely continued to put me off and I recognized that without divine intervention she would see to it that HB243 would die, regardless of how much she pretended to be fair.

Adding to my difficulty was that Paul Sanford, my Senate partner for Carly's Law and Leni's Law, had taken his position on term limits seriously and stepped away in 2018 after two terms. Without a champion in the Senate, we were dead in the water, until I could find another Republican senator crazy enough to stand up to the powerful religious right-wing Christian lobby and pick up the mantle.

When Senator Tim Melson stepped up and volunteered to carry the bill in the Senate to extend Carly's Law and fix Leni's Law, I was pleasantly surprised. It had never occurred to me that someone with Dr. Melson's extensive medical background might be as crazy as Paul Sanford. I still had my doubts when he asked me to draft a Senate companion bill for him to introduce.

By the time I handed him the blue-jacketed Senate folder a week later, it was apparent to me that my heavy lifting was done and it was time for medical professionals to refute the stigma with science. When I handed him the medical cannabis bill modeled after the Tennessee one that regulated growing, processing, and distribution of cannabis for medical purposes with seed-to-sale tracking, his eyes widened as he asked, "Are you sure?"

I replied, "It's the best I can do, but you are going to make it better," as the weight of the mantle moved from my shoulders to his. I'd brought it as far as my faith, experience, and prowess had prepared me to take it. For much of the five years I'd carried it, it felt more like a curse than a blessing. But it was never a curse, just a heavy blessing. It was not just good for the sick and afflicted who had been helped and would be helped—it was good for me, too.

Carrying the burden was like carrying bundles of shingles up a ladder under the watchful eye of my mentor Hack Ward when I was young. It was hard work, and it was tiresome, but it made me stronger. Physical labor is compensated with a physical reward, but spiritual labor receives a spiritual reward. In retrospect, it was worth the trouble, and I received far more than I gave to the cause.

The Master never gives us a burden that we haven't been trained and equipped to carry. If it gets too heavy, the Master knows when to send help to carry it when we need it. And He knows when we've reached our destination, even if it's just a transfer station. I doubt that Melson had an inkling of what he was getting into, but I did. It was comforting to know it was being placed on stronger, more stable shoulders than mine.

Dr. Tim Melson is an anesthesiologist, clinical researcher, and farmer who was elected to the Alabama Senate from Florence in 2014. His education and professional experience blended with his unique mix of humility and self-confidence, giving him an honest eye for the hypocrisy that permeates the world of politics. His wry and good-natured but self-effacing wit allowed him to diplomatically point out the pretentious prevarications of pandering politicians without being overly contentious. His open heart and mind would help him find the way.

A couple of weeks later, Senator Melson knew what he had to do and introduced SB236, the companion to my House bill, HB243. Very few political observers thought either bill had much chance, but I had been working on the issue a long time, and I knew the membership of the House and Senate were far more receptive than almost anyone realized.

The biggest problem was the stigma caused by decades of escalating political propaganda from opponents and proponents of the cannabis plant as they attempted to demonize one another in the public mind. The stigma was somewhat lighter since I introduced Carly's Law in 2014, but it was still caked on. It was our greatest obstacle, because in politics looking good usually trumps doing good.

Three weeks later, on April 25, a few ears perked up when SB236 passed the Senate Judiciary Committee with a six-to-three vote. It was the first time any of us could recall that a medical cannabis bill had ever even gotten out of a committee in either chamber of the Alabama Legislature. Although I recognized the significance, it didn't surprise me. I had known the committee chairman, Senator Cam Ward, since we were both elected to the House in 2002. He was a solid supporter of both Carly's Law and Leni's Law from the start and had been a longtime champion of helping afflicted children.

However, I was astonished, as were the gatekeepers in the House of Representatives, when Melson's bill came to the floor of the Senate two weeks later on May 9 and passed seventeen to nine with over one-third of the 2019 legislative session remaining. While Speaker McCutcheon was supportive, the rules chairman Representative Mike Jones was not, and neither was Representative April Weaver, the chair of the Health Committee, where the bill SB236 was assigned.

I counted a strong bipartisan supermajority of members who were supportive of Melson's bill and would vote for it if it got to the floor, but that was a very big "if." In the legislative process, some members are more equal than others, and the chair of a committee to which a bill has been assigned is most equal of anyone. Weaver had no plan to give Melson's bill a fair hearing in the Health Committee. But on May 12, Representative Weaver resigned her seat in the legislature to work for the Trump administration. Her replacement was Representative Paul Lee of Dothan. He was skeptical about medical cannabis but could be convinced if he had time to study the issue.

During the days that followed, support for SB236 continued to grow among House members and the public. Representative Lee wasn't ready to endorse the seed-to-sale medical cannabis legislation that we had hijacked from Tennessee. But he couldn't just let the bill die because it had authorization to extend the cannabis research at UAB.

As the waning days of the session approached, Lee recognized there was solid support for medical cannabis. He proposed utilizing the structure of the Alabama Medical Cannabis Commission to create a committee for studying the best practices in other states to determine *how* we were going

Senator Melson and I discuss amendments to SB46 during the final day of debate on the House floor.

to regulate the use of cannabis for medical purposes in Alabama, not *if* we were going to do it.

I was disappointed, but it was an offer that Melson and I couldn't refuse. We would live to fight another day, and the Medical Cannabis Study Commission would only uncover more evidence to nick away at the layers of the stigma that had been painted on the cannabis plant by lawyers, politicians, and bureaucrats for the past hundred years.

Our true adversary was the stigma itself, not the people who had been taken in by the powers that produce and perpetuate propaganda. The study commission provided an opportunity to shine a floodlight on the stigma and separate science from superstition.

The Alabama Medical Cannabis Study Commission began meeting during the latter half of 2019. Of the eighteen members, ten had a medical background (seven of which were MDs, including Dr. Jerzy Szaflarski), with only four lawyers, two of which were district attorneys. The chairman of the commission was Dr. Tim Melson and the vice chair was Dr. Steven Stokes, a radiation oncologist from Dothan, near the border of Florida, where patients can legally use cannabis to ease their suffering.

While the commission was heavy on the medical, scientific, and academic side, there were also members on the commission who fully embraced the stigma and would have an opportunity to publicly put forth their best arguments against the growing body of scientific evidence supporting the medical value of cannabis.

The two most strident stigmatists on the commission were Shelby County District Attorney Jill Lee and labor and employment lawyer Thomas Eden, two lawyers appointed to the commission by the attorney general to defend the stigma.

Blaming, shaming, and defaming has become such a part of our discourse that many of us don't even realize when we're doing it to others—but we sure know when it is done to us. When we feel the spiritual pain, we seek relief from it. For many people that unfortunately means transmitting it. If we can't get relief by striking back, we strike out at someone or something else.

Contempt is a contagious spiritual pandemic, exacerbated by the many avenues created by modern media for stigmas to propagate themselves. We can select whatever stigma suits our palate from an all-you-can-eat smorgasbord, open all the time on the internet or on television, no longer limited to personal contact. Stigmas are particularly pervasive in the political world, serving as quarries supplying stones for the persecutions that pave the path to power for the proud.

The best way to deal with a stigma is to illuminate it. When a stigma is confronted with truth and grace, it is transformed into wisdom and can no longer be used to transmit contempt. Jesus of Nazareth demonstrated using truth and grace to attack a stigma when he said from the cross, "Forgive them Father, for they know not what they do." Jesus wears the stigmas like a crown of thorns. When we stigmatize others, we also stigmatize the One who shares the burdens of those we oppress.

A prime example of Jesus's use of truth and grace to defy a stigma occurred early one morning as he was teaching on the grounds of the temple where he had gathered a crowd like a rock star. It wasn't long before the self-righteous learned men and religious authorities showed up with a fresh victim, a woman they had stigmatized with an accusation of adultery. People tend to automatically assume the woman was guilty because she'd been accused, but we don't know for sure.

People are so conditioned to blame, shame, and scapegoat that they immediately equate an accusation with a conviction, having little regard for evidence. Sometimes we don't even wait for an accusation and begin stigmatizing during the suspicion stage.

The only evidence of this woman's guilt is an accusation by her stigmatizing prosecutors engaged in a lynching under the guise of dubious legal or religious authority without regard for due process or a fair trial. Guilty or not, she had been unfairly stigmatized so she could be used as pawn in a political game to stigmatize Jesus as "soft on crime" and "against law and order."

Since they couldn't refute His message, they intended to stigmatize the messenger with a scheme that reminded me of something Wile E. Coyote might have read in the *Acme Book of Propaganda, Persecution, and Politics.*

They detested Jesus because he was the champion of those they oppressed, marginalized, and stigmatized. They used this shamed woman to lay a dilemma at the feet of the great moral teacher, forcing him to choose between the stigmatized woman or the shaming authorities. If he took the side of the shamed woman, they could stigmatize him with guilt by association.

Although blaming and shaming propagandists can be found anywhere on the political spectrum, these were tough-on-crime religious conservatives. If he defended the woman, they could expose him as a squishy, openminded, feel-good liberal, a blasphemer without regard for God's word according to their own interpretation. If he took the more common route and joined in stigmatizing her, they could discredit him before his primary base of followers, stigmatized outcasts. Without followers, he could easily be discredited as just another false prophet. But Jesus's way was something the self-accusers failed to consider.

They could have anticipated his response and avoided having their boneheaded scheme blow up in their faces like the famous cartoon coyote if they'd have listened to his Sermon on the Mount where he said, "Judge not that you be not judged, for with what judgment you judge, you shall be judged. And what measure you use, it shall be measured to you."

Instead of taking their bait, Jesus demonstrated his way with his response, "Let he that is without sin cast the first stone at her."

The way of Jesus does not provide for a double standard that qualifies us to stigmatize anything. Stigmatizing brings shame and disgrace to the object of scorn. It creates bitterness, resentment, and contempt that usually results in backlash. Stigmatizing is a form of spiritual repression that allows us to distance ourselves from people or things that cause us to feel uncomfortable. Stigmatizing makes us feel superior, while being on the receiving end makes us feel hurt and browbeaten. Neither way is Jesus's way.

Jesus's way illuminates our stigmas and washes them away. When his way becomes our way, our pain that had festered into the contempt we have been transmitting is transformed into God's love. Instead of transmitting stigmatizing contempt that hurts, we transmit His illuminating love that heals. That's what Jesus was talking about in his Sermon on the Mount when he said, "You are the light of the world," and sunshine is the best antiseptic for the corruption that stigmatizes.

I was confident the 2019 Alabama Medical Cannabis Study Commission report would be received by Governor Ivey and the Alabama Legislature differently than the federal officials did the Shaffer Commission Report in 1971, and it was. The commission passed the report twelve to three, with three abstentions, recommending legislation to the legislature to regulate cannabis for medical use, much like the one we hijacked from Senator Bowling in Tennessee. Two of the dissenting votes were attorney general's appointees Shelby County District Attorney Jill Lee and labor and employment attorney Thomas Eden. The final "no" vote was State Health Officer Scott Harris.

One member who strongly dissented recommended Alabama honor the tradition set by Harry Anslinger and Richard Nixon and continue to recognize cannabis as a Class 1 Controlled substance according to the federal Controlled Substances Act. When a stigma is set into law, it becomes legitimatized and socially acceptable. Being legal and being right are not always the same thing.

I doubt anyone in the Alabama Legislature has embraced the cannabis stigma more than Senator Larry Stutts. He was elected in 2014 and was one of only three Alabama senators to oppose Leni's Law in 2016. A former veterinarian, he became a successful OB/GYN, delivering thousands of babies in northeast Alabama. He is an intelligent, well-meaning, highly educated, church-going man who has lived a blessed life. All those things are desirable, but success is dangerous when it leads us to become self-righteous and self-important. A lifetime of accomplishment can easily give one an air of superiority and make it difficult empathize with the downtrodden and outcast, Jesus's primary constituency.

Soon after Senator Melson's 2019 medical cannabis legislation had passed the Senate, I was at an after-hours legislative reception sitting alone at a table munching hors d'oeuvres and trying to relax, when Senator Stutts strode to my table and said, "Marijuana Mike," as he towered over me and pinned the stigma on me. I took it as a simultaneous insult and challenge as anger flew over me. My first impulse was to tear into him, but I wasn't sure whether to punch his face or grab his throat.

But before I could decide, Dr. Fork's finger poked into my chest and his words, "You are a frigging genius," rang through my mind. My rage was transformed into pity for the counterfeit geniuses like us who display pride instead of gratitude for their blessings. It led me to call on the source of all intellect with perhaps the shortest but most effective of all silent prayers: "Now what?"

My prayer was immediately answered with a Bible verse (I Corinthians 1:27). I smiled at him and said, "Being a senator and a doctor might make you feel superior to a lowly fool like me, but God uses the foolish to confound the proud."

The proud senator muttered, "That he does," as he walked away. The entire exchange only lasted a minute or so.

Dr. Stutts probably means well and sincerely believes he is doing the right thing, but I seriously doubt as an OB/GYN that he has researched cannabis objectively as a treatment option for any of his patients, since nobody to my knowledge recommends cannabis for pregnant women. He has accepted the propaganda that Anslinger began promoting in the 1930s and Nixon institutionalized in the 1970s, and he has joined in propagating the stigma that has outlived them.

By doing so, Stutts's political agenda compels him to disregard those who know more about it than he does, like neuroscientist Dr. Jerzy Szaflarski, who conducted the UAB research, or the former vice chair of the Alabama Medical Cannabis Study Commission, Dr. Steven Stokes, who has used it in his practice to treat cancer patients. Dr. Stutts should know better, but pride is a deceiver that makes people think they know what they don't.

Human pride makes hard hearts, and hard hearts produce stigmas. Hardened hearts don't change until they are melted or broken.

CHAPTER 28

God Winks

With Senator Melson moving the medical cannabis bill through the legislative process at the beginning of the session, I turned my attention to legislation that addressed the outbreak of political corruption that plagued Alabama during the previous quadrennium. With Matt Hart, Alice Martin, Luther Strange, Spencer Collier, Mike Hubbard, and Robert Bentley out of office, the corruption issue had died down considerably. The system of checks and balances seemed to have worked to some degree. However, the flaws remained in our political system that allowed corrupt public officials within the Attorney General's Office to undermine the two most important lynchpins of a free society: the jury box and the ballot box. And the public was oblivious to it.

Until the flaws are acknowledged and exposed, they won't be addressed. It is much easier just to let that sleeping dog lie. But pride is a vicious animal that should always be kept chained or behind a fence. If not, that dog will awaken and indiscriminately attack whoever it pleases. I worked closely with the Director of Legislative Services Othni Lathram and senior Law Institute attorney Paula Greene to draft legislation that would update and clarify the Alabama Ethics Law. This legislation would also reform and empower the Ethics Commission and limit the ability of public officials to politicize the investigative process by adding some accountability on them.

Unlike the folks at the Attorney General's Office, the Executive Director of the Ethics Commission Tom Albritton and his staff were helpful and made themselves available to me for advice and feedback. Although it had been over a year since Matt Hart's departure under suspicious circumstances after the November 2018 election, I still felt like Typhoid Mary on the rare occasions someone from that office crossed my path. Of course, the attorney general's full-throated advocacy of the Anslinger/Nixon stigma put him in conflict with my support of access to cannabis for medical purposes, which didn't help mend any fences.

During the first week of the 2020 session, I introduced House Bill 179, which closely followed many of the recommendations from the Code of Ethics Clarification and Reform Commission chaired by Attorney General Steve Marshall and Executive Director of the Ethics Commission Tom Albritton in 2018. It was the same commission the previous Attorney General Luther Strange adamantly opposed in September 2016 at the urging of Matt Hart and Alice Martin when he falsely accused me of trying to "gut" the Ethics Law.

Also included in the legislation were updates to the Ethics Law in response to court rulings during the previous ten years since the last major changes were made by the newly elected Republican majority led by Speaker Mike Hubbard. One of the court rulings that needed to be addressed removed whistleblower protections. But the portion of HB179 that drew the most opposition was the part attempting to address the flaw in the investigative process that had allowed Matt Hart to politicize the grand jury and stigmatize his chosen targets.

The bill would require the nonpartisan Ethics Commission to screen all ethics complaints before they could be brought to a grand jury. This would make it more difficult for a partisan attorney general, district attorney, or their employees to utilize a grand jury to target political enemies with an ethics investigation. It would also prevent them from using the grand jury secrecy provision to promote a political agenda by shutting down potential critics while helping political operatives and media to stigmatize not only the targets of their investigation, but also their target's allies and associates.

HB179 was assigned to the House Ethics and Campaign Finance Committee that I chair. Since neither the legislature nor the public was ready to address the flaws in our system that had been made so obvious to me, I assigned the bill to a subcommittee chaired by Representative Allen Farley, himself a retired investigator who understood the problem. I hoped the subcommittee would hold public hearings and generate enough buzz to awaken the sleeping dog and goad him out in the open so he could be tamed or destroyed.

The ethics bill was ready to begin moving through the legislative process, but until there was enough public concern, any attempt to implement a legislative solution would be futile. If the people don't recognize corruption, it will continue to silently influence our political process like spiritual cancer. The devil's greatest trick is to convince the world he doesn't exist.

The medical cannabis issue was different. Public attention was on it and the deception surrounding the stigma was continuing to be steadily exposed by growing research and medical practice where it was allowed. However, a significant determined minority was still desperately holding out against the growing body of science indicating the value of cannabis as a safer, more effective treatment for many ailments than many more socially accepted drugs, like opiates. They were beginning to sound like those who don't believe Neil Armstrong walked on the moon, Lee Harvey Oswald killed President Kennedy, or that Elvis is dead. People believe what they want to believe, regardless of the evidence before them.

Senator Melson expeditiously moved his medical cannabis bill through the Senate on March 12 with nearly two-thirds of the 2020 session remaining. The bill had growing support from those in the House, including Paul Lee, the chairman of the House Health Committee where the bill was assigned. Unfortunately, it was the last day before the COVID shutdown. The medical cannabis bill and the ethics legislation were both dead for another year.

In 2021, I again introduced ethics reform legislation and this time moved it out of the Ethics and Campaign Finance Committee about halfway through the session. However, the Rules Chairman Mike Jones did not deem ethics to be a suitable issue to be placed on House calendar for a vote during the session. First as House Judiciary chairman and later as rule chairman, Representative Jones worked consistently but discretely against my efforts to expose the corruption I had witnessed. It's probably because he didn't want the legal profession's dirty laundry being aired out. But how do we know if it's clean unless we air it out occasionally?

In February 2021, Melson passed the Compassion Act out of the Senate with three-quarters of the legislative session remaining, even quicker than the year before. Although a significant majority of the House members supported the bill, the Rules Chairman Mike Jones was determined to kill it, despite a substantial majority of the legislature favoring it, even if it meant using Machiavellian tactics to prevent it from getting to the floor for a vote.

I had heard a persistent rumor floating around for over a year that Melson's bill would be sent through two committees in the House, Judiciary and Health, an almost unprecedented move. It deeply concerned me because it created an extra mechanism for lawyers on Judiciary collaborating with Jones, Attorney General Steve Marshall, and some of the more strident district attorneys to muck it up with amendments if they couldn't stop it. Although Speaker McCutcheon had repeatedly assured me that Melson's bill would go to Health Committee and be treated like any other bill, I was flabbergasted to see the rumor come true.

Speaker McCutcheon understood the medical cannabis issue and had been supportive of our efforts from the beginning, but he was a former hostage negotiator like me and was judicious and conservative in the use of force. His style of leadership was to be respectful of the process and let the system play out, which created opportunities for the opposition to undermine our effort. I saw the rules chairman's fingerprints all over the special double committee treatment.

Fortunately, Judiciary chairman Representative Jim Hill was a retired circuit judge who understood the medical cannabis issue and had experience managing shifty manipulative lawyers. Although sixteen amendments were offered in the Judiciary Committee, Chairman Hill deftly managed to help the committee winnow them down to ten reasonable amendments. However, it was April 7, and six weeks of the legislative session had passed. As each legislative day passes and the thirty-day session nears its end, the power of the rules chairman expands.

Although the clock was ticking, the Health Committee Chairman Paul Lee had learned a great deal about the issue since 2019 and was determined to move a clean bill expeditiously to the floor. Concerned about the filibuster being organized by Representative Jim Carnes of Birmingham who would talk it to death on the floor, Lee incorporated the ten judiciary amendments into a single substitute for the Health Committee to work from and clean up anything the lawyers might have slipped into the bill. The Health Committee made several tweaks and adopted the bill into a single clean substitute on April 15, giving plenty of time in the session for Melson's SB46 to pass.

The Rules Chairman Mike Jones was able to further delay bringing SB46 to the floor by moving a controversial gaming issue in front of it and allowing the filibustering opponents led by Representative Jim Carnes to kill two birds with one stone. Regardless of how anyone might feel about gaming, it is primarily about the desire for money and entertainment. The medical cannabis issue in Alabama was primarily driven by a desire to ease human suffering. It was a moral outrage to me that those issues were lumped together by our short-sighted adversaries and even some supporters intentionally ignoring the line between the use of cannabis for medical and other purposes. Politics muddles moral discernment.

As the session began winding down, my disappointment with Speaker McCutcheon began to grow. I felt a special bond with him knowing his moral compass pointed in the same direction as mine even though he had many more powerful political forces tugging at him in many different directions. I could accept that the rules chairman and others had been taken in and deceived by the Anslinger stigma, but Speaker McCutcheon knew better, and that brought with it a moral obligation.

When the proposed Rules Committee calendar came out for the twenty-eighth day of the thirty-day session without the Compassion Act, my heart was broken because we had once again squandered a perfect opportunity to help a multitude of suffering people. Making it worse was that my friend Mac had the authority to make it happen, but it appeared that he lacked the fortitude to exercise it. Rules adopted by the Alabama House give the Speaker broad authority to appoint or remove any chairman and any committee member at any time for any reason. Speaker McCutcheon had said repeatedly for weeks that he intended for HB46 to get a vote on the House floor, and it was time for him to make a stand.

I wasn't privy to their private conversation, but whether he came out and said it or not, it was evident that Speaker McCutcheon made Chairman Jones an offer he couldn't refuse and ordered him to call a special meeting of the Rules Committee to put SB46 at the top of the calendar for Tuesday, May 4, the twenty-eighth day of the thirty-day session.

Representative Jim Carns had been organizing a filibuster with several other devotees of the Anslinger stigma for weeks, and it commenced soon after the session day began. Carns was elected to the legislature in 1990 from an affluent lily-white Birmingham suburb. Birmingham politics takes racial divisiveness to an entirely different level than most other places in Alabama, and their legislative delegation reflects it. Carns is a product of that environment and has thrived as a politician in it for over thirty years.

When I was first elected to the Alabama Legislature in 2002, Carns was the chair of the House GOP Minority Caucus. Although we've had no open hostility to one another, we almost always fall on opposite sides of intraparty squabbles. Maybe it's because his engineering and manufacturing background and mine as a law enforcement officer from a disadvantaged childhood gave us an entirely different perspective and problem-solving mindset. Being a Marine, I wasn't inspired by his leadership style that seemed more about implementing a knee-jerk, right-wing, populist agenda for finding creative solutions to difficult problems for everyone's benefit.

In 2004, Mike Hubbard defeated Jim Carns for minority leader. The change in leadership marked the beginning of the rise toward Republican control of the Alabama Legislature. After sixteen years in the legislature, Carns ran for the Jefferson County Commission in 2006 and was elected. However, after a single term, he returned to his old seat in the legislature. In 2014, he ran against Mike Hubbard for the caucus nomination for Speaker of the House, but his effort fizzled.

Unlike me, Representative Carns has been a predictable right-wing politician throughout his career. So I was not surprised that he jumped on the right-wing, populist Trump bandwagon early. Hard left- and right-wing political movements are dependent on each other to provide fodder for the stigmas they use to stoke the fears that energize their respective bases of support. The fears stoked by the marijuana stigma has been part of the right-wing political playbook since it was institutionalized by Anslinger and reenergized by Nixon.

With about a dozen speakers taking a full twenty minutes on each motion, it came to hours' worth of talk per motion. Representative Carns and his crew could run the clock until midnight. Being Republicans, the majority caucus would not vote cloture and shut them down like they do to minority Democrats. The unusually circuitous route the bill had taken through two committees led to a concocted rule that created the necessity for an extra floor motion, giving the opposition another additional four hours' filibustering time. Although it appeared the deck was stacked against us, standing in the well on behalf of the Compassion Act was an honor for which I had spent much time in prayer and preparation.

Standing at the microphone as each opponent droned on throughout the day, I was strengthened by the power of hundreds if not thousands of prayers from those who had needlessly suffered because of the Anslinger stigma. The opposition's speechifying mostly consisted of monotonous, clichéd arguments more suitable to a discussion about recreational marijuana than the narrow bill before the body that would regulate cannabis for medicinal purposes. The most powerful and inspirational speeches came from ardent proponents such as Representative Debbie Wood and Representative Brett Easterbrook who shared their heartfelt personal testimonies.

As the evening wore on, a storm swept through Montgomery. The lights in the Statehouse flickered and went out. In the darkness, I remembered the storm that knocked out my opponent's get-out-the-vote phone calls the night before my primary runoff election in 2002 and the storm that knocked out the power in the Statehouse in 2016 the evening Leni's Law passed. There are those who don't believe in spiritual things who will say it was just a coincidence, but for those like me who have witnessed and experienced divine intervention many times, it meant something. It was a "God wink."

"God winks" provide believers with assurance that our Creator is always at work and that we are part of a greater work in progress. Even the filibustering opponents of the bill were part of that divine plan. Their opposition provided a platform to educate those who listened to the "debate" about the medicinal use of cannabis and what we were doing with the legislation that we had introduced. Even though they were running out the clock, I could feel support growing throughout the day. Standing at the microphone looking into the faces of the opposition, it was apparent that some of them felt uncomfortable and even a bit ridiculous. The filibuster exposed the absurdity of the Anslinger stigma to many.

As midnight approached, Representative Jim Carns was the final speaker as the clock approached midnight to end the twenty-eighth legislative day. He began by graciously commending me for my effort throughout the day but didn't seem to have much more to say. He spent much of his final ten minutes at the microphone silently with a grin as he peered at me standing before him, sadly watching time run out.

I was dejected and missed the House GOP caucus meeting the next day when Speaker McCutcheon announced that we would begin the twenty-ninth legislative day where we left off and stay on the Compassion Act until it received a final vote. The filibuster was broken, and it was apparent to everyone that we had the votes to pass the bill, but the opposition was still not ready to throw in the towel. I had been unable to consider accepting amendments while the filibuster was going on. However, when the opposition let it be known that they'd abandoned the filibuster after the Speaker spoke to the caucus, I agreed to consider amendments on the floor.

On Thursday, May 6, we resumed debating the Compassion Act where we left off the previous Tuesday. The amendments offered by opponents which would have undermined the purpose of the bill were rejected. However, some of the amendments were adopted with my approval. One amendment that I gladly accepted renamed the bill "The Darren Wesley 'Ato' Hall Compassion Act." Darren Wesley "Ato" Hall is the son of Representative Laura Hall. Seeing her son suffer and die from AIDS prompted Representative Hall to become the first Alabama legislator to introduce legislation authorizing the use of cannabis for medical purposes.

Hall was already a veteran legislator when I was first elected in 2002. I was fortunate to have been assigned the seat beside hers on the floor of the House of Representatives. I can think of no one who better epitomizes statesmanship than Laura Hall, and as a retired teacher, she couldn't resist helping a clueless freshman learn the nuances of the legislative process. Although I was a white conservative Republican and she was a black liberal Democrat, we quickly developed a special friendship and a spiritual bond. Although there were some questions of public policy on which we disagreed, we discovered a great deal of common ground as fellow travelers seeking the same truth, albeit from different perspectives.

Hall introduced her first medical cannabis bill in 2005 and continued to introduce it until 2009 when the mantle passed to Representative Patricia Todd, and then fell on me in 2014. During the years the Democrats introduced the legislation, I was a legislator who could always be relied upon to oppose their bills. Not that I needed to oppose it. The Democrats in control of the legislature until 2010 were just as committed to kill the bills as the Republicans who replaced them. Until Carly's Law in 2014, no cannabis bill had ever even passed out of a standing committee in the Alabama Legislature.

The Anslinger stigma was something that the establishment of both political parties in Alabama supported, and I watched with approval in my institutionalized ignorance as those in power ensured that bills which could have helped many suffering Alabamians were killed. When I look back at my attitude then with the benefit of twenty-twenty hindsight, I can't help but think of Saul of Tarsus watching the stoning of Stephen with approval. Pride makes those who are most wrong the most certain.

The greatest threat to the bill came from an amendment brought by a freshman legislator on behalf of the attorney general which would have automatically repealed everything we would have done immediately when the federal government finally removed cannabis from Schedule I. The amendment would have undermined our effort to create a mechanism at the state level to provide for and regulate the use of cannabis for medical purposes, after decades of abject failure at the federal level by politicians and bureaucrats.

The freshman who brought the attorney general's amendment was a talented former prosecutor with obvious political ambition. His deft presentation of the amendment minimized its true purpose, which was to protect the federal bureaucracy created by the Anslinger stigma by dismantling the Alabama Medical Cannabis Commission at the first opportunity. My motion to table the amendment failed by six votes.

It appeared that the amendment would succeed where the filibuster had failed. Our supporters began scrambling to quickly work the floor and educate legislators who were supportive of our efforts. The opposition had dominated the microphone for the past two days, but it was time for supporters to go to the well, not only to speak but also to buy time while we made sure we had the votes to kill the attorney general's amendment.

The tide turned in our favor when Speaker Pro Tempore Victor Gaston went to the well and made an impassioned plea on our behalf. Like Representative Hall, Gaston has been a shining example of statesmanship in the Alabama Legislature for many years. He was elected to the legislature in 1982 from Mobile as a Republican when the label carried its own stigma among most Alabamians. It is a testament to the respect he embodies not just that he has been re-elected nine times but had not even had an opponent since his first re-election.

It was no surprise that, when the Republican takeover occurred in 2010, the elder statesman was handily elected Speaker pro tempore by the new supermajority over the more politically ambitious Paul DeMarco from Birmingham. I had admired Gaston as a loyal conservative Republican in the tradition of Ronald Reagan for many years. He was not the sort of politician that allowed political philosophy to harden his heart and override his sense of common decency to others. After the usually gracious Gaston went a bit ballistic and gave the House a firm scolding for voting down my tabling motion, I renewed the motion and it prevailed sixty to thirty-nine, a twenty-seven-vote shift.

A little while later, it was even more lopsided when SB46 passed the House sixty-nine to thirty-one. Nearly half of those voting "no" had assured me they were supportive of the bill but needed to vote that way to appease their local district attorney and other hard-liners who had been lobbying against it. I didn't care, so long as it passed.

Governor Ivey signed the Darrell Wesley "Ato" Hall Compassion Act into law a few days later, as expected. Help was finally on the way for many Alabamians who had been innocent victims of the Anslinger stigma.

I am grateful to the one who controls the storms for choosing me to be in the middle of it and navigating me through it, but it is not something I'd like to do again. The discourse over government policy surrounding cannabis is far from over, but we had great success in that we exposed the stigma that had allowed it to be a one-sided discussion controlled from the top down. I was more than ready to move on to other things.

CHAPTER 29

The Blessing

During my final re-election campaign in 2018, I asked my seven-year-old granddaughter if she wanted me to win. "It doesn't matter,' she replied. "You've done it a long time. Maybe somebody else should take a turn." Her words confirmed what I already knew in my heart.

My sense of personal satisfaction with the outcome of the cannabis issue has been tempered by the futility of my efforts to expose the flaws I've discovered in our legal system that provide opportunities for it to be secretly corrupted by politics. The stigma created by the Mike Hubbard investigation and prosecution was successfully used to thwart any legislation I proposed regarding ethics, grand jury secrecy, legislative subpoena power, or anything else directed at preventing an unscrupulous prosecutor from abusing the power of their office and undermining the legislative branch of state government in the name of fighting corruption.

Soon after the 2021 legislative session ended, I made a report to the Alabama Bar Association of some of the corruption I'd witnessed in a final attempt to obtain closure by exposing it and seeing it properly investigated. The association received my complaint on June 1, and in an unsigned letter dated the same day from their Office of General Counsel, I received the following response:

> Thank you for contacting our office. We have received your complaint against the above referenced attorney. A copy is enclosed for reference purposes. Based on the facts you outlined in your complaint, the alleged incident took place more than six years ago. Pursuant to Rule 31, *Alabama Rules of Disciplinary Procedure,* there is a six-year statute of limitations for filing a bar complaint.

Discussing with the Speaker a particularly onerous amendment to SB46 during the final day of debate on the House floor.

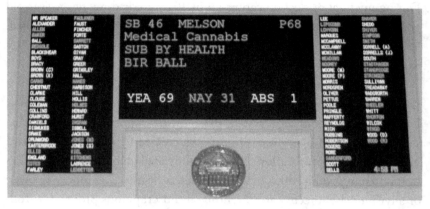

SB46 passed overwhelmingly 69-31. The 31 "no" votes are a clear indication that the Anslinger stigma is alive and well.

Maybe they would have properly investigated it if I had reported it to them in early 2016 instead of the secretary of state, the attorney general, the governor, and anyone else I could think of, but I doubt it. It's hard for me to believe the entire legal profession in Alabama was oblivious to what seemed so obvious to me. Maybe it's just a prime example of the story of the emperor's clothes—nobody is willing to even consider holding a prosecutor accountable for secretly misusing their authority or position to manipulate public opinion by affecting the outcome of elections or influencing a jury pool.

When I later learned that the Attorney General had allowed the Executive Director of the State Bar to plead guilty to seventeen ethics violations, avoiding a criminal investigation and possible jail sentence by paying $110,000 in fines and restitution, it reinforced my growing recognition of the double standard that permeates our legal system. It also forced me to accept that there was no state agency or legal mechanism that could or would objectively investigate misconduct within the Attorney General's Office.

For several years I have moved toward the sad conclusion that the prosecutorial misconduct I'd witnessed was not an anomaly as I initially thought it to be, but an indication of what is commonly accepted practice in public corruption cases. If that is true, then the legal profession itself has accepted that the end justifies the means and due process doesn't matter, only winning does.

It is certainly more expeditious to ignore corruption than to address it, but ignoring it only allows it to spread. But if due process is not actively protected, the United States Constitution becomes just a piece of paper that reminds us of the former American ideal that centered around the concept of creating a system of limited self-governance by the dispersion of power in a manner where the corruption it creates cannot be kept hidden for long.

Corruption always seeks darkness. The only way to subdue it is to expose it. In 1914, just before he was appointed to the U.S. Supreme Court, Louis Brandeis wrote, "Publicity is justly commended as a remedy for social and industrial diseases. Sunlight is said to be the best of disinfectants; electric light the most efficient policeman."

If we're serious about fighting corruption in Alabama, we must first shine the light on it. All of it. Sharing the rest of the story surrounding the circumstances that led to simultaneous ethical breakdowns at the highest levels of state government in Alabama appears to be my last hope for promoting a political atmosphere conducive to addressing the glaring flaws in our legal process that allow it to be tainted by political opportunists, propangandists, and zealots.

It's easy to forget that our political leaders are neither heroes nor villains. They're just humans—no more or no less vulnerable to being corrupted by their own pride than any of the rest of us. However, those who most aggressively engage in pursuit of political power are almost always primarily driven by the most insidious of all character flaws: spiritual pride. It is a treacherous parasite that feeds on the moral fiber of the souls it inhabits and can only be destroyed by exposure and acknowledgement by its host.

Nearly three hundred years ago, the work of the great revivalist preacher, philosopher, and theologian Jonathan Edwards played a significant role in helping to shape the thoughts that drove the founders of our nation to create our peculiar system of self-governance. In an essay about undetected spiritual pride, Edwards wrote, "It is by spiritual pride that the mind defends and justifies itself in other errors and defends itself against light by which it might be corrected and reclaimed."

Spiritual pride works like cancer that grows inside us undetected while we believe all is well. It deceives us all into thinking we are entitled to what we are not and that we know more than we do—and Speaker Hubbard was no exception. As his friend and former political ally, I watched firsthand as spiritual pride orchestrated both his dramatic rise to the highest plateau of political power in Alabama and his precipitous fall all the way to a prison cell. Contrary to what his stigmatizing critics would have us believe, he is not a devil, but just another victim of hell's favorite weapon against mankind since the dawn of civilization, spiritual pride.

Pride not only attacked Mike Hubbard from within as he accumulated power, but it also attracted the attention of others who were stricken by the same spiritual disease. They were resentful of the power he had accumulated and wanted it for themselves. Pride is the driving force of politics and an integral part of the complex system of checks and balances designed to control it.

In his essay, Edwards cited several symptoms of spiritual pride that are helpful to those with the courage to perform frequent self-examinations. The symptoms are obvious and rankle us when they are exhibited by others, stirring up our own pride, causing us to become the very thing we detest. I have discovered that by taking a moment to self-check for the symptoms cited by Edwards before confronting them in others, we can avoid being corrupted by the evil what we are resisting.

The first symptom is fault-finding. Pride magnifies the faults of others while camouflaging our own. Politics naturally exacerbates individual pridefulness, but it grows even worse when it is fed collectively by the tribalism of partisanship. Those who are constantly critical of others and unable to face their own failures and acknowledge them are surely infected.

The next is a harsh tone. Self-righteousness suppresses grace. Those who are most full of themselves have little regard for how their actions hurt others. They are quick to demand retribution and accountability for those they deem to be their inferiors, which is almost everyone. Pride promotes a feeling of superiority that causes people to demand the law is fully enforced with the most maximum penalties against those who they disagree with or dislike.

Putting on pretenses is the third symptom of pride cited by Edwards in his essay. It is said that perception is reality. That is only true for the prideful. Unfortunately, political decisions are almost always superficially driven by those more concerned with what looks good instead of what is good. Those who really believe in the Almighty God that is the source of all goodness recognize the fallacy of being overly concerned with what others think. But appearances are everything to the prideful.

The fourth symptom is easily taking offense. While the prideful are quick to point out the faults of others without regard to their feelings, it simultaneously makes them overly sensitive to every real or imagined slight. Their hypocritical double standard is clearly displayed by their inability to accept the same medicine they so freely dole out to others. Spiritual pride makes us overly defensive.

Presumptiveness is another common symptom of pride, particularly when it causes people to be unable to differentiate their opinions from God's word. Pride causes people to believe in themselves as the center of their universe. Unfortunately for them, only one god can occupy that space. The desperate craving of attention and neglecting to care about the needs of others round out the check list.

Like Edwards, the founders recognized pride as the spiritual force that drives the quest for power and ultimately leads to the downfall of almost all who are successful in attaining it. Recognizing that all humans are fallible, they strove toward the ideal of an infallible system built around using other prideful, self-serving power seekers as the primary means of protecting the public from their fallible leaders.

They created a hybrid system of governance seeking to limit corruption by dividing powers among three separate branches of government with each of them having vulnerability and power over one another, like the paper, rock, scissors game. The American Revolution led to a process that limited power by making it flow in different directions, pitting separate branches against one another.

Our American political system is a messy, convoluted process, but it is far better to have a clunky system that separates powers, holding its leaders accountable to one another, than a more efficient system that allows too much power to concentrate in the hands of flawed humans. If we fail to protect the delicate balance of the process that has been entrusted to us by clearly delineating the separation of powers and demanding that each be held equally accountable, it quickly denigrates into a less drastic version of the French Revolution with its guillotines.

Because it is comprised of elected representatives from separate districts, the power of the legislative branch was designed to be dispersed among many members and flow from the bottom up. It is also designed to be the most transparent, most openly political, and consequently messiest branch of government.

Because executive power is naturally concentrated and flows from the top down, the work of governance in a free society is more expedient from that branch, but power tends to gravitate toward the executive branch.

It is the responsibility of the judicial branch to act as a referee to protect the integrity of the process by ensuring the balance of power is maintained according to the rule of law. Corruption in any branch upsets the balance of power and undermines the credibility and effectiveness of all the branches.

In 2013, the Alabama Bicentennial Commission was created to acknowledge our past, celebrate our progress, and hope for our future as we celebrated our two hundredth year of statehood. I was honored to be appointed to the commission, although my effort had little to do with the splendid success of the commemoration, reflection, and celebration that spanned several years. Despite the many struggles we've faced in Alabama because of the deep divisions created by corrupt politics driven by fear and pride, it gave me hope for a brighter future.

Alabama's two-hundred-year birthday celebration culminated with a grand finale weekend that began on the evening of Friday, December 13,

2019, at the Montgomery Performing Arts Center with Dr. Condoleezza Rice delivering the keynote. She was brilliant, as usual, but the portion of her speech where she spoke about the Constitution and framework of governance the founders of our nation gave us particularly struck a chord with me.

She referred to the French political philosopher Tocqueville who contrasted the American Revolution with the French Revolution by saying, "The French believe in the perfectibility of man; therefore, they have perfect institutions. The Americans understand that man is imperfect, and they have therefore created perfect institutions."

Dr. Rice noted that the founders "gave to us a Constitution that delineated the rights of those who would be governed and the responsibilities and rights of those who would govern. They separated powers so that no one

Dr Condoleeza Rice delivers keynote address at the Alabama Bicentennial Celebration.

could be all powerful. The understood that human beings were not perfect, and so they gave us ways to challenge one another peacefully in courts."

Other important checks and balances the founders placed on those who hold power in our system of governance include free and fair elections and the First Amendment that guarantees freedom of thought and speech.

Dr. Rice ended the speech by saying,

> As Alabama enters its next century, there's a lot of work to do. A lot of work has already been done on our behalf, and this weekend as you take the time to celebrate that history, as you take the time to remember those who brought Alabama this far, ask yourselves one by one, individually, what have I done to make Alabama's next years better than its past? Because when it comes down to it, that is what democracy requires. Democracy is not a spectator sport. It requires each and every one of us to commit. It requires each and every one of us to act. It requires each and every one of us to believe, and that is a reason to celebrate.

After nearly half a century of participating in the process of public service, I still believe in the vision of those who framed the Constitution of the United States and the importance of striving toward an open and fair process in which everyone who holds political power is accountable to someone. Despite numerous shortcomings and many things that I could have done better, my service has been more a blessing to me than a burden.

I am fortunate to have escaped the clutches of politics with my conscience intact and look forward to enjoying the rest of my days with my loving wife Karen, sharing music and insight with friends who cross my path.

Dr. Rice's speech helped me better recognize the primary motivation that underlay my life of public service. It caused me to contemplate what I've done to make Alabama's future better than its past. I clearly recognized that by leaving public office, that purpose has not ended. It has just taken a different course and entered another arena. But it will always be guided by the same unseen hand.

~

Index

CPSIA information can be obtained
at www.ICGtesting.com
Printed in the USA
BVHW030706181022
649631BV00007B/8